NATIONAL COOKERY BOOK,

COMPILED FROM ORIGINAL RECEIPTS,

FOR THE

Women's Centennial Committees

OF THE

INTERNATIONAL EXHIBITION

OF

"For know, whatever was created needs
To be sustained and fed."—MILTON.

PHILADELPHIA:
WOMEN'S CENTENNIAL EXECUTIVE COMMITTEE.

APPLEWOOD BOOKS
BEDFORD, MASSACHUSETTS

National Cookery was first published in 1876, having been printed at the press of Henry B. Asmead of Philadelphia. It was registered at the Library of Congress that same year by Mrs. E. D. Gillespie, chairman of the Women's Centennial Executive Committee.

Thank you for purchasing an Applewood Book.
Applewood reprints America's lively classics—books
from the past that are of interest to modern readers.
For a free copy of our current catalog, write to:
Applewood Books, P.O. Box 365, Bedford, MA 01730

ISBN 1-55709-569-8

Library of Congress Control Number: 2004117888

This cookbook has been reprinted in cooperation with the Culinary
Trust, which is the philanthropic arm of the International Association of
Culinary Professionals (IACP). The Trust celebrates the culinary past and
future by funding educational and charitable programs related to the culinary industry (including scholarships for students and career professionals;
library research and travel grants for food writers), cookbook preserva-
tion and restoration; and hunger alleviation. Tax-deductible gifts to the
Culinary Trust should be sent to:
    The Culinary Trust
    304 West Liberty Street, Suite 201,
    Louisville, KY 40202
    Website: *www.theculinarytrust.com*
    Phone: (502) 581-9786 x264

Introduction
by

ANDREW F. SMITH

A number of cookbooks were published in celebration of the one-hundredth anniversary of the United States in 1876, but only one, *The National Cookery Book*, was directly associated with Philadelphia's Centennial Exposition. It was compiled by the Women's Executive Committee, chaired by Elizabeth Duane Gillespie. The committee solicited recipes from women throughout the nation. While not a scientific survey of American cookery, the recipes in *The National Cookery Book* are more reflective of American culinary traditions than those of any other nineteenth-century work. It was truly America's first "national" cookbook.

WOMEN'S EXECUTIVE COMMITTEE
President Ulysses S. Grant opened Philadelphia's Centennial Exposition on May 19, 1876. When it closed six months later, more than ten million visitors had passed through the gates, and the event was judged a tremendous success. Yet the Exposition almost didn't happen. An international fair held in New York City in 1853 had been a financial failure, discouraging the scheduling of other such events in the United States. The idea of a centennial exposition had been raised in 1867, but it wasn't until 1871 that Congress established a Centennial Committee charged with managing an "International Exposition of Arts and Manufacture" in Philadelphia in 1876. Along with officers and an Executive Committee, a Citizens' Centennial Board of Finances was created to guarantee the Exhibition's fiscal solvency in order to avoid the problems suffered by New York City's fair in 1853. The Centennial Committee planned to operate by selling stock, which was to be redeemed, after the Exhibition closed, with revenues collected through the sale of concessions and entrance fees paid by fair-goers. By 1873, however, few stock had been sold. Worse

iii

yet, a financial panic struck the nation in 1873, and its disastrous effects lingered through 1876. The Exposition was in serious trouble three years before it was scheduled to open.

Traditionally, women had taken the lead in organizing fund-raisers for religious and civic causes. However, the organizers of the Centennial Exposition had made a major mistake—no woman was appointed to any of the Centennial Committees. John Welsh, the President of the Board of Finance, decided to create a Women's Executive Committee to help generate the sale of stock.[1] On February 16, 1873, he invited thirteen women—one for each of the original thirteen colonies—to meet. Only nine showed up (the others declining to participate), but this small committee soon proved its value to the nascent Exposition.

When it came to selecting a president of the Women's Executive Committee, Elizabeth Duane Gillespie was the obvious choice. Born in Philadelphia, she was the great-granddaughter of Benjamin Franklin, who had been a member of the committee that drafted the Declaration of Independence in 1776. Her father, William J. Duane, had briefly served as Secretary of the Treasury during the presidency of Andrew Jackson. Gillespie had more going for her than just distinguished lineage. She was well connected in Philadelphia society, and her family was financially well off. What's more, she had administrative experience managing Philadelphia's Sanitary Fair, which had raised more than one million dollars to help soldiers wounded during the Civil War.

The first thing the Women's Executive Committee did was try to set up a network of representatives in each Philadelphia ward to help sell Centennial stock. Few women volunteered, although the committee did receive a letter from a local pastor asking their help in raising money for his church building fund! The committee became more aggressive in their recruiting, and by April 1873 there was at least one woman selling Centennial stock in each of Philadelphia's wards. Then, the committee established a national committee with chairwomen in thirty-seven states and territories.

To raise additional funds, the committee conducted a series of events to generate funds and heighten visibility, such as concerts, art shows, and bazaars. It also sponsored a highbrow tea on December 16, 1873—the hundredth anniversary of the Boston Tea Party, and held "Martha Washington Tea Parties," where tea was served in commemorative cups. Eventually, the Women's Executive Committee raised more than $126,000 for the Centennial Exposition.[2]

In addition to fund-raising for the Exposition, the Women's Executive Committee was responsible for preparing an exhibit of "women's work." For this, they had been allocated a modest space in one of the many exhibition halls. When told that they would have to relinquish some of their limited space to other exhibitors, the committee proposed that they be given a separate building. By this time, the committee had generated thousands of dollars in pledges, so their request was approved, provided they cover all expenses. They hired an architect, raised an additional $36,000 for the construction of the pavilion, solicited exhibitors, and filled the halls with exhibitions. The resulting Women's Pavilion was considered by many the most attractive at the Exposition.[3]

Throughout the Exposition, the committee published a newspaper, "New Century for Women," which "was entirely completed by women's labor—publishers, editors, contributors, and type setters all of that sex."[4] They planned the festivities surrounding Women's Day, which was ironically but intentionally scheduled for November 7, 1876—a national election day—because women were denied the vote. (Simultaneously, suffragettes met in Philadelphia demanding the right to vote.) The day's festivities included a reception at which Elizabeth Duane Gillespie announced that the Women's Executive Committee planned to assist in the creation of "a Museum of Art, in all its branches and technical application, and with a special view to the development of the art and textile industries of the state."[5] Exactly one year after the Exposition closed, the "Pennsylvania Museum and School of Industrial Arts" opened at Memorial Hall at Fairmont Park.

The last meeting of the Women's Executive Committee took place in April 1877, and shortly thereafter Mrs. Gillespie and her daughter left for Europe, where they spent the next four years. They returned to Philadelphia in 1881, when she immediately reformed the committee to assist in the further development of the Philadelphia Museum and School of Industrial Art. The committee decided that a larger facility was necessary for the museum, and they held fund-raising events to help cover the costs. This ancillary project of the Women's Executive Committee was later renamed the Philadelphia Museum of Art, now one of America's foremost art collections. Gillespie also contributed to World's Columbian Exposition, which opened in 1893, by assembling Colonial relics for a display in Chicago. Gillespie's autobiography, *A Book of Remembrance* (1901), was completed a few months before she died.

THE NATIONAL COOKERY BOOK

One fund-raising project for the Women's Executive Committee was the publication of a cookbook. This was not the first charitable cookbook. According to Margaret Cook, author of *America's Charitable Cooks: A Bibliography of Fund-Raising Cook Books Published in the United States (1861–1915)*, one of the first charitable cookbooks was Maria J. Moss's *A Poetical Cook-Book*, which was published in Philadelphia for the 1864 Sanitary Fair for which Elizabeth Duane Gillespie had been one of the managers.[6] Subsequently churches and civic organizations throughout the nation began issues cookbooks, and the proceeds went to some charitable causes. These were frequently compiled by the women in the church or civic organization submitting their own recipes.

The National Cookery Book did something similar, but on a much grander scale. The cookbook was intended to address the question asked by foreigners about America's "national dishes." It was to consist of "purely American recipes" excluding "the receipts common to all nations." To accomplish this end, the committee sent a letter to women in all the states and territories requesting recipes:

> *No receipt will be considered too homely, if characteristic of the country . . . Dishes peculiar to rich and poor,—to hunting, fishing, or exploring exhibitions, or to camp-life, etc., are desired. If comical and at the same time*

good, so much the better. Our aim is to give the true flavor of American life in all its varieties.

Soups, fish, shell-fish, meats, game of all sorts, cakes, pastries, puddings, sauces, preserves, canned fruits and vegetables in their endless varieties, give up unlimited resources. Of our beverages alone—already world-renowned—we hope to obtain a choice collection.

Thousands of recipes poured in from women all over the United States and its territories. The committee winnowed them down to about nine-hundred-fifty. These were then revised and loosely organized into twenty-seven chapters in the three-hundred-fifty-seven-page *National Cookery Book*. Unfortunately, the names and home states of the recipe contributors are not included in the book, but fifty-seven of the recipes contain a reference that reveals their geographic origin. Among these, twenty-one states, territories or regions are mentioned, from California to New England and from Idaho to Florida. The states with the largest number of mentions are Florida (11), Virginia (9), Maryland (7), and Pennsylvania and Idaho (5 each).

The most unusual state/territory recipes in the book come from Idaho and Florida. There are four Idaho recipes, three of which are for cooking game: "Idaho Method of Cooking a Deer's Head" (p. 135), "Idaho Smothered Quail" (p. 135), and "Idaho Method of Broiling Game or Meats" (p. 136). In the fourth recipe, "Idaho Roasted Onions and Potatoes" (p. 136), onion and potato are wrapped in moistened paper and cooked near hot ashes. The first cookbook published in Idaho did not appear until 1904, and so these recipes in *The National Cookery Book* may be the earliest recipes from that state.

FAMILIAR RECIPES

At its core, American cookery in 1876 still retained much of its English heritage. At least half the recipes in *The National Cookery Book* can be traced to traditional British sources. These include recipes for puddings breads, meats, soups, sauces, sweet pies, and other desserts. But in the two-and-a-half centuries since the establishment of English colonies, American cookery had been modified by climatic conditions in the New World, the addition of new ingredients, and numerous adoptions and adaptations from the cookery of diverse national, cultural, and religious groups, which had emigrated to America.

By far the most important ingredient in American cookery was corn, a grain native to the Americas. Europeans had imported wheat and barley, but these crops did not thrive in the new land. Without the quick adoption of corn, European settlements might not have survived. Corn plays an important role in virtually all nineteenth-century American cookbooks, but it is particularly emphasized in *The National Cookery Book*, in which an entire chapter, containing fifty-nine recipes, focuses on corn and corn products. In addition, many other recipes in the book include corn as an ingredient. While Native Americans introduced corn to early European colonists, American recipes using corn are not generally based on Native American foods. Instead, cornmeal was substituted for wheat flour in common English recipes.

For instance, the "Indian Pudding" recipes (pp. 196–198) were variations on British hasty pudding, which was made with different grains in different parts of the British Isles. In England hasty puddings were wheat-based, while in Scotland they were made from oats. The grain was boiled in water or milk until it formed a thick porridge, which was sweetened and spiced.[8] In America, most hasty pudding recipes used cornmeal, and Indian pudding was part of America's cookery repertoire from the earliest Colonial times.

Puddings (pp. 209–224) were an important component of American cookery in the nineteenth century. *The National Cookery Book* had a pudding chapter with fifty-nine recipes, and other pudding recipes appear elsewhere. Following English custom, puddings might appear at any course or meal. For instance, a visitor to the home of John Adams, the former U.S. president, in 1817 noted that Indian pudding was served before the meats; this odd-seeming course was intended to check the appetite. As the nineteenth century wore on, sugar was added to puddings and sweet puddings moved to the end of the meal as dessert.[9] This type of pudding became obsolete by the early twentieth century, and almost disappeared from the American culinary experience.

Game was extremely important in the diet of early Americans. At the time of European colonization, wild animals and birds were abundant in North America. They were relatively easy to hunt or trap. Unlike domesticated animals, wild game cost nothing to maintain. In addition, many birds and wild animals were crop pests, and killing them increased farm yields. Americans ate an astonishing array of game animals and birds. By the early nineteenth century, however, game was already dwindling east of the Mississippi. *The National Cookery Book*, like most nineteenth-century American cookbooks, has an entire chapter on game and another on "Open Air Cooking." These include recipes for canvasback duck, grouse, opossum, partridge, pheasant, pigeon, quail, rabbit, reed birds, snipe, squab, venison, and woodcock.

By far the most important game animal was the deer. Most nineteenth-century cookbooks included at least a few recipes for venison; some offered a dozen or more. In addition to being served at home, venison was served as a luxury in fashionable restaurants throughout the nineteenth century. However, by the mid-nineteenth century, venison had become a rarity in Eastern markets, and *The National Cookery Book* includes only three venison recipes (pp. 100–101). Deer meat remained an important food in rural areas, and in the South and West. Western hunters brought deer to market in eastern cities, although in an era before refrigeration and rapid transportation, many venison lovers complained about the condition of the meat when it arrived at market. By 1900, deer had become scarce even in many Western states, and state game laws had largely forbidden deer hunting. The result was the virtual disappearance of venison from the American diet by the early twentieth century.

One traditional American game dish was Brunswick stew (p. 138), which emerged in the mid-nineteenth century; both Georgia and Virginia claim it as their own. It was commonly made with leftovers and whatever meat was available, be it chicken, squirrel, or other game, along with onions, bacon, sweet corn, and other vegetables. Brunswick stew is still eaten today and many different recipes claim to be "authentic." Game gradually faded from the American culinary scene in the early twentieth century. Although venison, pheasant, quail and the like still occasionally appeared on the menu at swank restaurants, few ordinary cookbooks included recipes for game.

Foreigners visiting America often expressed surprise at the abundance of meat served. The longest chapter in *The National Cookery Book* covers the preparation of meat (pp. 59–84), with subsections on beef, mutton, lamb, veal, and pork. *The National Cookery Book* includes twenty recipes for beef (pp. 59–68) and an additional twenty for veal (pp. 72–79). It contains nine recipes for lamb and mutton (pp. 69–72) and thirteen for pork (pp. 79–84). Despite the imbalance between beef and pork, pork was the more important meat in America up to the twentieth century. Pigs ate virtually anything, and pigs were easy to manage, especially by farmers with limited acreage. Lard was America's choice frying medium well into the twentieth century. Perhaps most important, pork was easier to cure than beef. Beef did not surpass pork on American tables until the general adoption of refrigeration.

Another large chapter in *The National Cookery Book* is devoted to poultry (pp. 85–100), with subsections on turkey, chicken, goose and duck. Europeans introduced domesticated poultry into the New World, where they have thrived since Colonial times. Virtually every farm and plantation kept domesticated poultry. The birds required little care, roaming freely about the farm to find their own food. They were easily transported. Their feathers were used for bedding, and their eggs were a nutritious (and sometimes profitable) bonus. Chickens were by far the most common poultry in America followed by turkeys; there were far fewer domesticated ducks and geese. Reflecting this hierarchy, *The National Cookery Book* includes twenty recipes for chicken (pp. 89–98), seven recipes for turkey (pp. 85–88), and one each for duck and goose (pp. 98–99). There is also a separate chapter devoted to eggs (pp. 125–127). One recipe, "To Fry Eggs as Round as Balls" (p. 127), dates to 1794.

Soups were a significant component of English cookery, and many traditional English soups appear in *The National Cookery Book*. But there are also unusual soups, such as pepperpot, gumbo, and peanut soup, that reflect more exotic origins. Pepperpot is a West Indian stew made with meat or fish and vegetables, vigorously spiced with red pepper and thickened with the juice of the cassava root. Recipes for it were published in British cookbooks by the mid-eighteenth century and some of these were reprinted in American books. However, pepperpot was probably known in America prior to this time, having been brought to British North America by African slaves who had lived in the Caribbean. American pepperpot was made with a variety of ingredients, the common element being the seasoning—crushed peppercorns or red pepper. Pepperpot recipes were published in America by the early nineteenth century. Pepperpot recipes all but disappeared in the twentieth century, but commercial pepperpot was sold in cans up to the mid-twentieth century, and the dish has been kept alive in culinary fakelore claiming that it was first prepared at Valley Forge by the Continental Army. The recipe for "Pepper Pot" in *The National Cookery Book* (p. 22) is mild compared to other recipes published in American cookbooks. It includes beef suet, veal, tripe, and sweetbreads, along with mild cayenne pepper and seasonings.

Gumbo was likely first developed in New Orleans. "Gumbo," an African word for okra, was used in the United States by the early nineteenth century. Little evidence has surfaced about the origins of this complex stew. It usually incorporated okra and/or filé (powdered dry sassafras leaves), both of which have mucilaginous thickening properties when cooked. Filé, which also adds a spicy flavor, is thought to have originated with the Choctaw Indians in Louisiana. Principal ingredients in gumbo might include chicken, turkey, squirrel, rabbit, crab, oysters, or shrimp, as well as cabbage or other greens. Gumbo recipes migrated quickly throughout America, popularized when they appeared in agricultural publications. The first known recipe was published in *The American Farmer* in 1830, and it was quickly reprinted elsewhere. The first gumbo recipe to appear in an American cookbook is in Eliza Leslie's *Directions for Cookery* (Philadelphia, 1838), which included okra, but no filé. *The National*

Cookery Book has three gumbo recipes (p. 23), one with okra, one with filé, and one with both.

Peanut soup, or "Groundnut Soup" (p. 26), probably originated with slaves. The peanut plant had originated in central South America, but had been introduced into Africa by Europeans in the sixteenth century. As ground peanuts had been used in soups in Africa, it is likely that this dish had been made for years by African-Americans. On the eve of the nineteenth century, peanuts were grown in Philadelphia gardens.[11] The plants were likely introduced by French Creole refugees, who had settled in Philadelphia after escaping the 1791 slave insurrection in Haiti. *The National Cookery Book* records (p. 269) that these families "brought slaves with them as nurses and attendants," and these slaves introduced peanut cookery to Philadelphia. Wearing bright madras turbans, they sat on low stools on Philadelphia street corners and sold peanut cakes.

The National Cookery Book has four recipes for chowder: "Chowder" (p. 350), "Clam Chowder" (p. 30), "Rhode Island Chowder" (pp. 36–7), and "Lobster Chowder" (p. 56). Whether chowders were introduced into New England by French, Nova Scotian or British fishermen is undocumented, but chowders were important dishes by the beginning of the eighteenth century in America. The word "chowder" comes from the French *chaudière*, meaning kettle. The first known American recipe was published in Boston in 1751. Chowders, composed of fish, shellfish, and vegetables, were quite distinct from broths soups, or stews. They were cooked with the aim of producing a thick dish without reducing the ingredients to the consistency of a purée. Cooks in America built on this basic concept, and in 1867 New York Cooking School director Pierre Blot write that chowder could be made a hundred different ways.[12]

The Fish chapter of *The National Cookery Book* contains thirty-four recipes. Eight are for shad (pp. 32–34), a fish native to American waters occurring along the Atlantic coast from southern Labrador to northern Florida. American shad undertake extensive seasonal migrations, moving into rivers for spawning beginning in January in southern climes, and continuing until July in the northernmost portion of their range. After spawning, shad migrate north along the coast to Canada, where they feed during the summer. A southward migration occurs later along the continental shelf, where the fish overwinter prior to spring spawning migrations to their natal rivers. Shad have been exploited for their fatty flesh and rich, delicious roe since prior to European settlement. Once plentiful along most east coast rivers, today shad is caught only in small quantities. Virtually all nineteenth-century American cookbooks had one or more recipes for shad, but these recipes have all but disappeared as did the shad, although recently shad have made a comeback in America.

Shellfish were an important food in nineteenth-century America. *The National Cookery Book* includes an entire chapter on "Shell-Fish" with eighteen recipes for oysters, five for lobster, three for crabs, and two for clams and shrimp. Shellfish recipes are found in other parts of the book as well. In "Open Air Cooking," for instance, is found one of the first descriptions of an American "Clam Bake" (pp. 129–132). Despite repeated statements from recent writers that the clambake dated to pre-Columbian times, what we think of today as a clambake dates only to the mid-nineteenth century.

Reptiles make an appearance in this chapter as well: There are recipes for "Turtle Steaks" (p. 52), four recipes for terrapin (pp. 52–3), and one for "Terrapins' Eggs" (p. 53). Turtles were found in abundance in the New World and they were consumed from the beginning of European settlement. Terrapins were particularly prized, but most types of sea turtles were consumed. Prior to the Civil War, turtles were considered slave food in the South. In the North, turtle meat and soup were delicacies, and extensive directions for making turtle soup were published in American cookbooks. The meat, which came from female or "cow" turtles, was prepared in numerous ways. Male or "bull" turtles' meat was tougher and generally was used only for making soup.

A chapter titled "Little Dishes" is a catchall for recipes that do not easily fit into other parts of the book. Two intriguing recipes in this section are for "Brother Jonathan" and frogs' legs. "Brother

Jonathan" (p. 111) consists of rounds of cornmeal mush layered with grated cheese (Parmesan is suggested) and browned in the oven "as you do macaroni." The name "Brother Jonathan" was a then-common term for the people of the United States. Only a few references to "Brother Jonathan" as the name of a dish have been located, and all were published around the time of the Centennial.

Readers may be surprised to find a recipe for "Frogs" (p. 117) in *The National Cookery Book*. The United States had acquired an abhorrence of eating frogs from the British, who traditionally scorned all things French. On the American frontier, however, frogs' legs were eaten when nothing else was available. Beginning in the mid-nineteenth century, frogs' legs became fashionable at the tables of the wealthy. Recipes for frogs' legs frequently appeared in American cookbooks in the mid-nineteenth century. The recipe in *The National Cookery Book* broils just the legs, and seasons them with mushrooms or ketchup. To assure readers about the taste, the recipe informs readers that the frog flesh resembles chicken.

The Vegetable chapter (pp. 143–162) in *The National Cookery Book* contains sixty-one recipes for an impressive variety of vegetables: artichokes, asparagus, beans, beets, cabbage, carrots, cauliflower, celery, corn, cucumbers, eggplant, Jerusalem artichokes, kale, mushrooms, okra, peas, peppers, potatoes, rice, turnips, spinach, squash, sweet potatoes, tannia, and tomatoes. Most recipes will seem fairly familiar to modern readers, with the possible exceptions of those for Jerusalem artichokes, tannia, and Saratoga potatoes.

The Jerusalem artichoke *(Helianthus tuberosus)* is closely related to the sunflower *(Helianthus annuus)*. These were the only two plants domesticated in Eastern North America in pre-Columbian times to be widely disseminated. In the seventeenth century both were carried to Europe, where they became fad foods. The Italian word for sunflower—girasóle (sun turner)—was corrupted by the English to "Jerusalem" and, as the tuber tasted vaguely like a globe artichoke, it came to be called Jerusalem artichoke. *The National Cookery Book* has two recipes for "Jerusalem Artichokes" (p. 150), one for boiling them, the other for baking them.

Tannia *(Xanthosoma sagittifolium)* is native to tropical South America, but in pre-Columbian times was introduced to the Caribbean, and from there into Florida. Tannia has a starchy corm similar to that of taro *(Colocasia esculenta)* and it is used in similar ways. *The National Cookery Book*'s recipe (p. 148) is for making fritters of mashed tannia.

Potatoes had been consumed in America since the mid-seventeenth century. Recipes for paper-thin potato slices fried in deep fat had appeared in American cookbooks since the early nineteenth century, and they became all the rage when they were dubbed "Saratoga Potatoes" (p. 145) in the early 1870s. Saratoga Springs, the upstate New York resort, was also the site of an important American victory during the Revolutionary War. Today, Saratoga potatoes are better known as potato chips.

The National Cookery Book has forty-one recipes listed under "Sauces," such as recipes for mayonnaise and ketchup. In 1876 "Mayonnaise" (p. 273), a thick sauce made by whipping oil, vinegar, and seasonings into beaten egg yolks, was known only to the upper crust in America. Mayonnaise recipes appeared in cookbooks published in the United States by 1829, but it did not become an important condiment until the end of the nineteenth century. The major reason for this delay was the high cost of imported olive oil, a necessary ingredient. When less expensive olive oil began to be shipped from Florida and California, mayonnaise was commonly used on salads and as an accompaniment to cold fish and meats.

Ketchup recipes were first published in England in the early eighteenth century. Derived from Southeast Asian fermented sauces, early ketchup recipes were highly piquant condiments made from seafood (notably anchovies and oysters), mushrooms, or nuts (especially walnuts), enhanced with vinegar and a multitude of spices. British colonists brought ketchup recipes to America. The first known reference to tomato ketchup was not published until the early nineteenth century, and although a late arrival, tomato ketchup caught on in America. Ketchup recipes in general, and tomato recipes in particular, became the rage in the United States during the pre-Civil War years.

The National Cookery Book contains thirteen recipes for ketchup (pp. 276–280), including ones based on walnuts, mushrooms, cucumbers, oysters, and barberries, and four recipes for tomato ketchup.[13]

The National Cookery Book contains forty-four recipes in its beverage chapter. These include an "Egg Nog" recipe (pp. 300–301) and "Sangaree" (p. 301). Eggnog was an American invention. According to the *Oxford English Dictionary*, the first reference to eggnog appeared in 1825. The first located recipe appears in Lettice Bryan's *Kentucky Housewife* (1839). Most recipes use rum or brandy. The potent recipe in *The National Cookery Book* includes both brandy and rum.

Sangaree—sweetened, spiced wine served over ice—likely originated in Spain, but it was widely disseminated in the eighteenth century and was commonly consumed in the West Indies and North America. Recipes for it appear in American cookbooks regularly throughout the nineteenth century. In the late twentieth century, with fruit and fruit juice added—and under its Spanish name—*sangria* once again became popular.

Bread was a staple food in America, as it is in much of the world. *The National Cookery Book* includes fifteen bread recipes, but in the introduction the editors confess that theories of bread-making are so varied that "it would be impossible to fix upon any one receipt as the best." Hence they included only those that were "highly recommended." Of those recipes, three (pp. 166–167) were identified with Sylvester Graham, a preacher and temperance advocate who cultivated a devoted following in the 1830s. Graham was the first American to formulate a systematic dietary regimen that he believed would assuage many illnesses. Specifically, Graham believed that "stimulation led to debility." Hence, he advocated the exclusion of all stimulants, such as spices and alcohol, and the adoption of a bland, meatless diet, with an emphasis on coarsely-ground whole-wheat flour, which was called "Graham flour." During the 1830s, Sylvester Graham lectured widely, wrote books, and changed the lives of thousands of people. He died in 1851, but his ideas inspired further investigation of therapeutic diet throughout the nineteenth century.

In addition to the three recipes mentioned above, two additional recipes for "Graham Gems" appear elsewhere in the cookbook, and several other recipes specify that Graham flour be used. That so many recipes attributed to Graham appeared in *The National Cookery Book* is a testament to his continued influence.

The National Cookery Book includes a generous selection of cake recipes, divided into breakfast cakes (pp. 169–182) and dessert cakes (pp. 253–272). The former grouping includes recipes for biscuits, muffins, brioches, waffles, flannel cakes, rice cakes, and tea rolls. It includes one for "General Washington's Breakfast Cake" (p. 169), although it does not attribute the recipe to him. The latter section offers a variety of cheese cakes, coffee cakes, cookies, crullers, cup cakes, doughnuts, fruit cakes, ginger snaps, jelly cakes, jumbles, macaroons, pound cakes, rusks, short cake, sponge cakes, and wafers.

The National Cookery Book, like many other nineteenth-century household manuals, provides "Preparations for the Sick," as well as recipes for preserves, canning, and pickles. These last were particularly important during the nineteenth century, when food could not be kept chilled for long and had to be processed in some way so it would keep. Sugaring fruit in preserves, salting meat in canning, and fermenting vegetables in pickling were common ways of preserving fresh foods for future seasons. One recipe in the pickle section has a Benjamin Franklin connection: "Poke Melia—A Russian Pickle" (p. 328) was reportedly given to Benjamin Franklin on his departure from Paris in 1785 by an unnamed Russian. This recipe was likely contributed by Elizabeth Duane Gillespie.

Unusual Recipe Collections

Two unusual assortments of recipes are also found in the National Cookery Book. The first are twelve Jewish recipes scattered throughout the book. Two are for "Kugel" (pp. 24, 62–63). The first of these is a savory boiled suet pudding served in chicken soup. The second recipe actually describes *cholent*, a hearty casserole traditionally put in a communal oven on Friday night and slow-baked overnight for consumption on the Sabbath day. "Passover Soup Dumplings" (p.

24), made from pounded "biscuit" (i.e., matzo meal) are an Eastern-European Jewish tradition. According to culinary historian Mark Zanger, the first recipe for them appears in an American cookbook in 1857. The "Stewed Fish, with White Sauce for Passover of Friday Nights" (p. 40), is clearly a version of gefilte fish. The "Purim Round" (pp. 64–65) is pickled (corned) beef. "Soaked Passover Bread" (p. 116) is fried in butter to make the Passover breakfast dish commonly known as matzo *brei*. "Passover Fritters" (pp. 228–29) and "Crimslech for Passover" (pp. 238–39), are fried and baked versions of little sweet cakes spiced with cinnamon and raisins. "Queen Esther's Toast for Purim" (p. 239) is simply french toast; a similar recipe was previously published in Sarah Rutledge's *Carolina Housewife* (1847). According to Mark Zanger, this may be the first Jewish recipe in a general American cookbook.[14] "Haman's Ears for Purim Night" and "Kichlers for Purim Night" (p. 239) are little fried pastries. "Prealaters for Passover" (p. 270) are meringues, made without flour in observance of the Passover dietary laws.

Jewish recipes had been previously published in the United States. Jennie June's *American Cookery Book*, first published in 1866, included a chapter on Jewish cookery, and Mrs. Levy's *Jewish Cookery Book* was published in Philadelphia in 1871.[15] But the recipes identified as Jewish in *The National Cookery Book* did not come from previously published sources, which suggests that they had long been used in families.

The second unusual group of recipes are seven attributed to an "Oneida Squaw." The Oneida Iroquois lived west of Syracuse in central New York. Two recipes use bear as the main ingredient: "Baked Bear's Meat" (p. 141), and "Bear's Meat" (p. 141). In pre-Columbian times, bears *(Ursus Americanus)* had been numerous and their meat was an important food source. In addition to their meat, bear fat was used in Native American cookery. By 1876, bears had largely disappeared from New England. Three other recipes use fairly unfamiliar game: "Woodchuck" (pp. 141-2), "Mud Turtle" (p. 142), and "Muskrats" (p. 142). The woodchuck *(Marmota monax)* or groundhog was relatively scarce in Colonial times, but as farmland replaced forests, woodchucks multiplied, and today they are among the most common mammals in eastern North America. Their meat was commonly consumed by both Native Americans and Anglo-Americans. The mud turtle *(Kinosternon subrubrum)* is a small turtle indigenous to the eastern United States. It lives in fresh or brackish water. The muskrat *(Ondatra zibethicus)* is an aquatic rodent common throughout eastern North America; its fur, as well as its meat, were prized by Native Americans. The final two Oneida recipes (p. 142) are corn-based: "Indian Bread," small cakes composed of ground corn and beans, and "Hulled Corn" (p. 142), a method for preparing corn for eating by removing the outer shell and boiling the kernels with lye. These recipes are unusual, and do not appear in other cookbooks. Two other recipes in *The National Cookery Book* are identified as "Indian": "Sweet Corn as Prepared by the Indians" (p. 188), in which dried corn is used for making soup, and "Succotash" (p. 158), a dish of finely chopped sweet corn and beans boiled together. As noted in the recipe, Anglo-Americans added flour and butter for taste to this dish. For most present-day Americans, succotash is seen only on the Thanksgiving table—a nod to the Indians' contribution to the survival of the European settlers.

· · · · ·

How such a significant cookbook could have been overlooked by scholars and historical cooks is puzzling. There are several possible reasons for this oversight. Not many copies of *The National Cookery Book* were printed. The acidic paper and binding used for the book have not enhanced its longevity: The pages of surviving copies are usually brown and brittle, and the covers easily separate from the pages. As previously noted, *The National Cookery Book* was published by the Women's Executive Committee, which had many other responsibilities at the Exhibition. The committee was not geared up to engage in selling, promoting or marketing its book—it was simply one activity among many sponsored by the committee during a very hectic and event-filled year. No reviews or references to the cookbook have been located, and the compilers had no interest in printing additional copies or editions after the end of the Centennial Exposition.

Another problem with the history of *The National Cookery Book* is its very title, which still confuses researchers and cookbook collectors today. In 1850, Philadelphian Hannah Mary Peterson published a book with a similar title, *The National Cook Book*. During the subsequent decades this book went through at least eleven editions or printings and was still available in bookstores in 1876. Another Philadelphian, William Vollmer, had published yet another cookbook with a similar title, *The United States Cook Book*, in 1856. It, too, went through subsequent editions or printings, and it was still being sold in Philadelphia in 1876.

Other cookbooks published had in their titles the word "Centennial"—a hot word in 1876, but a word absent from the title of *The National Cookery Book*. Ella Myers' *Centennial Cook Book and General Guide* was sold in Philadelphia and other cities. It was published by the author's husband, who actively promoted its sale through extensive advertising. This cookbook was republished several times with various titles through the 1880s. *The Centennial Buckeye Cook Book*, compiled by Estelle Woods Wilcox, began as a recipe collection from the women of an Ohio church. It had remarkable staying power, going through nine major editions under various titles, including *Practical Housekeeping* and *The Dixie Cook-Book*. It eventually sold more than one million copies, becoming by far the best-selling cookbook in nineteenth-century America.[16]

Despite its partial eclipse by more aptly-titled works, *The National Cookery Book* was not forgotten. When the Bicentennial rolled around in 1976, Deborah J. Warner, curator of "The Women's Pavilion, 1876: A Centennial Exhibition," at the Smithsonian Institution, edited a 24-page booklet with some original recipes.[17] The entire book has been microfilmed by the Library of Congress and Research Publications of Woodbridge, Connecticut, and is available in some libraries. Those scholars lucky enough to locate a copy have found the recipes extremely valuable. This reprint makes one of America's greatest cookbooks available to all.

AFTERWORD

If *The National Cookery Book* reflected what America ate in 1876, the Centennial Exposition was a harbinger of the future. Many new foods and drinks were introduced—either displayed or sold—at the Exposition. As Francis A. Walker, the Chief of the Bureau of Awards, exclaimed, the Exposition was filled with ". . . barricades of hams, pyramids of canned meats and fruits, stores of pickles, sauces and jellies, assortments of coffees, teas and tobacco . . . the display of food products, animal and vegetable, at Philadelphia was enormous in quantity, and almost incomprehensible in variety. After all, it is by food we live."[18]

Although not mentioned in *The National Cookery Book*, many foods and culinary products would become American favorites within a few years. In the Horticultural Hall, a forty-acre display of tropical plants included banana trees. While bananas had been imported into the United States since the 1840s, they were known mostly to dwellers in port cities. There are no banana recipes in *The National Cookery Book*, but bananas were sold for ten cents apiece outside the exhibit and were destined to become one of America's favorite fruits.[19]

Flavored soda water is not mentioned in *The National Cookery Book*, but it was a major attraction at the Exposition. James W. Tufts and Charles Lippincott had their own building fitted with a thirty-foot soda fountain and dozens of soda dispensers ready to refresh thirsty fair-goers. They paid $20,000 for the soda concession, plus two dollars per day royalty for each soda dispenser. This totaled an estimated $52,000—an astronomical sum in 1876. But it was a worthy investment: Temperance supporters had banned the sale of hard liquor at the Centennial and the summer of 1876 was an extremely hot one. The counters were crowded throughout the run of the Exposition. After the Exposition closed, Tufts and Lippincott made a fortune selling soda fountains to drug stores around the nation. With the soda fountains went serving counters, which soon became social gathering places in towns throughout America.[20]

California wines were served at a small California restaurant at the Centennial Exposition. One observer reported that

California wine had not yet succeeded in matching the light, fragrant product of Burgundy, or of the Bordeaux region.[21] California vintners made a major promotional effort at the 1893 Columbian Exposition in Chicago, which sparked considerable attention, but California wines did not begin to compete with French wines until long after World War II.

Commercial snack foods are conspicuous by their absence in *The National Cookery Book*. Yet popcorn and peanuts were highly visible at the Exposition. Both had been sold on the streets of American cities and in trains since early in the nineteenth century, and both were sold by vendors at the Exposition. Red and white popcorn balls were offered at a booth in Machinery Hall, and it "was crowded all day, and thus showed the attractiveness of the exhibitor's peculiar wares and machinery." I. L. Baker, who sponsored the exhibit, had paid the steep price of $8,000 for the exclusive popcorn concession throughout the grounds. Baker set up several of his "curious and attractive furnaces and selling booths" and sold popcorn for five cents a bag.[22] Today it is one of the most popular salty snacks in the United States.

The National Cookery Book makes no mention of canned food. Commercial canning had been underway in America since the 1820s, but it had not taken off until the Civil War, when government contracts spurred development of canneries in Northern states. The manufacturing of canned goods made solid progress after the Civil War, but its heyday was begun in the 1880s and following decades, when millions of canned goods were manufactured. Many canners were present at the Exposition, and most received awards for their products. One small Camden, New Jersey, canner that received an award was the Joseph Campbell Preserve Company (later renamed The Campbell Soup Company). Although 12,000 awards were given out at the Exposition, Campbell proudly cited its award for years.[23]

The Vienna Bakery was one of the most popular food establishments at the Exposition. In 1873, Eben Norton Horsford, one of the founders of the Rumford Chemical Works in Providence, Rhode Island, was appointed a member of the United States Scientific Commission held in Vienna. Horsford concluded that the bread made in Vienna was superior to that made in America, and published his findings in a government publication.[24] This led to the inclusion of a Vienna Bakery at the Centennial Exposition. The concession for the bakery was acquired by a small company, Gaff, Fleischmann & Co., which manufactured "German Pressed Yeast." The company had been launched in 1868 by Charles and Maximilian Fleischmann, immigrants from Austro-Hungary, and Cincinnati brewer and yeast maker James F. Gaff. They intended to set up Vienna Bakeries in New York and Philadelphia after the close of the Exposition. Yet their building was "crowded to repletion during every day of the Exhibition, hundreds frequently waiting for the opportunities to obtain a seat at one of the marble-top tables, and a chance at the limited but most excellent bill of fare."[25] Fleischmann bought out Gaff, and changed the name to Fleischmann Company, which had a major influence on American bread making during the late nineteenth and early twentieth centuries.

Elizabeth Duane Gillespie's autobiography, *A Book of Remembrance* (1901), was completed a few months before she died. In it she claimed *The National Cookery Book* still found favor with old-timers, and she was probably right.[26] Few of the recipes that appear in *The National Cookery Book* survived into the twentieth century. The main reasons for this were three massive shifts that rocked the United States during the second half of the nineteenth century. The first two were demographic: an internal migration from rural areas to urban centers, and a massive immigration into American cities by newcomers from Southern and Eastern Europe. These immigrants added new ingredients and new cooking styles to America's proverbial stew pot, although these changes were not apparent until decades later. The third big change was the American industrial revolution, which provided employment for those arriving in American cities and created vast quantities of goods to purchase. These shifts affected every aspect of American life, especially food production, distribution, and consumption.

Throughout the nineteenth century, most Americans grew a substantial portion of their own food on farms or in garden plots.

Small general stores catered to those who were not self-sufficient or who desired luxuries not grown or raised in the local area. Food was mainly sold as generic products measured out from unmarked barrels, sacks, and jars. This changed as food production was industrialized. Food processors and manufacturers grew rapidly after the Philadelphia Exposition as massive agricultural surpluses flooded the market and technology lowered the cost of production. The result was the rise of large food manufacturers, who needed to persuade Americans of the superiority of branded products over generic groceries. To accomplish this, food companies began advertising their products regionally and nationally through newspapers and magazines, and locally via circulars, billboards, and in-store promotions. Food advertising became a major source of American opinion and action regarding what, when, and how to eat.

While *The National Cookery Book* is valuable from an historical standpoint, it also offers wonderful recipes that can be re-created today by anyone willing to include some trial and error in the cooking process to allow for changes wrought in ingredients and kitchen technology by the passage of more than a century. Enjoy!

ACKNOWLEDGMENTS

Many thanks for Barbara Kuck, director of the Culinary Archives and Museum at Johnson & Wales University, Providence, Rhode Island, for providing a copy of *The National Cookery Book* for this reprint. Many thanks also to Mark Zanger, who offered advice about the Jewish and Florida recipes, and Bonnie Slotnick for her editing of, and comments on, this introduction.

ABOUT ANDREW F. SMITH

Andrew F. Smith is the author or editor of eight books on food history. He teaches culinary history at the New School University, and currently serves as the general editor of the University of Illinois Press's Food Series and the editor-in-chief of the *Oxford Encyclopedia on Food and Drink in America*.

END NOTES

1. Mrs. E.D. Gillespie, *A Book of Remembrance* (Philadelphia and London: J. B. Lippincott Company, 1901), 271–2,

2. Frank Norton, ed., *Frank Leslie's Historical Register of the United States Centennial Exposition, 1876* (New York: Frank Leslie's Publishing House, 1877), 268; Library Company of Philadelphia,

3. J.S. Ingram, *The Centennial Exposition* (Philadelphia: Hubbard Bros., 1876), 112, 116; Frank Norton, ed., *Frank Leslie's Historical Register of the United States Centennial Exposition, 1876* (New York: Frank Leslie's Publishing House, 1877), 268.

4. Frank Norton, ed., *Frank Leslie's Historical Register of the United States Centennial Exposition, 1876* (New York: Frank Leslie's Publishing House, 1877), 268.

5. Mrs. E. D. Gillespie, *A Book of Remembrance* (Philadelphia and London: J. B. Lippincott Company, 1901), 372.

6. See Margaret Cook, *America's Charitable Cooks: A Bibliography of Fund-Raising Cook Books Published in the United States (1861–1915)* (Kent, Ohio: np, 1971); Maria J. Moss, *A Poetical Cook-Book* (Philadelphia: Caxton Press of C. Sherman, Son & Co., 1864). The dedication in Maria J. Moss's *A Poetical Cook-Book* reads: "When I wrote the following pages, some years back at Oak Lodge, as a pastime, I did not think it would be of service to my fellow-creatures, for our suffering soldiers, the sick, wounded, and needy, who have so nobly fought our country's cause, to maintain the flag of our great Republic, and to prove among Nations that a Free republic is not a myth. With these few words I dedicate this book to the Sanitary Fair to be held in Philadelphia, June, 1864."

7. Mrs. E. D. Gillespie, *A Book of Remembrance* (Philadelphia and London: J. B. Lippincott Company, 1901), 294–295.

8. Andrew F. Smith, "In Praise of Maize: The Rise and Fall of Corny Poetry," in Harlan Walker, ed., *Food in the Arts, Proceedings of the Oxford Symposium on Food and Cookery 1998* (Devon, United Kingdom: Prospect Books, 1999), 194–205.

9. Richard J. Hooker, *A History of Food and Drink in America* (Indianapolis & New York: Bobbs-Merrill, 1981), 122.

10. [Lafcadio Hearn], *La Cuisine Creole; A Collection of Culinary Recipes from Leading Chefs and Noted Creole Housewives, Who Have Made New Orleans Famous for its Cuisine* (New York: Will H. Coleman, 1885), 18–22; *American Farmer* 12 (April 16, 1830): 39; *New England Farmer* 8 (May 21, 1830): 352; *New England Farmer* 9 (September 24, 1830): 24; [Sarah Rutledge], *The Carolina Housewife* (Charleston: W. R. Babcock & Co., 1847), 43.

11. Bernard McMahon, *The American Gardner's Calendar; Adapted to the Climates and Seasons of the United States* (Philadelphia: Printed by B. Graves for the Author, 1806), 581.

12. *The Boston Evening Post*, September 23, 1751, as cited in Richard J. Hooker, *The Book of Chowder* (Boston: The Harvard Common Press, 1978), 27; Pierre Blot, *Hand-Book of Practical Cookery* (New York: D. Appleton and Co., 1867), 159–160. I am indebted to Karen Hess who brought this reference to my attention.

13. For more information about ketchup, see Andrew F. Smith, *Pure Ketchup: The History of America's National Condiment* (Columbia: The University of South Carolina Press, 1996).

14. Mark H. Zanger, *The American Ethnic Cookbook for Students* (Phoenix, Arizona: Oryx Press, 2001).

15. J. C. Croly, *Jennie June's American Cookery Book* ((New York, American News Co., 1866); Esther Levy, *Mrs. Esther Levy's Jewish Cookery Book* (Philadelphia: W. S. Turner, 1871). Levy's cookbook was reprinted by Applewood Books in 1988.

16. Estelle Woods Wilcox, comp., *Centennial Buckeye Cook Book*. Reprint. Introduction and Appendices by Andrew F. Smith (Columbus: Ohio State University Press, 2000).

17. Deborah Jean Warner, ed., *The National Cookery Book: Compiled from Original Receipts, for the Women's Centennial Committees of the International Exhibition of 1876* (Washington, D.C.: Legado Press, 1976).

18. Francis A. Walker, *World's Fair Philadelphia, 1876. A Critical Account* (Chicago: A. S. Barnes, 1878), 56.

19. Frank Norton, ed., *Frank Leslie's Historical Register of the United States Centennial Exposition, 1876* (New York: Frank Leslie's Publishing House, 1877), 82; *Visitors Guide to the Centennial Exhibition and Philadelphia 1876* (Philadelphia: J. B. Lippincott & Co., 1875), 16; Frank Norton, ed. *Frank Leslie's Historical Register of the United States Centennial Exposition, 1876* (New York: Frank Leslie's Publishing House, 1877), 219; Richard J. Hooker, *Food and Drink in America: A History* (Indianapolis/New York: Bobbs-Merrill Company, Inc., 1981), 232; Virginia Scott Jenkins, *The Fruit with A-Peel: The Impact of the Importation of Bananas on American Culture* (Washington, D.C.: Smithsonian Institution Press, 2000).

20. J. S. Ingram, *The Centennial Exposition* (Philadelphia: Hubbard Bros., 1876), 287–291; "Centennial Concession, or Extortion?" *Manufacturer and Builder* 8 (March 1876): 53; John J. Riley, *A History of the American Soft Drink Industry, Bottled Carbonated Beverages 1807–1957* (Washington, D.C.: American Bottlers of Carbonated Beverages, 1958), 10–11, 60–61; J. H. Snively, "Soda-Water," *Harper's New Monthly Magazine* 45 (August 1872): 341–6; "Druggist Circular," as in *Confectioner's Gazette* 34 (August 10, 1913): 34, 36–37; Richard J. Hooker, *Food and Drink in America: A History* (Indianapolis/New York: Bobbs-Merrill Company, Inc., 1981), 273–74.

21. Ben Beverly, *What Ben Beverly Saw at the Great Exposition* (Chicago: Centennial Publishing Co., 1876), 139–140; Donald G. Mitchell, "In and about the Fair," *Scribner's Monthly* 13 (November 1876): 117.

22. J. S. Ingram, *Centennial Exposition* (Philadelphia: Hubbard Bros., 1876), 758; *Frank Leslie's Illustrated Newspaper* 153 (November 18, 1876): 179, 186; *Frank Leslie's Illustrated Historical Register of the Exposition 1876* (New York: Frank Leslie's Publishing House, 1877), 56, 210, 306. For more information about popcorn, see Andrew F. Smith, *Popped Culture: A Social History of Popcorn in America* (Columbia: University of South Carolina Press, 2000).

23. Francis A. Walker, ed., *International Exhibition, 1876; Reports & Awards; Groups 1–36;* edited by (Philadelphia: Lippincott, 1878). For more information about canning and the Campbell Soup Company, see Andrew F. Smith,

Souper Tomatoes: The Story of America's Favorite Food (New Brunswick: Rutgers University Press, 2000).

24. Eben Norton Horsford, *Report on Vienna Bread* (Washington: Government Printing Office, 1875).

25. Frank Norton, ed., *Frank Leslie's Historical Register of the United States Centennial Exposition, 1876* (New York: Frank Leslie's Publishing House, 1877), 213.

26. Mrs. E. D. Gillespie, *A Book of Remembrance* (Philadelphia and London: J. B. Lippincott Company, 1901), 294.

THIS VOLUME

IS

DEDICATED

TO THE WOMEN OF AMERICA,

BY THE

WOMEN'S COMMITTEES

OF THE

CENTENNIAL INTERNATIONAL EXHIBITION

OF

1876.

CONTENTS.

PREFACE.

THE Women's Centennial Committees of the International Exhibition of 1876 respectfully offer this volume to their countrywomen, and solicit their patronage.

Among the many enterprises planned by the committees to carry out the objects of their organization, was a National Cookery Book. It was thought proper in a department exclusively devoted to "women's work," that cookery—an art which has been consigned so largely to her—should not be forgotten. It was also believed that it would not be thought presumptuous to endeavor to afford the visitors from abroad, who might honor the Exhibition by their presence, an opportunity of judging of our progress in this art, and also of the resources of our country.

"Have you no National Dishes?" is a question that has been asked by foreigners travelling in this country.

The Committees believe that the answer to this question may be found in their unpretending book.

Hotels, with their French cooks and gregarious customs, are not the true exponents of the inner life of a people!

To carry out their plan in the most efficient manner, a printed circular was forwarded to all the corresponding committees in every State and Territory of the Union, asking for contributions to this object. The response has been gratifying, and the result is here given to the reader.

It would be impossible to thank individually each contributor who has kindly aided in this work. From the most remote as well as from the nearest States, the same desire to aid has been shown, the same lively sympathy exhibited. To each and all the cordial thanks of the Committees are tendered.

The size of the book has necessarily limited the number of receipts accepted; many were duplicates, and a large number came too late.

INTRODUCTION.

GOOD cooking is necessary for the enjoyment of one of the great pleasures of life. It enables us to make the best use of the endless variety provided by Providence for our gratification and sustenance. It promotes health, contentment and kindly feeling.

The man who returns hungry and weary to his home, to ejaculate between his teeth the old proverb about who sends the victuals and who the cook, is not in a contented state of mind, nor are his listeners; but he who sits at a table where knowledge and skill have combined to make even the simplest fare wholesome and acceptable, is unconsciously soothed and calmed. The frets and cares of daily life fade before the comforts of home, and lend to it an additional charm. Insensibly he is made happier—the influences of a well-ordered household render him complacent.

This man finds himself able to give an impromptu invitation to a friend to dine with him, without the gloomy dread upon his mind that the "pot luck" may prove anything but luck.

On the other hand, the smiling appreciation which daily
rewards her whose care and attention has made all this so
pleasant for him, serves in its turn to brighten the golden links
that bind a household together.

In the matter of health, there can be but one opinion. Food
that is tough, indigestible, crude or half burnt, must be unwholesome.

In a country like ours, where generous living is universal, it
is of great importance that the food should be properly prepared, and that the simplest housewife should know the broad
principles necessary to that end.

Economy, applied to cooking, is one of the offspring of
knowledge. On this point Americans have much to learn.
There is no country in the world where there is so much waste.
This arises, in great measure, from the habits which have de-
scended to us from a period when food was so cheap and plenty
that "it was not worth while to save." That which is utilized
and made into wholesome dishes in other lands, was, and still
is, too often thrown away with the garbage. The knowledge
and skill which can turn to account cold meats, vegetables,
and dessert left from yesterday's dinner, stale bread, &c., &c.,
are comparatively little known. All intelligent foreigners
who have seen our home life observe this.

The most fruitful source of waste in this country comes from
the incompetence of our servants. Painstaking and time are
required to plan and carry out the details of economy, intelligence and a willing mind to guide; but these are too often
wanting. To destroy or throw away that which would help
out to-morrow's dinner, is easier than to take the trouble of
making it useful. The "little dish" which, if properly pre-

pared, would have been appetizing, and all sufficient in its place, has been left unmade, wasted or destroyed, and something fresh must be substituted. This evil bears heavily upon the housewife, but there is no help for it. She must submit to her fate, if she will not make the sacrifice of seeing more of her kitchen than suits her taste.

A housekeeper should visit her larder every morning. If she asks for information, she will most probably be told that there is nothing fit for use. If she examines for herself, her intelligence, and even a very little knowledge of cooking, will enable her to see at once that the elements of two or three " little dishes " are before her.

Bread need never be wasted in a family. Cut into small pieces and dried, it may be pounded, sifted, and put away, in a dry place, for daily use.

Fat or drippings should always be saved. Do not allow it, as is too often the case, to be skimmed into a general "fat crock," where it is left to spoil, but keep each kind separate. This is easily done by using a little system. Boil the fat of each day, strain it, and pour it into a bowl of hot water. Set it away to cool. The next day a cake of pure drippings will be found. Scrape the under surface free from sediment, wipe it dry, and set it away for future use. Or, have little earthen cups or bowls for the purpose, and make them hot on the range. Put the cake of fat into a cup of the proper size ; it will melt and take form, and you will, by doing this, keep a supply of drippings, moulded in small forms, and can select the kind and size you require.

This applies to beef and veal only. Mutton fat, or tallow, is fit only for the soap pot.

Care must be taken in using ham to flavor meats, soups, &c., that the outside is not made use of—it is apt to impart a smoky flavor.

Wine, in cooking, should be added last; heat causes the fine flavor to fly off.

Modern cooks are greatly benefited by the numerous little machines and implements invented for kitchen use, to be found in the kitchen-furnishing establishments in our large cities. Much of the old laborious work of chopping, sifting, stoning, paring, beating, &c., may now be done with magic celerity and in great perfection by their aid. Among them are the various "water baths," commonly called "Farina Boilers," now indispensable in our kitchens. In all preparations of milk, and in those in which eggs are an ingredient, a water bath should always be used. It is difficult to boil milk in any other way without scorching it; eggs are also rendered safe from curdling.

NATIONAL COOKERY BOOK.

SOUPS.

THE best soups are made from fresh beef or veal. Very good soup, however, may be made from the scraps and bones of one or both of these meats when left from the day before.

Mutton should not be used with other meats. It makes a good soup by itself for those who are fond of mutton, but it does not mix well.

Soup meat is never selected from the choicer parts of the animal. In beef the shin is commonly used. Its flavor differs a little from that of the other pieces; if preferred, the butcher can supply other cuts suitable for the purpose.

In boiling fresh beef intended for "bouilli," the water should be reserved for soup. If the piece is large, the liquor reduced by boiling will be strong enough. If it is small, beef or veal bones boiled with it will be necessary.

Soup meat should always be boiled the day before the soup is needed, that the fat congealed on the top may be removed. Nothing can be more inelegant than grease swimming on soup. It is an evidence of coarse and careless cooking.

Meat for soup should be put on the fire in cold water, in order more thoroughly to extract the juices. It should boil till the bones fall apart and the meat is exhausted. If the liquor

2   (17)

diminishes very fast, fill it up with boiling water, always keeping the meat covered with the water; when done, strain it through a sieve and set it away to cool for use.

For vegetable or *Julienne* soup, stock must be used that has had no vegetables boiled in it. In this case the vegetables must be boiled, cut into little slips and added to the stock, to be used for the day's soup, adding the water, also, in which they were boiled.

Spices are seldom used in soup delicately made, except in the cases of calves'-head, turtle, and a few other rich dark soups. Dried herbs also are used only in calves'-head soup and pepper-pot. Seasoning must depend upon the judgment of the cook or the taste of the family. A cook should always remember that salt and pepper may be added if required, and that there is no remedy when there is an excess of either.

When wine is required in soup, add it only a short time before serving.

If the stock for a clear soup is too pale, add a little browned sugar; this not only improves the appearance, but it gives a mellow flavor that is greatly prized in vermicelli and vegetable soups.

When, in preparing for a party, a large number of turkeys and chickens have been boiled for "chicken salad," the water in which they were cooked should be set aside. When the salad is made, all the bones and fragments not used should be thrown into this water,—omitting the skin,—more water added, and the whole boiled till exhausted. Strain it and set it away to cool. When cold, remove the fat from the top, and you have the stock for chicken soup, adding rice, barley, vermicelli, or sippets of toast.

Barley requires many hours to boil, and should always be put in water to soak all night before using it. Vermicelli and other Italian pastes require about fifteen minutes to cook. The pastes made in the United States need a longer time. The hard-grained wheat used in Italy for this purpose differs from our own. All the various forms of this article are made from the same paste. The yellow vermicelli differs only in having saffron as an ingredient.

For making soup stock in cool weather to last for many days, use the shin of beef, beef bones, and a small knuckle or shoulder of veal. Boil these in plenty of water for half a day until the meat is exhausted. Strain it and put it away to cool. The next day remove the fat, and for each day's use take as much of the jelly for the basis of the soup as may be required.

Some persons prefer to boil the vegetables with the meat when first put on to cook. This is done when their flavor only is required. It is best, perhaps, always to boil the onions thus, as they dissolve entirely, and leave only a mild, though essential, flavor.

The vegetables should be carrots, onions, a little fresh parsley, a few lettuce leaves, and a little celery, not enough of the last to make the flavor predominate. In using celery seed, be careful; it is very strong, and a very little will be sufficient to give that "suspicion," as the French call it, that alone is necessary. One great art in soup making is not to suffer any one flavor to override the others. Turnips and cabbage are too strong for stock, and are only good in rather coarse soups.

For soups made from stock, the only spice admissible is a small quantity of mace. The use of nutmeg in any soup or meat dish is a mistake. It belongs properly only to cake and desserts.

When the vegetables are boiled and exhausted with the meat, they are strained off with it and rejected. When it is cold and the fat removed, the stock is ready.

STOCK FOR SOUP.

Boil the day before you want to use it a shin of beef and as many beef bones as your pot will hold. Cover them with water, and let boil till the meat falls from the bones. Strain it and set it away to cool. The next day remove all the fat from the top, and you will find it a stiff jelly, which will serve for stock for several days. For a family of six, a quart of the stock will be enough for dinner. Boil in a large saucepan two or three carrots, a good-sized onion, one turnip, a sprig of celery and a sprig of green parsley. Let them boil till quite soft. An hour before dinner put the stock on the fire to cook; add a quart of water, a blade of mace, and pepper and salt to taste. Mash the vegetables when soft, in the water they have been boiled in, and strain this water into the soup. About twenty minutes before dinner throw in the vermicelli.

If preferred, the vegetables may be put on at first with the meat, obtaining their flavor thus, and straining them off when put aside to cool. This is well if you require stock for only this kind of soup. If you want a vegetable soup, you must boil your vegetables as above, but not so soft. Cut them up in little pieces about an inch long and scarcely thicker than a straw, and throw them into the pot when half done. This is *Julienne* soup. If only a clear soup is wanted the vegetables must be boiled alone and not too soft, the water only in which they have been boiled added to flavor it. If you wish your soup very clear, use the white of an egg to clear it as for jelly.

BEEF SOUP.

A gallon of water to four pounds of beef. It should boil at least six hours; put the meat into cold water with a little salt. Let it boil slowly but steadily, and skim it well. When no more fat rises to the top, add six potatoes, some pieces of celery, three cloves, a tablespoonful of cayenne pepper and salt mixed, some parsley, some pieces of sweet potato and three dozen boiled chestnuts.

SHIN OF BEEF SOUP.

Boil a shin of beef for several hours, till the meat falls from the bones. Remove the bones and meat and set away to cool. Next morning take the fat from the top, put it on the fire and add a small cabbage, cut fine, half a dozen carrots, cut small, four or five turnips, two or three potatoes, and a couple of onions. If tomatoes are in season, add three or four. Season with thyme, parsley, pepper, salt, allspice and a little mace. When the vegetables are well boiled, strain off the liquor through a colander, mash the vegetables till they are a smooth pulp, and return them to the soup. If you like small pieces of the meat in the soup, they can be put in the day the soup is required. By using beef bones to boil with the shin you make the soup richer, in which case do not boil the shin so much, but set it away to become cold; the next day, by making a rich bread stuffing with onions and spices, you can make a good baked meat dish of the shin meat, using some of the soup to moisten it, and covering it with bread crumbs before setting it in the oven. If you have on hand some pork or ham fat, place some slices on the top with the bread crumbs.

CALVES'-HEAD SOUP.

The calf's head must be what is usually called a "dressed head;" that is, it must have the skin on, the hair only having been removed. Have it split down the middle by the butcher. Wash it well, and take out the eyes. Then put it on to boil in about two gallons of water. Let it boil slowly until the bones are ready to fall out. Then take it from the fire, take out the bones and gristle, skin the tongue, and set the whole away to cool. The next morning remove all the fat from the top of the liquor, cut up all the head into spoon pieces, and put them and the liquor into a soup pot over the fire, with two small onions, a small teaspoonful of sweet marjoram, a little powdered cloves and allspice, salt, black and cayenne pepper, and a large tea-spoonful of sugar. Let the soup simmer slowly for several hours, adding to it little dumplings made of shortened dough and a little thickening of flour and butter, mixed. If you like, before putting the meat into the liquor again, you can fry the pieces a rich brown and add them. If you wish force meat balls, save a little of the brains to chop up with any cold meat you may have, and add a little pork fat or ham to flavor them; bind them together with egg and flour, and fry them in lard. If you like wine in this soup, do not add it until it is in the tureen, as it loses its fine flavor in cooking. Stir it well while adding the wine. A calf's head will make soup enough for two or three days, if the weather is cold enough to keep it. If you wish the soup very rich, boil from two to four calves' feet with the head.

PEPPER POT.

Take a knuckle of veal and from three to five pounds of tripe—half honey-comb and half leaf. Boil them all day in about two gallons of water. If the water wastes a great deal, add more. Strain off the liquor and set it away till next day; it will form a jelly, and the fat on the top must be carefully removed. Set the jellied liquor on the fire in the soup pot; add three or four small onions, a few potatoes, and a bunch of dried sweet herbs. Cut the tripe into small squares; add a dozen cloves and two dozen pepper-corns, some cayenne pepper and salt, and, if you like the flavor, a little fresh celery. Then take about a handful of the glutinous and tender parts of the boiled veal, half this quantity of beef suet, and a pair of sweetbreads; chop all together and mix with an egg or two. Season them with sweet herbs, pepper and salt; roll them in flour and fry them a light brown. If you have any cold boiled pork, add some to the balls. Taste the soup, and if it requires more seasoning, add it. Throw in the balls just before serving.

COLD TURKEY SOUP.

Take the remains of a turkey left from dinner, with the stuffing, gravy, &c. Crack the bones and let them boil in about two quarts of water. Add two spoonfuls of butter, a few sprigs of celery, and black and cayenne pepper and salt. Remove all the turkey bones, and just before serving throw in three pints of oysters. Omit the oysters if you choose, but be careful when putting on the turkey to remove all the skin, as it is apt to impart a strong oily flavor to the soup.

OKRA GUMBO SOUP.

Put about three quarts of ripe tomatoes into a stew pan ; cover them with water and set them on the fire. When done through, take them out of the water and remove the skin and cores. Return the tomatoes to the water and let it simmer on the fire, adding an onion. Fry a chicken, which has been cut up in pieces of convenient size for " helping," sprinkling it well with flour, and adding to it okras, sliced. When the chicken and okra are well done, place in the pan with the stewing tomatoes, and let all cook together, carefully skimming off the grease that rises ; add sufficient sugar to the soup to give it a pleasant flavor, and salt and pepper enough to season it. To be eaten with boiled rice.

SASSAFRAS GUMBO SOUP.

Boil one or two chickens in as much water as you will require for your soup. Cut them first in small pieces, convenient for helping. Let them cook till they nearly fall to pieces. Add minced onion, salt, and black and red pepper. To a quart of soup allow a half tablespoonful of powdered sassafras leaves. Oysters added will make a delicious oyster gumbo. To be eaten with boiled rice.

NEW ORLEANS GUMBO SOUP.

Fry chicken or turkey cut up in pieces, with slices of bacon and an onion. Then place them in the soup kettle ; cover them with water ; add the seasoning according to taste, and let it boil slowly. Just before serving the soup, add the "fillet," which is simply pulverized sassafras leaves, or, if you prefer, okra pods, which also give the mucilaginous character so much prized in this soup. Serve it with boiled rice.

Kugel for Soup.

Soak a loaf of stale bread without the crust. Strain off the water, and season it with pepper, salt and ginger. Add three quarters of a pound of suet, well shredded and chopped, and six eggs beaten light. Make a clear beef soup, flavored with onions, parsley and salt. Place the above mixture in a floured bag; tie it tight and put it in the soup. When the soup is done, turn out the kugel into the tureen whole, and pour the soup over it.

Passover Soup Dumplings.

Pound the biscuit fine; season it with pepper, salt and ginger, and scald it with boiling water. Then melt a quarter of a pound of fat and throw over it. Let it get cold; then add eight eggs, beaten light, and make it into dumplings. Throw them into the soup about fifteen minutes before it is served.

Michigan Pea Soup (Without Meat).

Three pints of shelled peas, one small onion, minced. Put a tablespoonful of butter into the soup pot, and when it is boiling hot add the peas and onion. Stir them until they become a bright green. Add five quarts of water, and let it boil till the peas are tender. Add three tablespoonfuls of flour, mixed in a quart of milk. Draw the soup pot from the fire, and when it stops boiling put in the yolk of an egg, beaten in a tablespoonful of milk. Salt and pepper it to your taste. Do not boil it after the egg is in.

Green Pea Soup (Without Meat).

Boil three quarts of shelled peas in six quarts of water. When quite soft, mash them through a sieve or colander. By pouring some of the water over them, the pulp will pass and leave the skins behind. Return the pulp to the water in which it was boiled and set it again on the fire. Add a head of lettuce, chopped fine, and salt and pepper. Thicken the soup with two or three ounces of butter, mixed smoothly with flour. Half an hour before the soup is served, add a pint of young peas, and let them boil till soft. The peas from which the pulp is extracted should be large old peas. This soup requires five hours to make. Little sippets of toasted bread may be served with it. The soup should be about as thick as a very rich cream. Salt, it and use plenty of black pepper. It is a delicious soup.

WINTER PEA SOUP.

Boil one pint of split peas in three quarts of water till quite soft. Then add half a pound of beef and a slice of bacon, with a handful of spinach, a few cloves, a little mace, pepper and salt. Let all stew for two hours longer; strain and serve, with small dice of fried toast on a separate dish.

BEAN SOUP.

Take one pint of dried beans and half a pound of salt pork. Put them into four quarts of cold water, and boil slowly for four hours; then strain them through a colander till all but the skins have passed through. Season with pepper and salt. Throw away the skins, return the soup and pork to the pot, and boil another hour.

BLACK BEAN SOUP.

Soak three teacupfuls of beans in a gallon of warm water for four hours. Then put them on to boil in the same water, with a pound and a half of beef. Let it boil till the beans are soft enough to mash through a colander. Return the beef to the liquid with the pulp of the beans, adding an onion, chopped fine, a little parsley, and a few cloves. This soup should be put on five hours before dinner. Tomatoes are a great improvement. If you have none, use tomato ketchup. Before serving, stir in a little butter. A ham bone is sometimes boiled in it for an hour. Avoid putting in any portions of the ham that may impart a smoky flavor.

GROUND-NUT SOUP.

Have parched three pints of shelled ground-nuts, and remove the skin; then pound them to a smooth paste, adding salt to taste. Then mix in a large bowl, very gradually, the paste, in about two quarts of boiling water, and season it with black and cayenne pepper. Allow it to simmer until it thickens.

You may add one quart of oysters just before serving, and one saltspoonful of celery seed.

TOMATO SOUP.

Boil a small quantity of meat, with some cabbage, parsley, celery, onion, salt, pepper and allspice. When well boiled add one dozen tomatoes, cut in pieces, and thicken with butter, rolled in flour. Then strain through a colander and serve, with small squares of bread fried in butter on a separate dish.

TOMATO SOUP.

One can of tomatoes, or twelve large fresh ones. Skin and boil them in one quart of boiling water until very tender; then add half a teaspoonful of soda. When effervescence ceases, pour it into the tureen, and add one quart of milk, thickened with flour or bread crumbs, and a small piece of butter. Season with salt and cayenne.

ARTICHOKE SOUP.

Boil very soft, and peel one quart of artichokes, and drain and squeeze them through a colander. Mix together one tablespoonful of butter and one of flour, and add to this one quart of good clear broth, made of beef, veal or chicken. Let the mixture come slowly to a boil; then add one quart of fresh milk and the artichokes, and let all boil up once, stirring constantly to prevent curdling or burning.

CORN SOUP (FOR LENT).

Three pints of water to each quart of young corn, freshly cut from the cob. When tender, add two ounces of sweet butter, mixed with one tablespoonful of flour, and let all boil ten or fifteen minutes longer. Just before taking up the soup, add an egg, well beaten, with salt, pepper and half a pint of milk.

EGG SOUP (FOR LENT).

Make a rich custard; instead of sweetening it, season it with salt, pepper and savory herbs. To every quart add a piece of butter as large as a walnut.

BARLEY SOUP.

Three quarters of a pound of barley, well picked and washed, and soaked all night in cold water; a gallon and a half of water to eight or ten pounds of beef. Put it on early, and when thoroughly boiled and skimmed, take it off the hottest part of the fire and let it stand where it will simmer gently till done. Season it with salt and pepper, and if you like you may add tomatoes or tomato ketchup.

SOFT SHELL TURTLE SOUP.

The turtle should be carefully killed and cut up, in order that it may taste perfectly sweet, and also to save the eggs. Cover the meat with water, and boil it until the skin comes off and the bones fall out. Then take the meat out and chop it fine with onions, rejecting the undesirable parts. Strain the soup and return it with the meat to the pot, with as much cold water as will make the quantity of soup desired. Add a quarter of a pound of butter, mixed with enough flour to keep it from oiling, and six eggs. Tie up in a piece of thin muslin a few cloves, allspice and a little mace, and add them. Skim the soup until the scum ceases to rise. The longer it boils the better it will be. Just before serving, slice three lemons into it, and add half a tumbler of claret and half a tumbler of sherry wine. Reserve some of the turtle meat when boiled, for force meat balls, which should have beef added to them. Throw these in when it is served.

New Bedford Oyster Soup.

In one quart of milk boil one head of celery and a small onion, cut in pieces. After these have boiled for twenty minutes, add half a teacupful of pounded crackers, half a cupful of butter, a teaspoonful of Worcestershire sauce, and a very little cayenne pepper. Just before serving, put in the oysters and let them boil up once; the soup will then be ready to serve. It should be made in a farina kettle, to prevent the possibility of its burning or of the milk curdling.

Oyster Soup.

Strain the liquor from two quarts of oysters. Put on the liquor to boil with one quart of water. Thicken two table-spoonfuls of butter with flour, well rubbed in; stir it in the liquid smoothly, adding salt, black and cayenne pepper to taste, and a blade of mace. Skim it, and then put in one pint of sweet cream and the same of milk. Let all boil, but not too long, lest the milk should curdle. About twenty minutes before serving throw in the oysters, and cook them till the fins shrivel. If you like the flavor, throw in a sprig of celery.

Baltimore Oyster Soup.

Two quarts of oysters; three pints of milk; three ounces of butter; one and a half ounces of flour; two stalks of celery, chopped; pepper and salt to taste. Strip the oysters by drawing them carefully through the thumb and fingers, dipping the fingers frequently into a basin of cold water. Lay them in a dish. Strain the liquor through a hair sieve or thin muslin and put it over the fire to boil, being careful not to burn it. At the same time put the milk into a vessel over a pot of boiling water, or in a farina boiler, allowing it to boil from the steam. Mix to a smooth paste the butter and flour, and as much seasoning as you like; when quite smooth, thin it with some of the hot milk. When the milk boils, pour in this thickening, and stir until the milk begins to thicken; then add the oyster liquor, and when all comes to a brisk boil add the oysters and celery. When the oysters are well curled on the edges and look plump, serve it in a hot tureen. Eat it, if you like, with tomato soy and crisped crackers. Ordinary oyster soup is made without celery, and seasoned with mace and cayenne.

Clam Soup.

To every pint of clams and their juice add three pints of water. Put them into the soup pot with a knuckle of veal. When these are well boiled, add a bunch of sweet herbs, thyme, parsley and marjoram, tied well together, so that they can be removed before serving. This soup will require six or eight hours, and must be well skimmed. If convenient, it would be better to boil the veal the day before, so as to remove the fat when cold. About an hour before serving stir in a quarter of a pound of butter, well mixed with flour and some cayenne pepper. When you serve it, stir in half a pint of white wine.

Clam Soup.

Cut up fine twenty-five large clams; add clams and juice to two and a half quarts of water; add half an onion and a large tablespoonful of flour, rubbed in two tablespoonfuls of butter, and let all boil for fifteen minutes; then pour it into the tureen and stir in the yolks of three eggs, beaten in a pint of milk, and serve. Season with salt and pepper.

CLAM CHOWDER.

One quart of clams; eight potatoes; eight onions; one table-spoonful of sweet marjoram; the same of summer savory; half a teaspoonful of cloves; two tablespoonfuls of sugar; salt and pepper to taste; half a dozen slices of salt pork; two quarts of water. Boil the onions forty-five minutes; then the potatoes and then the raw clams. Soak three quarters of a pound of pilot bread and throw it in before serving.

MISSISSIPPI CRAB SOUP.

Boil from three to four pounds of beef or fowls five hours, together with onions, carrots, parsley, three or four tomatoes, and a little spice. Strain the soup and add to it half a dozen crabs, chopped fine, and salt and pepper to taste.

CRAB SOUP.

Pick one dozen of crabs with great care. Season them with salt and red pepper to your taste. Put two quarts of new milk into a porcelain kettle and let it come to a boil; then add a quarter of a pound of butter, rubbed smoothly into two table-spoonfuls of flour, and then put in the crabs. Boil them for half an hour and serve.

FISH.

FISH, to be wholesome and palatable, must be fresh. They should be scaled and cleaned immediately. This should be done on a dry table, and not in a pan of water, as is often the case. As little water as possible should be used for the insides. Keep them in ice until it is time to put them on the fire.

Fish should be put on the fire in boiling water. About ten minutes for each pound is usually allowed for boiling. A regular "fish kettle," with a suspended perforated tin for the fish to rest on, ought to be used. It is almost impossible otherwise to take up a large fish without breaking it. Wrapping in a cloth is often resorted to, but this is an imperfect method.

As soon as the fish is done, lift it out of the water. If it is a little before time, empty the kettle and suspend inside of it the tin with the fish upon it, and cover it with the lid till needed.

A little curled parsley is usually served as a garnish for boiled fish.

Salt fish should never be allowed to go beyond a gentle simmer. It is hardened by boiling.

In frying fish, the lard must be deep in the pan and boiling. As soon as the fish is plunged into it, a crust is formed and the juices kept in. A little fat at the bottom of a pan soon burns, and the fish becomes sodden before it is cooked.

Small wire baskets made for this purpose are much used for frying. The fish are laid at the bottom and immersed in the boiling fat, and run no risk of falling to pieces.

(31)

Some persons use olive oil for frying fish.

To broil fish a quick fire is necessary and the gridiron should be well greased to prevent sticking.

Nearly all fresh fish, of the larger kinds, are boiled for table use. The smaller are baked or broiled. The very small ones are fried, and are called "pan fish."

Very large fishes, such as halibut, pickerel, salmon, &c., are cut in pieces of convenient size and sold by the pound.

It is impossible to enumerate the great variety of fishes known on this continent. Among the choicer kinds are the shad, the sheep's head, the Spanish mackerel, the golden mullet of the South, trout, salmon, bass, in great variety, blue fish, and the cisco of the Western lakes. The rules which apply to the cooking of one will apply to nearly all.

Sheep's Head.

This highly-prized fish is said to take its name from the resemblance its teeth bear to those of a sheep. The best are found on the Atlantic coast, in the bays and estuaries of the Middle States. As it never ascends the smaller streams, and is only eaten in perfection when freshly caught, it cannot be enjoyed by those who are remote from the sea. It is sometimes called the American turbot, and weighs from four to twenty pounds. Those of the middle size are best for the table. It is usually boiled, and served with butter or egg sauce. Sometimes it is stuffed and baked, but this method does not do justice to this fine fish. Cold boiled sheep's head, flaked and served with a *Mayonnaise* dressing, is excellent, and resembles a lobster salad, but "with a charm all its own."

Shad.

To eat this delicious fish in perfection it must be "planked." Heavy slabs of oak, with cross-fastenings of wire, can be procured in our large cities for this purpose. If not provided with one of these, the primitive method, though rather rough, will serve the purpose quite as well. Take the head of a flour barrel, and secure the shad with two or three nails upon it; set it in front of the fire and broil it till thoroughly cooked through. The shad must be fresh, well scaled and cleaned. It must be cut entirely open, and laid with the outside next the plank. The head must be removed and the roe fried in a frying-pan. When the shad is removed from the "plank," rub some butter over it and add a little salt and red pepper. Serve it on a hot dish without delay.

Corned Shad.

A favorite mode of eating shad is to have it corned for breakfast. Nothing in the way of fish could be finer.

After cleaning and preparing the fish for cooking, sprinkle it well with salt, inside and out, and set it away in a cool place. In the morning broil it, serving it with a little butter, to moisten it, and red pepper.

The roe must be fried. In a cool place a corned shad may be kept for two or three days if a whole one is too much for one meal. As shad come in season in the early spring, and last only about six weeks, there is but little time to enjoy this great dainty.

Shad are salted for winter use like mackerel, but lose much of their flavor. They are also smoked like salmon. Salt shad must be soaked all night before being used.

Fried or Broiled Shad.

Those who will not take the trouble, or do not see the merit of "planking," broil shad on a gridiron, or fry it in lard in a frying-pan. In these cases rub it well with butter, as above, before serving, and pepper and salt it.

3

Boiled Shad.

Shad is excellent boiled. When it is cleaned and ready for cooking, place the roe inside of it and tie the fish firmly in several twists of cord; then roll it in a cloth, put it into the fish kettle and let it boil about twenty minutes. Serve it with butter or egg sauce, and sprinkle it with capers in serving it.

Baked Shad.

Make a rich bread stuffing, mixing it with egg, beaten light, pepper, salt and a little mace. Stuff the shad; sew it up and put it in a quick oven and bake it. Serve it with mushroom or tomato ketchup.

Potted Shad.

Clean the fish well, reserving the roes to pot with the shad. Remove the heads and tails and split them in two. Cut each half of the fish crosswise into three pieces. Rub each piece with salt and pepper. Lay the fish in the bottom of a jar in a layer; then scatter over it sliced onions and a few cloves and allspice; then add another layer of fish, with onions and spices as before, and so on until the jar is full. Pour strong vinegar upon the fish till they are covered. Cover the mouth of the jar with a piece of old muslin and tie it; then spread over the muslin a cover of thick dough made of flour and water, pressing it in at the edges to keep in the steam. Set the jar in an oven after the bread has been drawn, and let it remain five or six hours, or till the oven is cold. In cities this is best done at a baker's. The jars must be stone, as earthenware would be dangerous to use with vinegar. When the jars are thoroughly cold, take off the dough and cloth and cover them with a plate. They are fit to eat as soon as they are cold. When using it, lift each piece out carefully, as it crumbles very easily. You will find all the bones dissolved. Shad should be potted only in small quantities, as it does not keep long. For a small family two or three at a time. The mouths of the jars should be wide.

To Pickle Shad.

Clean the fish and split them in two, and lay them in several waters until quite free from blood. Rinse them in strong salt and water, and place them in a deep stone jar in layers, adding salt and saltpetre to each layer. Fill the jar to three or four inches from the top, and be sure to have the fish quite covered with brine. Put a weight on top to keep them down.

To Salt Shad for Summer Use.

Get the largest shad. Have them nicely cleaned and remove the heads. Put them in a large tub. Sprinkle them with fine salt as you place them. Let them stand till next morning; then drain them and pack them in the vessel they are to be kept in, putting plenty of coarse salt under and between them, and a large quantity on the top. Place a board inside of the vessel and a weight on the top of it. About twelve or fifteen shad are sufficient for a family.

Chowder.

Cut half a pound of salt pork in slices, and fry them with two large onions, sliced. Boil two pounds of potatoes and cut them in pieces. Cut six pounds of fresh fish into slices. Place them in layers in a broad flat stew-pan. Sprinkle the layers with two tablespoonfuls of summer savory and thyme, powdered together, half a teaspoonful of mace, cayenne pepper, cloves and black pepper. Add six quarts of water, and boil it gently two hours. Before serving, add two large pilot biscuits and a pint of wine. Salt it to taste.

This dish is usually made of fresh cod. Halibut or any firm fish may be substituted.

Rhode Island Chowder.

Take six slices of good pickled pork, (pig preferred,) and fry them in the bottom of a good sized-dinner pot, turning the slices till they are brown on both sides. Take out the slices of pork, leaving the drippings in the pot. Take seven pounds of "tautaug," dressed (leaving the heads on), or ten pounds of "scup" (tautaug to be preferred), and cut each in three pieces, unless small, when cut them in two. Place in the pot, on the drippings, as many pieces of fish as will fairly cover the bottom of the pot. Throw into the pot, on the fish, three handfuls of onions, peeled and sliced in thin slices. Do not be afraid of the onions! Put in this salt and pepper to taste, as in other soups. Then lay on the six slices of pork, on the top of the pork the rest of the fish; cover this with three handfuls more of onions, peeled and sliced. (Nine or ten onions in both layers will suffice, though more will not injure it.) More pepper and salt to taste. Then pour into the pot water enough just to come fairly even with the whole, or partly to cover the same. Put the cover on the pot, place it on the fire. Let it boil gently and slowly for thirty minutes. It is to BOIL thirty minutes, not merely *to be on the fire* thirty minutes, and at all events let it boil until the onion is done soft. Pour in at this point about a quart (a common bottle) of best cider or champagne, and a tumblerful of port wine, and at the same time add about two pounds of sea biscuits.

Note.—If, when the onion is done, you find there is not liquor enough in the pot, soak the sea biscuit in water for a few moments before putting them in. This practice may be generally recommended.

After the cider, wine and crackers are put in, there is no harm in stirring the whole with a long spoon, though it is not necessary. Then let the whole *boil* again (not merely be over the fire) for about five minutes, and the chowder is ready for the table. Before dishing up, let the cook taste it and see whether it lacks pepper or salt, when, if it does, it is a good time to add either.

NOTE.—Also, never boil a potato in chowder. If you want potatoes, boil them in a separate pot, and serve them in a separate dish on table.

TO STEW HADDOCK.

Take a haddock with the skin on. Cut it down the back bone. Then cut it up into square pieces. Salt and pepper them, using both red and black pepper, and a little mace if you like it. Rub the saucepan well inside with butter, that the fish may not burn. Cover it up and set it on a slow fire for ten or twelve minutes. Then add a tumbler of wine, a large spoonful of anchovy sauce and one of ketchup. Stir in a little butter and flour, well mixed. Shake the saucepan from time to time, that the fish may not burn. Cover it well and let it stew about fifteen minutes. Serve the gravy round it in a deep dish.

HADDOCK FRICASSEE.

Remove the bones and cut the fish in small pieces. Put them in a saucepan with the skin side up and without any water. Sprinkle ground mace and salt and pepper on each layer. Cover it and cook for twenty minutes. Then add a quarter of a pound of butter, rolled in flour, and one cup of sherry wine. Let it remain fifteen minutes longer on the fire.

HADDOCK AND OYSTERS.

Cut the fish in pieces and put them in a saucepan, with mace, pepper and salt on each layer. Cover them with water, and stew gently for fifteen minutes. Then add a quarter of a pound of butter and thicken with flour. Add to this one quart of oysters, without the liquor, and, as soon as the oysters are cooked, half a cup of sherry wine, and serve.

Scalloped Haddock.

Cut the fish in pieces, taking out as many of the bones as possible. Place them in a deep tin baking pan, with bread or cracker crumbs in alternate layers. Sprinkle salt, pepper and mace upon the layers of fish, and plenty of butter upon the bread. Let the last layer be crumbs. Cover the pan and set it in the oven. Remove the cover in about fifteen minutes, and let the fish remain to brown about half an hour. It can be turned out on a platter for the table.

To Cook Salmon.

Salmon is generally boiled, either whole or in pieces. This should always be done in a regular fish kettle, otherwise it is difficult to remove the fish without breaking it. It is almost impossible to tell when the fish is sufficiently done if wrapped in a cloth. The water should have salt in it.

Salmon is sometimes baked. A choice way of cooking it is to broil it in slices on the gridiron. Salmon, like most fish, should be handled as little as possible.

It is eaten with ketchup or lobster sauce.

To Souse Rock Fish.

Use the water in which the fish was boiled—the quantity must be regulated by that of the fish. Put the water on the fire with salt, whole pepper, allspice, a few cloves and a blade or two of mace. Let it boil until the flavor of the spices is extracted. When done, add as much vinegar as there is liquor. Let the spices remain in it. Cut the fish into pieces, put them in a stone jar, and pour the liquor over hot; this will keep for some days in cool weather. It is a good and economical way of using boiled fish left from dinner. Salmon may be treated in the same way.

To Cook Halibut.

Halibut is often boiled and served with egg sauce. It is also flaked, laid in a dish in layers, with white sauce between, sprinkled with bread crumbs and baked. The most usual method is to cut it in small pieces and fry it in bread crumbs, like oysters or veal cutlet.

To Boil Trout.

Trout, after being drawn, should be boiled in a strong cloth. Add a little salt to the water. Fish of a pound weight will not require more than eight or ten minutes to boil. To be served with melted butter or egg sauce.

Smelts.

Clean and dry them with a towel. Beat up an egg or two in a dish and dip them into it; then roll them in bread crumbs or cracker dust, seasoned with pepper and salt. Fry them in plenty of boiling lard. When of a delicate brown, they are done. Place them on soft paper to drain and serve them hot.

To Bake a Fish.

Take a small fish, or the tail end of a large one. Skin the upper side, and lard it with salt pork. Fill it with a rich stuffing of bread, pepper, salt, spice, and a little butter or chopped pork, with a little onion, minced fine. Slice two onions thin and lay over it. Sprinkle it with black and red pepper and salt, and a spoonful of bread crumbs. Add a gill of white wine when about half done. If your kettle is deep, lay two broad strips of cloth under the fish, to enable you to lift it out without breaking. It will take about an hour to bake. When the fish is taken up, add to the gravy in the kettle some butter, red wine or ketchup, and a little flour if not thick enough. Serve it with sippets of toast.

BROWN GRAVY FOR FISH.

Mince fine an onion and set it on the fire, in a pint of water, to boil, with six cloves, a blade of mace and a little cayenne pepper. Mix well together a quarter of a pound of butter with a large tablespoonful of flour; stir it in the water and let it boil about twenty minutes longer, adding a little brown coloring. If you have no coloring made, brown some sugar in an iron spoon or ladle, and stir it in. Lastly, add a tablespoonful of ketchup and the same of anchovy liquor.

STEWED FISH, WITH WHITE SAUCE. (FOR PASSOVER OR FRIDAY NIGHTS.)

Boil six or eight onions in water until tender; strain and cut them in slices. Put five pounds of rock or other fish, cut in pieces, in a stewpan with a quart of water, a little salt, cayenne pepper, ginger and mace to your taste. Strew the onions on top. Let it boil fifteen minutes; skim it, and have ready a mixture of chopped codfish or haddock (about two pounds), carefully boned; eight ounces of grated stale bread (during Passover use ground matzoth); one small onion, chopped fine; a little parsley, cut fine; dried marjoram, rubbed; mace, pepper, salt and ginger, to your taste; a tablespoonful of melted butter; six eggs, well beaten. Mix the whole well together and form it into balls in a tablespoon. Drop them one by one into the stewpan with the boiling fish. When all are in, cover closely and boil for ten minutes; then take the pan off the fire. Have ready six eggs, well beaten, the juice of four lemons, and chopped parsley; stir this into the beaten eggs. Then take from the stewpan the gravy, and stir it gently into the egg and lemon. Pour the whole back into the stewpan, and carefully simmer it until the sauce thickens, keeping the pan in constant motion to prevent the fish from scorching or the sauce from breaking. Serve when cold, decorated with parsley and sliced lemon.

To Stew a Rock Fish.

Rub the fish well with butter, to keep the skin from breaking. Brown three or four onions in slices, and spread them on the bottom of the fish kettle. Place the fish upon the onions, with pepper and salt. Pour over it about three pints of water (according to the size of the fish and the kettle), and let it simmer very slowly. Just before serving, add a wineglassful of wine and the same of mushroom or tomato ketchup. Stewed tomatoes may be substituted for the latter.

To Crab Rock Fish.

Pick cold boiled rock into small pieces. Put it in a stewpan with a gill of water. Add salt, a large spoonful of pepper, vinegar, a lump of butter, and a little cayenne pepper. Shake it over the fire until very hot.

To Stew Black Fish or Sea Bass.

Clean and scale the fish. Fry them whole and then remove them to a stewpan. Next pour some water into the frying-pan in which you have fried the fish, and thicken it with a little flour, mixed in cold water. When sufficiently cooked, throw this gravy over the fish and let it stew. Season it with cloves, mace, pepper and salt, and a little green parsley, chopped fine. About twenty minutes before serving it, add a gill of ketchup and a gill of port wine. A little stewed tomatoes may be added, if you choose.

To Barbecue Fish.

Clean the fish thoroughly; wipe it dry, and cut it across as if for frying. Salt it inside and outside and lay it in a baking dish. Strew over it a seasoning made of bread crumbs, parsley, sweet marjoram, thyme, salt, pepper and a few cloves. Add two or three tablespoonfuls of water, and lay on top a large piece of butter. Bake it well, and just before serving add a teacupful of port wine.

SCALLOPED FISH.

Three pounds of halibut, bass or cod, boiled with plenty of salt. Remove the skin and all the bones, and flake it with a fork. Boil a bunch of parsley and a large onion in milk, to extract the flavor. Take them out. Add one quart of milk, or milk and cream together, thickened with three tablespoonfuls of flour. Moisten the fish with some of the sauce until quite smooth, and then add a large piece of butter. Butter a deep dish. Put in the fish and sauce in alternate layers, with sauce on top. Cover with bread crumbs and bake a rich brown.

SCOLLOP FRITTERS.

Chop one pint of scollops. Add two beaten eggs, one tablespoonful of flour and a little salt. Fry a tablespoonful at a time in hot lard.

FISH CROQUETTES.

Pound in a mortar any kind of cold boiled fresh fish. Chop finely a hard boiled egg and mix it smoothly with the fish. Make a batter of egg, milk, flour, and half a tablespoonful of anchovy sauce, and make the fish into balls and fry. To make the batter, allow one tablespoonful of milk and two of flour to one egg.

DRIED CODFISH.

Take from three to four pounds of desiccated codfish for a family of six persons. Put the fish to soak in a deep pan over night, with the skin downwards. Three hours before dinner pour off the cold water and pour on boiling water, enough to cover it well. Keep a close cover on the pan. Let it stand an hour. Pare and boil potatoes enough to make an equal quantity, when mashed, with the fish. Some persons like more potatoes, but one half is usual. Pour the water off the fish. Pull it to pieces, throwing away bones and skin. Break the potatoes with the masher. Add the fish by degrees, beating it thoroughly. Beat into it a quarter of a pound of butter, four large spoonfuls of olive oil, two or three spoonfuls of mixed mustard. Put the mixture into a pudding pan. Place it in a moderate oven for three-quarters of an hour to brown it. Egg sauce is served to eat with it. For breakfast it is made up into small cakes, browned, and called fish balls.

FISH CAKES.

Freshen salt codfish. Put it in the kettle in which it is to be cooked and let it stand where it will be warm for some hours. About an hour before using it, place it where it will scald without boiling. Chop it fine, and mix it with mashed potatoes. Melt a small piece of butter in a little milk, and when you have stirred it into the fish, make it up into little flat cakes like biscuits. Roll them in a plate of flour, and fry them in the fat of fried pork.

SALT FISH AND CREAM.

Take some fish that has been softened in warm water for a few hours and pick it to pieces with a fork, taking out the bones. Put it in a saucepan with a pint of cream and a piece of butter. Let the cream boil; then add a tablespoonful of flour to thicken it, which has been made smooth in a little cold milk. Beat up three eggs, and stir them in just before removing from the fire. Milk may be used instead of cream.

NEW ORLEANS COURBOUILLON.

Slice three green onions with three cloves of garlic,—just enough to give it a flavor. Fry them, and when sufficiently done, mix a tablespoonful of flour, half a bottle of claret wine, and half a bottle of beef tea. Cut the fish in slices and put in the pan, with five whole tomatoes. Season it to taste and let it simmer till done.

The fish must be fresh.

SHELL-FISH.

OYSTERS should be eaten when fresh. If it is necessary to keep them for any length of time, put them in a cool cellar, and occasionally sprinkle the shells with salt and water.

This favorite bivalve, so plentiful and of such acknowledged superiority in the United States, is prepared in an endless variety of ways. A great many receipts are given here of the most popular methods. Fashion, the great regulator, gives the preference sometimes to one and sometimes to another.

Raw oysters are commonly served as a first course at dinner on ceremonial occasions. Fashion now ordains that they should be served on ice. When any portion of the dinner is placed on and carved upon the table, a large block of ice, selected for its clearness and beauty, is shaped in a rocky form, while a basin, hollowed in the middle, contains the oysters.

When the dinner is carved and served from side tables, the oysters are placed before each individual in small plates composed of ice. These articles are made by the confectioner by means of chisels and hot irons. They are troublesome to make for those not accustomed to them, and it is best not to undertake them at home. Ice blocks and plates are served on napkins, to absorb the water.

Lobsters and crabs should be boiled as soon as possible after they are caught. The most humane manner of killing them, and that which is generally adopted, is to drop them into a full kettle of boiling water. Terrapins and turtle are killed in the same manner.

(45)

To Stew Oysters.

Put two ounces of butter into a stew pan, with a small table-spoonful of flour; stir them well together over the fire until quite thick, but do not let them boil for more than a minute; then add a half-pint of cream, a little nutmeg, a very little mace, cayenne and white pepper. Stir the ingredients over the fire for five minutes; then add fifty oysters, drained from the liquor. When cooked, just as you take them off the fire, add the yolks of two eggs, well beaten.

To Stew a Hundred Oysters.

Drain them and let cold water run over them through a colander. When washed and drained, put them in a saucepan with a little salt and a large blade of mace. Let them stand in a cool part of the range about fifteen minutes, stirring them occasionally with a wooden spoon. Mix a quarter of a pound of butter and a little flour together, and stir it smoothly into the oysters. Let it simmer long enough to cook the flour; then add a teacupful of cream and some cayenne pepper, and let them remain on the fire until the oysters begin to curl.

To Boil Oysters.

Wash the oysters very clean. Put them in a basket and immerse the basket in a pot of boiling water. As soon as the shells open, remove the basket from the water as quickly as possible, to preserve the juice. Take off the upper shell, and serve them on large dishes, hot, in the lower shell.

To Broil Oysters.

Select the largest and finest oysters. Dry them in a towel and season them with pepper and salt. Lay them inside of a folding broiler, made of wire, close together. Turn the broiler frequently from side to side, to keep the juice from flowing out. Have ready a dish quite hot, and as you place them in it, put little pieces of butter upon them and serve them immediately.

To Steam Oysters.

Drain the oysters well, washing each one in the liquor to remove the pieces of shell. Put them in a tin plate inside of a steamer already placed over a pot of water that is boiling. Cover the steamer tight with its lid, and leave the oysters in the hot steam until they begin to puff up and curl. Serve them in a hot covered dish, with butter, salt and pepper.

To Pan Oysters.

Drain the oysters and put them on the fire in a hot pan with pepper and salt. When the oysters are puffed, pour them into a hot dish with some lumps of butter.

To Griddle Oysters.

Take the largest and finest oysters; dry them in a cloth. Heat the griddle as for baking cakes, and grease it. Have close to the fire a dish with butter, pepper and salt in it. Lay the oysters from the cloth upon the griddle; they will brown almost immediately. Brown them on both sides and then drop them in the dish with the butter; the juice will soon flow and make the gravy.

Oyster Omelet.

Mix a teaspoonful of flour with milk enough to make it as thick as cream, and beat into it two ounces of melted butter. Beat six eggs well. Chop a dozen large oysters fine, and beat them with the eggs. Add pepper and salt to season it. Fry it as you would any other omelet, and just before it is put in the pan add a teaspoonful of chopped parsley in a tablespoonful of melted butter.

MINCED OYSTERS.

Mince twenty-five oysters fine in their own liquor; stir in bread crumbs, sweet oil, salt, pepper and vinegar. Put alternate layers of the mince, and soda crackers wet with wine, into a deep dish, and bake for half an hour, or until nicely browned.

OYSTER SALAD.

Strain the juice of the oysters and boil it. When boiling, throw in the oysters, well washed, and let them become plump. Then drain them very thoroughly through a colander. When they are perfectly cold, place them in the dish they are to be served in and cover them with a rich creamy salad dressing.

TO FRY OYSTERS.

Use only the largest oysters for frying. Wipe them dry with a cloth. Dip each one separately into beaten egg and cracker, or stale bread crumbs, and fry them quickly in plenty of boiling lard. Many persons use Indian meal instead of bread or cracker crumbs.

TO SCALLOP OYSTERS.

Put a layer of bread crumbs with butter in the bottom of a dish, then a layer of oysters, and so on, alternating till the dish is full. Use pepper and, if the oysters are fresh, salt. When the dish is full, add a gill of wine. Bake for about twenty minutes.

SCALLOPED OYSTERS. (BAKED IN THE HALF SHELL.)

Fill the deep sides of large oyster shells with oysters and bread or cracker crumbs, prepared with small bits of butter, and spice and salt to taste. Place the shells on a pan and bake them a short time in the oven. Clams, with the hard parts removed, may be done in the same manner.

To Pickle Oysters.

Open as many oysters as will fill a gallon measure without the liquor. Wash them well in the liquor, carefully cleaning away the particles of shell. Strain the liquor. Set them on the fire and pour the liquor over them, adding salt, if they are fresh. Let them remain on the fire till they are ready to boil and the fins much shrivelled. If the oysters are large they may boil a minute or two. Then take them out and set them to cool on large dishes. Add some mace and whole pepper to the liquor, and let it boil for some time, carefully skimming it till the scum is entirely removed. Pour the liquor into a large pan, and when perfectly cold add a pint of white wine and half a pint of strong vinegar. Place the oysters gently in a jar and cover them with the liquor.

Virginia Spiced Oysters.

Strain the liquor from one gallon of oysters. Boil it up quickly and skim it thoroughly. Add one tablespoonful of whole allspice, one saltspoonful of powdered mace, one tablespoonful of whole pepper, and a pint and a half of vinegar. Let it boil once more.

Plunge the oysters into cold water. Let them drain well, and then throw them into the hot spiced liquor. Give them a quick boil and set them away in a stone jar. If fresh water oysters, salt must be added. Do not cover them until cool. Before serving, add small angular pieces of lemon.

Fricassee of Oysters.

Scald fifty oysters in their own juice. Remove the scum, strain off the juice and reject it. Put the oysters into a hot tureen, cover and set it aside in a warm place.

Rub well together six ounces of butter, three tablespoonfuls of flour, with as much scalding milk, into a fine smooth paste. Stir this mixture into a quart of hot milk in a stewpan on the

4

fire. Season it with salt and pepper, and a very little ground allspice and mace. Stir it until it thickens. Then stir in four well-beaten yolks of eggs, taking care that the mixture is not hot enough to curdle the eggs. Pour this over the oysters in a baking dish, cover them thickly with fresh bread crumbs and brown them in a quick oven.

BALTIMORE OYSTER PIE.

Make a puff paste of one pound of butter, or butter and lard mixed, flaked into one pound of sifted flour, wet to a stiff dough with ice water and rolled out on a marble slab, or in a very cold room. Handle it as little as possible. Line the sides of a deep dish, holding more than two quarts, with this paste. Having stripped your oysters, season them thoroughly with pepper, salt, and a blade or two of mace. Cut up six ounces of butter into little bits, and stir through the oysters with a half teacupful of cracker crumbs or grated bread. Then strain the oyster liquor carefully, and put all in the dish. Cover it with the paste, rolled about one-fourth of an inch thick, and with an opening in the centre. Cut out with a cake cutter, or jagging iron, ornamental bits of paste, and arrange around the edge and above the opening. Have the oven hot, and bake from a half to three-quarters of an hour. If the crust browns too quickly, cover it with paper. A teacupful of cream poured in through the opening on the top, just before the pie is done, is a great improvement, but not essential. Two quarts of oysters make a good-sized pie.

OYSTER PIE.

Two slices of bread, soaked and mashed ; one cup of milk ; two eggs, well beaten ; two spoonfuls of butter, pepper, salt and nutmeg ; one quart of oysters mixed with the bread. Bake in a deep dish in a good rich crust.

OYSTER PATTIES.

The most elegant mode of serving oysters in crust is to use " shells" of puff paste made for this purpose by the cake bakers. For dinner parties these are always preferred. The large ones can be made to hold from fifty to two hundred oysters. The smaller are about as large as the top of a tumbler, and hold from four to five oysters each. Both large and small are provided with a flat top, to be laid on when filled.

Stew the oysters, and make the sauce much thicker than for stewed oysters. Warm the shell, or shells, on a tin, and when ready to be served, put in the oysters and lay the lid lightly on the top.

TO FRY CLAMS.

Split them open and take out the hard part. Dip them in the yolk of egg, and when the butter in the pan boils, drop them in. They cook as quickly as oysters.

BAKED TURTLE.

The turtle found in the Mississippi lakes is very delicious. Its local name is "coutah." It is made into soup, stewed, or baked in the shell. Clean carefully either the soft or hard shell turtle. While cutting it up, preserve as much of the juices that flow out as possible to stew it in. Put it in a stewpan with an onion minced, a little cloves, allspice, mace, and pepper and salt. Dust enough flour on a large lump of butter as will keep it from oiling, and stir it in while stewing. When nearly done, mix a small quantity of bread crumbs with it, some sherry wine, according to the quantity of turtle, and a few drops of lemon juice. Sprinkle it thick with bread crumbs and bake it. Place the turtle-shell, with the mixture in it, on a napkin in the dish in which it is to be served.

To Dress Turtle Steaks.

The steaks are taken from the thick part of the turtle's fins. Season them with pepper, salt and mace. Flour and fry them quickly in butter and lard, mixed. Then pour over them a little water and let them simmer for a quarter of an hour. Just before serving, squeeze a lemon over the steaks.

Terrapins.

HINTS ON THE CARE OF TERRAPINS.

A supply of terrapins may be obtained in the fall and kept all winter in a barrel or cask, in a cellar where they are not liable to freeze. They need not be fed, although they will be fatter, and consequently better, if you throw the kitchen waste (vegetable parings, &c.) into the barrel. As they become torpid in winter, if you should fear that any of them may be dead, have the barrel removed to a warm room for a few days; you will then be able to discover if it is so. Before cooking them, put them in a tub and cover them with strong salt water. Let them remain in it all night; this removes any odor in boiling.

A Maryland Receipt for Cooking Terrapins.

Put the terrapins, alive, in boiling water, and let them remain until the sides and lower shell begin to crack; this will take less than an hour. Then remove them and let them get cold. Take off the shell and outer skin, being careful to save all the blood possible while opening them. If there are eggs in them, put them aside on a dish—the eggs are considered a very choice part of the terrapin. Take all the inside out, and be careful not to break the gall, which must be immediately removed, or it will make the rest bitter. It lies within the liver. Then cut up the liver and all the rest of the terrapin in small pieces, adding the blood and juices that have flowed out in cutting up. Add about half a pint of water. Sprinkle a little flour over them as you place them in the stewpan. Let them stew slowly for ten minutes, adding salt, black and cayenne pepper, and a very small blade of mace. Then add a gill of the best brandy and half a pint of the best sherry wine. Let it simmer over a slow fire very gently. About ten minutes before you are ready to dish them, add half a pint of rich cream and half a pound of sweet butter, with flour to prevent oiling. Two or three minutes before taking them off the fire, peel the eggs carefully and throw them in whole. If there should be no eggs, use the yolks of hens' eggs, hard boiled, and cut up in small pieces. This receipt is for four terrapins.

A PHILADELPHIA RECEIPT FOR COOKING TERRAPINS.

Drop the terrapins, alive, into a pot of boiling water. When dead, take off the outside skin from the shells and the nails from the claws. Wash them in warm water, and boil them till they are quite tender and soft. Throw a handful of salt into the water. When they are ready to be taken out, take off the shells and pick them carefully, removing the sand bag and gall without breaking them. Cut the meat and entrails into small pieces. Place them in a porcelain-lined saucepan, adding the juice which has flowed in cutting them, but no water. Season them with salt, cayenne and black pepper. To each terrapin allow a quarter of a pound of butter, mixed well with a handful of flour for thickening. After stewing a short time, add four or five tablespoonfuls of cream and half a pint of good Madeira wine to four terrapins. The yolks of two boiled eggs and one raw one may be added before serving.

A SUBSTITUTE FOR TERRAPINS' EGGS.

Beat the yolks of three hens' eggs in a mortar and make them into a paste with one raw yolk. Roll into balls and throw them into boiling water to harden. These are excellent if the terrapin eggs are deficient.

A Delaware Receipt for Cooking Terrapins.

The meat of what are called "counts" is too coarse. Terrapins, to be delicate, should be of medium size; two, or even four, to make a "count" are much the best.

To one dozen terrapins (four to a "count") allow three-quarters of a pound of butter; one tablespoonful of flour; the same of mustard; one saltspoonful of cayenne; one teaspoonful of salt; half a pint of good wine; six yolks of hard-boiled eggs. Never boil terrapins without watching each one to see that it is perfectly tender before taking it from the water, which should be boiling when they are put in. At the end of half an hour begin to examine them; some will take half an hour, some an hour and a quarter. Never put a terrapin in the stew that is not entirely tender. You had better chop it fine to thicken the gravy. The claws should come off with a little effort, and be tender. No subsequent stewing out of the shell will make them fit to eat. If boiled too much, they will be stringy and flavorless. While hot, remove the skin and nails. Open each one carefully over a bowl to save the gravy. Against the upper shell lie two sand bags, which are spongy. Remove these, and the head, and gall bladder from the liver. Put the meat into a deep bowl with one half of the livers, cut up, and cover them with the wine several hours before it is wanted. A tablespoonful of brandy may be added to the wine if it is of inferior quality. Rub the other half of the livers, the six eggs and the butter well together until very smooth. Add the flour, the mustard and cayenne. If terrapins are torpid, as in the winter, you may use the entrails, chopping them very fine, to add to the gravy. When they are feeding, as in the spring and summer, they must be thrown away.

The dressing must be made very smooth. When ready for serving, let one person especially attend to them. They are easily spoiled by burning or over-cooking. They should only come to a boil to scald the flour, and be served at once very hot.

The meat, steeped in wine, should be first put in the stewpan, the dressing added, and be stirred constantly.

The quantities required of mustard and cayenne entirely depends on the strength of the material furnished, and the cook should be discreet in the use of them. The quantity of salt varies with the quantity of meat turned out from the terrapins. Those who prefer the small ones, get a large one for its eggs, as they are considered a delicacy; but no terrapin epicure would ever prefer the larger meat. The larger terrapins may be boned and the meat very carefully stewed up.

There is a red-legged terrapin in the market, the eggs of which are very delicate, and by many considered superior to the eggs of the diamond back, though the meat is very poor.

For an invalid, terrapins stewed in cream, with salt and pepper, are nourishing and appetizing.

LOBSTER SALAD.

After carefully picking the lobster, remove the stomach, the blue vein down the back, and the spongy pieces; cut it into small pieces. Mash all the green and white fat and the red coral into a smooth paste. Season it well with salt and cayenne pepper. Mix it with an equal bulk of salad dressing or *Mayonnaise* sauce. Stir it all together. A short time before serving, place on a flat oval dish alternate leaves of tender lettuce and endive in a border, fill the middle with the lobster, placing occasionally a lettuce leaf. Pour *Mayonnaise* dressing over the top.

TO STEW LOBSTER.

Plunge the lobster alive into boiling water. When the shell begins to turn red, take it out. Clean and pick it. Put it in a saucepan with cream enough to stew it in. Season it with red pepper and salt. Mix about an ounce of butter with enough flour to prevent oiling, and stir it in. Just before removing it from the fire, add the yolks of two eggs, beaten, and a tablespoonful of vinegar.

Lobster Curried.

Mix together a piece of butter, one tablespoonful of curry powder, two tablespoonfuls of flour, a little salt and pepper, the soft parts of the lobster, and a cup of hot water. Stir and boil these together. Then add a cup of cream and throw in the lobster, which must be cut up. Let it then simmer a few minutes.

Lobster Rissoles.

Chop lobster meat fine and mix it with four hard boiled eggs, seasoned with pepper and salt. Make a batter of three eggs, three tablespoonfuls of milk, and the same of flour. Stir into it the lobster and egg. Make it into balls, and fry them brown in butter.

Lobster Chowder.

Pound three crackers very fine, mix them with a piece of butter the size of an egg, and the soft fat of the lobster. Season it with pepper and salt; this will form a paste. Boil a quart of milk, and add the paste to it by degrees. Chop the meat of the lobster, and stir it in with the milk and paste. Boil it once, and it is done.

Soft Crabs.

Open them and remove the sand bag. Wash and season them inside and out with salt and cayenne pepper. Fry them in butter or lard; or, if you prefer, in cracker dust, dipping them first in yolk of egg.

DEVILLED CRABS.

Put a quarter of a pound of butter into a saucepan with a
little flour, and cook it together. Stir it without stopping, to
prevent burning. Add to it a tumblerful of cream. Season it
with cayenne pepper and salt. Then add an onion, boiled or
mashed to a paste, and a little cayenne pepper. Then the crab
meat and one raw egg. Stir it all together and let it cook for
a few minutes, or till it begins to thicken. Then pour it into a
flat dish and let it remain till cold. Fill the back shells of the
crabs with the mixture, then egg them on the top with a brush,
and cover them with bread crumbs or cracker dust. Lay them
in a baking pan, put a small piece of butter on the top of each,
and bake them in an oven till browned. If you prefer, fry
them in deep lard.

TO STEW CRABS.

Pick the crabs carefully and season them with spice, cayenne,
mustard and salt. Mix together the yolks of two eggs, a tablespoonful of butter and one of flour; add two glasses of white
wine. Stir in the crabs and stew for half an hour.

SHRIMP PIE.

Shell two plates of boiled shrimps. Squeeze off all the heads
while shelling. Place them in a stewpan with a little of the
water from the dish they have drained on. Add four ripe
tomatoes, from which the seeds have been removed, chopped
fine, two spoonfuls of butter, black and cayenne pepper, and a
little allspice, and stew them gently together. When stewed,
stir in two wineglassfuls of wine. Turn it into a baking dish
and sprinkle it with grated bread, forming a thin crust on the
top. Put it in a quick oven, and let it bake only long enough
to brown on the top.

Shrimp Paste.

Shell two plates of boiled shrimps. Pound them to a paste perfectly smooth, pounding a little at a time. Add gradually one and a half pounds of butter. Season it with black and cayenne pepper, nutmeg and salt. Place the paste in moulds, or small deep bowls, pressed close, and then bake them until the top becomes a nice brown—about twenty minutes.

MEAT.

IT is extremely difficult to give directions as to the time required for roasting or boiling meats, so much depends upon circumstances. The size of the piece, the kind and degree of the fire, even the season of the year, must be considered. The heat from an anthracite coal fire is more intense than from one of wood. In winter frost must be overcome.

About fifteen minutes to a pound is usually allowed for roasting meats, with the exception of veal, which requires a longer time. Poultry needs more time than beef; ducks less than either turkey or chicken; venison and bear about as long as beef.

Roasting should be done before a steady hot fire. Place the roaster close to the fire at first, and let it brown rapidly. The quick heat in the beginning stops the flow of the juices, which are consequently kept within the meat. It should be frequently turned and basted. Roasted meats are greatly superior to those that are baked; the flavor is finer, and they are more tender and juicy. This is a point on which a cook is prone to deceive—it is so much easier to slip a piece of meat into an oven than to watch and baste it before the fire.

Gravies should be entirely free from grease. The flour used in basting is usually sufficient to prevent the gravy from being watery. If you wish a large quantity to be served in a boat, the gravy must be put on the fire in a skillet with a very little flour, some browned sugar and seasoning, and a little water.

Flour browned is frequently used for thickening gravies or

(59)

stews. It is difficult to brown it properly, and it is apt to impart a scorched flavor, however well done. The best and only true gravy is that which flows from the meat itself while being carved or in basting.

Sugar browned in an iron ladle is the best coloring. It is well to keep browning on hand, and not wait till the hurried time before dinner to prepare it. This may be done by browning a large quantity at a time in a skillet and then diluting it with water, bottling it and putting it away for use. For gravies in which wine is required, the sugar may be diluted with wine. The dregs of the wine bottles when decanting may be used for this purpose. It will keep longer made with wine.

Browning sugar requires great care. If it is suffered to burn, a bitter taste is imparted, and the sweet nutty flavor so desirable is lost.

To ensure tenderness in boiling, the process must be very slow. Plunge the meat into the water when it is boiling hot, then set it in a corner where it will simmer slowly. By this means you harden the albumen of the meat on the surface, and prevent the flow of the juices into the water. Time and slow cooking will make almost any meat tender. Rapid boiling makes it fall to pieces and become stringy.

These remarks apply in even greater force to stewing. No stewed meat need be tough. Time enough to cook it slowly is all that is required.

A little sugar is a great improvement in cooking meats in any form. Used judiciously, it is not detected, while the meats are richer in flavor. A heaped teaspoonful to a large pot of soup will be sufficient. The sweetness imparted by browned sugar is the chief reason why it is so desirable in gravies, soups, &c.

ROAST BEEF.

The best pieces for roasting are the sirloin and the ribs. The fat should be evenly dispersed through the meat; very lean meat is not good. The most perfect method of roasting is with a jack. When this is not obtainable, a "tin kitchen" or roaster is the best. The beef should be dusted with flour when put to roast, and constantly basted. When first put before the fire, it should be placed very close. When the outside has scorched a little, and the juices are thus prevented from flowing out, draw it back a little and let it cook more slowly. The time required depends upon the size of the meat, the fire, &c. If the pure juices of the meat alone are wished, skim the gravy in the roaster thoroughly and serve it without any addition. If the gravy is made in a skillet, thicken it a little, as water must be added; brown it with browned sugar and season it with salt and pepper.

BOUILLI.

The rump is the choicest piece for this purpose. Put it on in boiling water. Then set it on the side of the fire where it will simmer slowly. The water must cover it. Throw into it it three or four carrots, two or three onions, pepper, salt, and a dessertspoonful of sugar. Skim it from time to time. If it is to be served without browning, watch it closely, and when the bone loosens it is ready to serve. If you wish it browned, take it out of the water a little while before the bone loosens, put it in a baking pan, dust it lightly with flour, and let it brown slowly.

For the sauce, have ready two carrots and two small onions, well boiled; the onion may be soft enough to mash. Cut the carrots in small pieces. Take some of the liquor in which the beef was boiled and put it on the fire in a skillet with the carrots and onions. Thicken it with flour, and make the gravy a fine brown by adding sugar carefully browned. Add pepper and salt. Pour some of this sauce over the beef when it is served, and send the rest to table in a sauce-boat. Sprinkle some capers on the top. It will require four or five hours to simmer.

Beef Bouilli.

Take the thigh bone of a rump of beef, wash it well, pour over it a gill of vinegar, and dredge it well with flour; put it into a pot with three pints of water and let it come slowly to a boil. Season with finely-chopped cabbage, carrot, potato, turnip, onion, parsley, spice, salt and pepper. After the whole begins to boil, place it where it will simmer slowly for five hours, keeping the pot closely covered.

To Broil Beef Steaks.

The best way to cook beef steaks is to broil them on a gridiron. Let the coals be hot; grease the bars of the gridiron; keep the steak-tongs in hand and turn the steak incessantly from side to side, that the juices may not run out; when it is glazed on the outside, they will no longer do so. Then cook it more slowly, and do not turn it so often.

To Fry Beef Steaks.

Make the frying-pan hot on the fire. Place the steak in it, and turn it rapidly from side to side to glaze it well. When this is accomplished, the steak will be nearly done. Throw a little butter, water, and pepper and salt in the pan; dust a little flour into it. Let it cook till the gravy is done, and serve it.

If the gravy can be dispensed with, the steak will be better if the turning process is continued until it is done. Then serve it on a hot dish, butter it and season it with pepper and salt.

Kugel.

Soak one pint of Spanish peas and one pint of beans all night in three pints of water; take a leg of beef, cracked in three pieces, and three pounds of lean beef. Put the whole into a deep earthenware baking pan, seasoning with pepper, salt, ginger, and a little cayenne pepper. Make the kugel in the following manner: Take one pound of flour, half a pound of chopped suet, a little nutmeg, grated, with a small quantity of ground ginger, cloves and allspice. Add one pound of coarse brown sugar, a quarter of a pound of stale bread, soaked in water and pressed dry. Mix all these together into a paste, and put into a quart bowl, well greased with suet. Cover it with a small plate and put it in the middle of the pan with the peas and beans, and with sufficient water to cover the whole. Tie a coarse paper over the pan, and put it into a very slow oven, where it should remain all night—in all some fifteen hours; add a little water, if necessary, from time to time. The pudding must be turned out of the basin; a sweet sauce, flavored with lemon and brandy, is an improvement.

BEEFSTEAK PIE.

Cut the steak into small pieces, with a very little fat. Dip each piece into flour and put them in layers into a pie dish, seasoning each layer with salt and black and red pepper. Fill the dish with the pieces of steak so as to raise the crust in the middle. Half fill the dish with water or gravy, and a teaspoonful of Worcestershire sauce. Put a border of paste round the wetted edge of the dish; moisten it and lay the crust over it. Cut the paste even with the edge of the dish all round, and brush over it the beaten yolk of an egg. Make a hole with a knife in the top and bake in a hot oven.

BEEFSTEAK AND OYSTERS.

Put into a stewpan one and a half pounds of beefsteak, with a little water and a large piece of butter. When the meat is nicely browned, pour in half a pint of water, a little pepper and salt, and the oyster liquor. Set the stewpan over a moderate fire and let the meat stew gently; then add five dessertspoonfuls of port wine, a piece of butter, rolled in flour, and twenty-

five oysters. Stew all together until the edges of the oysters
are shrivelled, and serve very hot.

BEEF A LA MODE.

Take a rump of beef. Remove the bone at the end and half
of the chine bone. Put these on to boil, to help make the gravy.
Take some parsley, thyme, and a small piece of lemon peel;
mince them fine. Add salt, pepper, nutmeg, and six cloves,
pounded fine. Rub all these in the places from which the bones
have been removed, and also in the partings of the meat. Put
some butter into your pot, and when it is hot, flour the fat side
of the meat and fry it of a light brown. Then add to it a quart
of weak gravy, six onions, four carrots and two turnips. Cover
the pot close, and let it stew slowly for three or four hours.
When it is tender, take out as much of the gravy as you think
will be wanted for sauce; remove the grease from it. Add some
small onions, turnips and carrots, cut in pieces and previously
boiled. Mix some flour and butter for thickening, and a little
scorched sugar for browning; let it stew together well. Just
before it is ready to be removed from the fire, stir a quarter
of a pint of red wine and a tablespoonful of ketchup in the
gravy. Taste it to see if there is salt and pepper enough.
Serve it in a deep dish, with some of the gravy around and
over it.

PURIM ROUND.

Remove all the bones from a plate of fine beef and put it in
the following pickle: Two buckets of water; salt sufficient to
make it strong enough to bear an egg; a pint of molasses; two
pounds of brown sugar, and six ounces of saltpetre: to be well
skimmed before the beef is put in. Let it remain in the pickle
four weeks. Remove all the ragged pieces. Wash and dry it
with a cloth and lay it flat on a board. Grate a loaf of stale
bread; season it with pepper, salt, ginger, cloves, and chopped
parsley. Strew this over the beef and roll it up very carefully.

Skewer and tie it well. Wrap it in a cloth. Boil it for four hours. Put it on a flat dish with a board on top, upon which place heavy weights, till it is quite cold. Take off the cloth; trim it and serve it with a garnish of parsley. It should be cut very thin.

DELMA.

Chop cold roast beef or mutton fine, as for force meat. Boil half a pound of rice until it is perfectly dry. Season the meat well with pepper and salt, parsley, onion, and sweet marjoram, and mix it with the rice. Make a rich gravy of the bones and scraps of the meat. Have ready some cabbage leaves. Dip them in boiling water. Make the meat and rice up into balls the size of an apple, and tie up each one in a cabbage leaf. Put the balls into a stewpan with the gravy already prepared and let them stew. The meat and rice should be in equal proportions. When you serve them, untie them and throw away the cabbage leaf. They will not taste of the cabbage if properly done. Pour the gravy over them.

FRICADILLOES.

Mix equal quantities of cold beef, chopped, and mashed potatoes, with a small onion, minced, two or three ground cloves, pepper and salt. Moisten it with an egg and make it up in little pats. Fry them in lard.

BEEF OMELET.

Chop fine two pounds of raw beef. Powder two soda crackers, and mix them well together with two eggs, well beaten. Add a small piece of fat pork, chopped fine, and season it with sage, pepper and salt to taste. Make it up in a round ball, and bake it three hours in a slow oven. It is well to try a little piece in a pan on the stove to see if the seasoning suits your taste. It should be basted from time to time with butter.

5

An Old Friend with a New Face.

Cut beef that is left over into slices. Slice an onion very thin, and lay a few pieces in the bottom of a pie dish; then a layer of beef. Dredge in a little flour, and fill in the dish with layers of sliced onion, sliced beef, pepper, salt and flour. Add the cold gravy. Scald and peel as many tomatoes as will cover the dish. Lay them on, and dust with bread crumbs, pepper and salt, adding some small pieces of butter. Set in the oven, and when the tomatoes are cooked through, serve it.

To Dress Cold Beef.

Cut cold roast beef in very thin slices. Season with pepper, salt, sliced onion, and chopped parsley, and put all together in a stewpan with a large piece of butter and nearly a pint of good broth or gravy. Let all simmer slowly; when quite hot, stir in the yolks of two well-beaten eggs, a teaspoonful of vinegar or lemon juice, and a glass of port or white wine. Stir it briskly over the fire and pour into a hot dish.

Brown Ragout.

Take five pounds of veal cutlets and six pounds of lean, tender beef; separate two pounds of each for the balls. Cut the remainder into moderate-sized pieces. Flour and fry them in melted fat over a brisk fire, so that the meat is brown without being thoroughly cooked. Prepare the balls as follows: Chop the meat fine, and add eight ounces of grated stale bread, five eggs, and one small onion, chopped fine. Season with pepper, salt, ginger, mace, marjoram, rubbed fine, with a little chopped parsley. Mix all well together. Form them into balls in the hand, using flour to prevent their adhering; then put them into the pan of boiling fat and brown them like the meat. Take a quart of meat gravy, seasoned with ground allspice, very little cloves, and salt to your taste, one onion, chopped fine. Stew the whole together slowly for two hours; then add six pickled walnuts, mashed with a silver spoon, the juice of two lemons; thicken with brown raspings of bread. Boil the whole fifteen minutes longer before serving.

SPICED TONGUE.

Parboil a fresh neat's tongue and remove the skin. Then rub it with powdered allspice, pepper, ginger and carraway seed, and stick it with cloves. Chop a piece of onion and brown it in fat. Flour the tongue and put it in this fat to brown. When this is done, make a gravy by adding as much water as will stew it, though not cover it. Then add a dessert-spoonful of sugar, a handful of raisins and another dust of flour. Lastly, put three-quarters of a tumbler of Madeira wine. Let all stew together. Serve with some of the sauce and raisins poured over it.

BOILED CORNED BEEF.

Corned beef should be simmered slowly. The choice pieces are the rump and the round. The meat should be kept covered with water. Let it boil until the bone loosens. When it is done, take it immediately from the water. Meat left to grow cold in the water will mildew on the surface very quickly. Slow boiling is the secret of tenderness. If the meat is not very tender in itself, by very slow and long simmering it will become so.

PRESSED CORNED BEEF.

Take a piece of corned beef—the "plate" is usually selected—and boil it till the bones loosen. When done, take out the bones. Wrap it in a cloth and place it between two slabs of marble or wood while it is warm. Place a heavy weight upon it, and let it remain under pressure two days. Cut it in thin slices for luncheon or breakfast.

To Make Meat Jelly.

Put a knuckle of beef and other fresh beef bones, obtained from your butcher, in a large pot. Cover them with water and boil them slowly six or seven hours, till all the meat falls from the bones. Strain off the liquor through a sieve or colander. While the meat is boiling, set two or three carrots and an onion on the fire in a saucepan. Let them boil till they are soft enough to mash. Do not mash them, but strain the water off into your beef liquor, adding a teaspoonful of sugar and stirring it well. The next day remove carefully all the fat from the top, wiping it finally with a cloth. If the jelly is not clear enough for your purpose, clear it with white of egg, as for calves'-feet jelly, and strain it through a jelly-bag. This jelly had better be made two days before needed, as it may require to be cleared, and will have to stand another night to become firm again. If you like a little acid flavor, strain into it, when you finally set it to cool, as much lemon juice as suits your taste—let there be no rind flavor. If you like a spicy flavor, add two or three cloves in the last boiling. If the jelly is not stiff enough for your taste, add some gelatine also.

This jelly is intended to serve with cold turkey, chicken, or game. If you wish to ornament a ham with it, throw into it before straining a few tablespoonfuls of the liquor in which the ham was boiled, to give it the ham flavor,—this must be cold so as to contain no grease,—but be careful not to put in too much, else it will taste smoky. To serve a cold boiled turkey with this jelly, a little of the water in which the turkey was boiled, added to the jelly while hot and unstrained, will give it the turkey flavor; but if you have stuffed the turkey, it is best to avoid this, as the stuffing may have thickened the water, which will prevent the clearing of the jelly.

This jelly is an improvement to any cold meat, and is highly ornamental. It may also be used for soup by diluting it with water, and adding what you prefer to thicken it,—chopped vegetables, vermicelli, barley, &c. If you wish a clear soup, serve it with sippets of toast.

MUTTON AND LAMB.

MUTTON should be young and fat. The latter shows it to be in good condition. In cold weather it should always be hung in a cold dry place, where there is a good circulation of air, for several days before it is required. If frozen, it can be kept with advantage much longer.

Lamb, with the exception of the chops, is always roasted. When the shoulder is cut away from the breast at table in carving it, epicures think it an improvement to pepper and salt the opening freely, pour a glass of Madeira wine over it, and lay the shoulder back again for a few minutes. The juices that flow in the cutting mix with the wine, and make a very rich gravy. Some persons eat mint sauce with lamb.

In roasting mutton it should not be overdone, and great care should be taken to remove the grease from the gravy before serving it. It is very unpleasant to see it lying congealed on a plate. Currant jelly is served with roast mutton, especially if it be a saddle.

In boiling a leg of mutton, a large onion dropped in the pot will be found an improvement. It imparts a sweetness to the meat without revealing itself.

BOILED LOIN OF MUTTON.

Procure a tender, good loin of mutton. Wash it and roll it in a cloth. Put it on to boil with a little salt in the water and one small onion in the bottom of the pot. Let it simmer slowly all the time. When done, lay it on the dish with the smooth side up, and serve it with a sauce of eggs, flour and water. (See Sauces.) Pour a little over the top, and sprinkle a very little chopped fresh parsley over it. A few capers will improve it. This is a very choice dish if well done. The sauce cannot be distinguished from melted butter. Be careful to have the mutton well jointed by the butcher.

Mutton Chops.

Trim the chops, and throw the trimmings into a saucepan to simmer with a little onion. Season some grated bread or cracker with salt and pepper. Dip each chop into melted butter, or nice drippings, and then into the crumbs. Broil them slowly on a gridiron. Then make the sauce. Strain off the water from the trimmings after all the substance is stewed out of them. Skim off the fat, and thicken the liquor with flour and butter rubbed together. Boil it up, and add a small teacupful of tomato ketchup, a couple of anchovies, if you like the flavor, a pickled cucumber, cut fine, or two small spoonfuls of capers. If your sauce is not thick enough, add a few bread crumbs. Give it another boil, and dip each chop into the sauce as it is taken hot from the fire. Place the chops in regular order round the dish and pour the remainder of the sauce in the middle.

Stuffed Leg of Lamb.

Take off the fat and cut off the shank. Make deep incisions in various parts. Fill them with stuffing, made of bread crumbs, and chopped salt pork, seasoned with sweet marjoram, pepper and salt, moistened with an egg. Put the meat into a large saucepan, and put hardly water enough to cover it. Add an onion, a carrot, cut in dice, and some ground cloves. Let it simmer steadily three hours. When done, dish it; thicken and boil up the gravy, and pour it over and around the meat.

To Stew Lamb and Peas.

Take a neck or loin of lamb; put it on to boil with sufficient water to cover it, seasoning it with pepper and salt. When partly done—in about half an hour—put in the peas and let them stew together, adding two tablespoonfuls of sugar after the peas have boiled. If a whole peck of peas are used, and the lamb is not very rich, put in a small piece of drippings or veal fat. It will take about two hours to cook.

HARICOT.

Cut a breast of mutton into pieces easy to help with a spoon. Brown them in a frying-pan, and put them into a pot with some carrots and an onion or two, and cover them with water. A few potatoes cut up may be added. Stew very gently. It will take a long time to cook the carrots. If they are not young summer carrots, they had better be boiled a little before putting them in with the meat. Season with pepper and salt and a pinch of sugar.

MINCED MUTTON.

Take some cold mutton, either boiled or roasted. Remove the skin and outside parts. Mince it very fine, with a small onion. Put a small piece of butter into a stewpan. When melted, add half a tablespoonful of flour. Stir it well several minutes, and add about a gill of stock, with salt, pepper, a dash of nutmeg, a little thyme and the yolk of an egg. Throw in the mince. Stir it on the fire for some minutes. Serve it with toasted bread under it, or potato balls round the dish.

MUTTON STEW.

Cut up the mutton and boil it with an onion in a little water. Skim it well. Add six or eight tomatoes, and season it with pepper and salt. About an hour before serving it, stir in two tablespoonfuls of flour mixed with water.

FRIED LAMB.

Cut a loin of lamb into thin slices, and lay them in water to extract the blood. Then fry them in butter, anchovies and lemon.

To Prepare Lamb or Mutton. (For the Invalid or
the Epicure.)

Take of the leg of either lamb or mutton (other portions
where lean meat prevails may be substituted for the leg), and
with a sharp knife remove every particle of fat and all the white
tissues and sinews, leaving nothing but the pure red flesh or
fibre. It will then be in fragments. Pile them on the steak-
board and pound them with an iron steak-hammer. Turn the
mass, and heap it up under the hammer as fast as it spreads out
thin. Continue pounding until it becomes a pulpy mass, almost
a jelly in its fineness, then gather it once more in a pile and tap
it gently with the hammer to flatten it into a slice one-half or
five-eighths of an inch in thickness. Remove it from the board
with the back of a knife, and roll it up as fast as lifted—this
prevents tearing it apart. Lay the roll on the buttered broiling wires and unroll it there. Cook it close over the coals from
half a minute to one minute on each side. It should be slightly
rare, but less rare than beef. Add a little salt and butter when
it comes off the fire, pressing them into the meat with a knife.

VEAL.

Veal, in good condition, should be fat. Like most meats, it
is better for hanging some time, when the weather is cold enough
to admit of it. Veal requires a great deal of cooking, and must
never be served with the flesh or gravy tinged in the slightest
manner with red. It is excellent cold, and makes a good salad
dressed as chicken salad. It is never boiled.

To Dress a Fillet of Veal.

Skewer or tie the flap well round the fillet. Make incisions
in the upper and lower surfaces with a sharp knife. Prepare a

stuffing of grated bread, minced onion, salt, pepper, and a little mace. Wet this stuffing with a little meat jelly or broth, or if you have none, with some butter. Work it well together, and fill the holes which you have made, with the stuffing. If you like a little pork or ham fat, add it to the stuffing. Dredge it well with flour, and put it in a deep stewpan or pot on the fire. It will take about three hours to stew. If you prefer to bake it, it will not require so long a time. The gravy must be made by adding broth or water in the bottom of the pan and letting the meat stew in it. If the gravy is not brown enough, add browned sugar. If it is sufficiently brown, throw half a teaspoonful of white sugar into it.

BREAST OF VEAL RAGOUT.

Take a breast of veal. Cut out half the long bones. Half roast it at a quick fire. Then cut it in pieces of a convenient size for helping. While it is roasting, let the bones, with the shreds and clippings of the veal, boil over a quick fire, adding to them an onion, a blade of mace, red pepper and salt. When the bones are thoroughly cooked, strain off the liquor, and thicken it with flour and butter rubbed together. Put the veal into this gravy, and with browned sugar make it a rich brown. Let it stew very slowly till quite tender. Remove, by skimming, the grease from the gravy as it rises.

VEAL CUTLETS.

Cutlets should be small—about the size of fried oysters. Dip the pieces in the yolk of egg, well beaten; then roll them in bread crumbs or cracker dust, and fry them in boiling lard. A brown gravy must be made in the pan, with broth thickened with flour, and colored brown with browned sugar; seasoned to taste. A white gravy is made by thickening a little cream or milk in the pan and seasoning it. Pour it in the dish in which they are to be served before putting the cutlets upon it.

GUNDINGA (A FLORIDA DISH).

Take two pounds of calf's liver, and let it boil, with a little salt in the water, until it is tender. Then chop it up fine. Take two large onions, two cloves of garlic, five ripe tomatoes, and a small piece of pork; let these fry together. After they have been well fried, add the chopped liver and a quart of the water in which it was boiled, a few grains of allspice, black pepper and salt. Let all boil together till it becomes thick.

GOHOTE.

Take two or three pounds of the fillet of veal, according to the size of your family. Mince it very fine on a chopping board, with an onion. Season it with salt and pepper and a small piece of fresh parsley. Add a teacupful of grated bread, some slips of pork fat, and a little butter. Beat the yolks of two eggs. Stir and mix all well together. Make it up in a ball, or mould it in a bowl; put it in a baking pan; cover it with bread crumbs and some small pieces of butter, and brown it in the oven. If raw veal is used, it will require more baking than meat already cooked. This dish is usually made from the remains of the cold veal of the day before. All the scraps and bones must be boiled up in a stewpan, with a little onion, pepper and salt, for gravy. Thicken the gravy with a little flour, and brown it with sugar, burnt brown in a large iron spoon or ladle over the fire. Remove the mould from the pan to the dish in which it is to be served, and pour the gravy over and around it in the dish.

VEAL POT PIE.

Take the long and glutinous parts of the veal. Cut it up in small pieces, half the size of your hand. Make a paste and roll it out in one sheet. Cut the centre out to fit the bottom of your pot; then line the sides of it with the paste. Let it be thicker on the bottom. Then put in your veal, with the bones, and, if you like it, some slices of pork. Have ready a half dozen of potatoes, cut in quarters, three onions, sliced, and pepper and salt. Intersperse these with the meat. Add a pint of water. Cover the whole with a layer of the paste, and let it simmer quietly on the fire two or three hours, or even longer; in which case you must add more water. If you like, add a few little dumplings made of the paste.

To Dress a Calf's Head.

Let the calf's head be what is called "dressed;" that is, with the hair removed but the skin on it. Boil the head till you are able to remove the bones without cutting. Season it with salt, pepper, mace and cloves. Make a rich stuffing of bread and chopped meat, with dried herbs to flavor it, and a little minced onion. Put the meat into the baking dish, and put layers of the stuffing with it. Rub the top over with yolks of egg beaten, and sprinkle it with bread crumbs. Moisten it with some of the liquor in which the head was boiled, and bake it about twenty minutes.

Calf's-Head Stew.

Parboil a calf's head the day before it is needed in as little water as will cover it. When taken off the fire, cut the meat off the bones, and set the water in which it was boiled away for making the gravy. Skin the tongue. Slice it and fry it with the rest of the meat till a light brown. Place enough of the water reserved in your stewpan, thickening it with flour and browning it with burnt sugar, and seasoning with pepper, salt and mace. Put the browned meat into this and stew the whole, adding, lastly, a wineglassful of wine. The brains, which must be boiled in a cloth when the rest of the head is boiled, are to be mashed fine, with eggs, and flour and seasoning, and then fried in little fritters and served with it.

BAKED CALF'S HEAD.

Chop the nose off, and split the head down the middle and take the eyes out.

Tie a string tightly round the head, and soak it in salt and water for an hour or two; then place it in a pot with cold water, without removing the string, and boil it until the tongue is very tender. When sufficiently cool, cut the string, take out the tongue, and remove from it all the hard white skin. Place it in a dripping-pan. Take the brains, some fat, and all the meat you can find, and chop them together very fine, adding salt and pepper to taste. With a spoon spread all nicely over and around the tongue; then take half a teaspoonful of ground cloves, the same of allspice, and sprinkle over this. Beat two eggs quite light, and add to them three or four crackers, rolled fine. With a knife spread a thick layer of this over the whole. Place small lumps of butter here and there. Add a little water to keep it from burning, and place it in the oven a few moments, or until nicely browned.

CALF'S HEAD AND LIVER.

Soak it in cold water half an hour. Scrape it clean. Take out the brains. Put the head into a floured cloth, pinned tightly, and into boiling water to boil three hours. After it has boiled an hour, add the liver, heart, tongue, and a piece of salt pork. Put in the brains, after being well washed, and boil them about half an hour. When done, take the head from the kettle and remove all the bones, which will slip out easily. Flour and salt it, and lay it in a frying-pan, skin side down, and brown it in butter. Dish it with the brown side uppermost, with the liver, heart, tongue, and pork on another dish. Mash up the brains, and add them to butter sauce. A part of the brains may be seasoned with a tablespoonful of sage, a bit of butter, salt, and a tablespoonful of vinegar. Be sure to choose from the market a head with the skin remaining.

Veal Balls.

Two ounces of beef suet; two ounces of veal; the yolks of one raw and one boiled egg; a small onion; pepper, salt, mace, a dash of nutmeg, and grated lemon peel to taste. Mince all the above. Beat them well together. Make them up in balls. Fry them, and serve them with the gravy.

Scalloped Veal.

Mince cold roast veal. Butter a baking dish. Put in layers of the veal, seasoned with salt and pepper and bread crumbs, with butter. On the top layer pour some milk and a beaten egg. Put in a little of the gravy. Bake three-quarters of an hour.

Veal Rolly-Poly.

Two pounds of veal, chopped fine; one pound of pork, chopped fine; two eggs; a small onion; a little sage, salt and pepper to taste. Roll it into shape. Sprinkle with egg and cracker dust. Bake it from twenty minutes to half an hour. Slice it cold.

The onion can be dispensed with.

Sweetbreads (Brown).

Lay six sweetbreads in hot water and parboil them for half an hour, adding salt, pepper, and a very little mace. Let them cool. Remove the large sinews and the fat, and fry them in a quarter of a pound of butter, a tablespoonful of flour, and one onion, cut up. When quite brown, add the liquid mixture to a gravy made of veal or beef stock, seasoned with mushroom ketchup, celery seed, or fresh celery, parsley, and sweet marjoram. In summer, fresh stewed tomatoes may be substituted for the mushroom ketchup. Stew the sweetbreads very slowly in this gravy for an hour; then strain the gravy. Pour it over the sweetbreads and serve on a flat hot dish.

Fricasseed Sweetbreads.

Clean half a dozen sweetbreads thoroughly. Put them in a stewpan with enough water to cover them. Boil them till tender and then take them from the water. Stir into the water a quarter of a pound of butter, mixed well with flour, and add mace, pepper and salt. When near the dinner hour, return the sweetbreads to the gravy and let them warm through; when you are about to serve them, stir in two or three eggs, beaten well, with a little fresh parsley, chopped fine. Garnish with brown meat balls.

Sweetbreads and Veal Balls.

Take two pounds of a fillet of veal. Chop it fine, with a small piece of onion. Season it with pepper, salt, cloves and mace. When chopped, add bread crumbs, one third the quantity of the meat, and mix all well together, with the yolks of two eggs, beaten light. Roll this into balls the size of a walnut, and fry them a light brown. Then put them into a stewpan with a little gravy, previously made from the shreds and bones left from veal, and which must be well seasoned. Let them stew very slowly for two hours. Have already prepared two or three sweetbreads thus: Boil them slowly till tender, though not enough to fall to pieces; then throw them into cold water. Twenty minutes before it is time to serve them, add the sweetbreads to the balls, and let them stew. Flavor the gravy with tomatoes or mushrooms, according to taste.

To Dress Sweetbreads.

Let six sweetbreads simmer gently for half an hour, with a little salt and mace. Then prepare a sauce of thick, smooth-drawn butter, adding to it a well-beaten egg and a gill of cream. Lay the sweetbreads in a hot dish and pour the sauce over them.

SWEETBREAD SALAD.

Boil the sweetbreads. When cold cut them into little dice. As you arrange your salad dish, place in each leaf a piece of sweetbread; then throw over the whole your thick salad dressing.

CROQUETTES OF CALVES' BRAINS.

Wash thoroughly and boil the brains. Beat them up with bread crumbs soaked in milk, a little finely-powdered sage, salt and pepper. Make it into balls and fry it, dipping each ball into beaten egg.

FRICASSEED CALVES' FEET.

Boil four calves' feet until tender; then remove the long bones and cut the feet in two. Put them into a pan with a small quantity of the water in which they were boiled. Add the yolks of two eggs, beaten light, half a nutmeg, a wineglassful of sherry wine, and a lump of butter half the size of an egg, a teaspoonful of salt, and pepper to taste. Let them remain until the gravy thickens.

PORK.

PORK is an article of food in such common use that few directions for preparing it are necessary. The general instructions for roasting and boiling will apply to it. It is a meat that requires a great deal of cooking, and is never considered fit to eat if underdone. A young pig is roasted in the same manner as a turkey, the stuffing differing somewhat in having more onion and a good deal of dried and powdered herbs. It is generally eaten with apple sauce. Pork chops and steaks are cooked as those of mutton and beef.

A loin of fresh pork is generally scored across the skin, and is sometimes stuffed with a rich stuffing of bread, onion and herbs. Pickled pork, if it has been long in salt, should be soaked all night before boiling it.

BAKED PORK AND BEANS.

Pick over and wash one quart of small white beans. Soak them all night. In the morning pour off the water and put them in an iron pot or earthen crock, placing in the middle a piece of salt pork, the inside of which has been deeply scored. Place this a little above the beans, that it may brown and crisp. Cover the beans with water. Some persons put a little soda in the water, others a spoonful of molasses and black pepper.

Make a stiff dough of flour and water, and roll it into a thick cake, large enough to cover the beans, leaving a hole in the middle for the pork to brown. Bake it all day, very slowly, in a cool oven. Lift the dough occasionally, to see if there is enough water. If too dry, add boiling water. Towards the last the beans must soak up all the water.

Remove the paste which is useless, and place the pork in a dish and surround it with the beans.

Earthenware crocks are to be had in New England, diminishing in size at the top, made expressly for this purpose.

TO BOIL A HAM.

A ham should be put into cold water, enough to cover it. As soon as the water boils, set it on one side, where it will only simmer, for eight hours. Then take it out, remove the skin, and put the ham again into the kettle and let it remain in it until the water has cooled. Then take it out, trim it nicely, sprinkle over it pounded cracker and a little brown sugar, and brown it in an oven.

To Bake a Ham.

Wash and put to soak over night a medium-sized ham. Early in the morning put it on to boil, well covered with fresh water. Let it just begin to boil over a brisk fire, then move it back, and keep it simmering only until it is done—this ought to be in about four hours—filling the boiler as it needs it with boiling water. Then take it out, and skin it while hot. Trim off carefully the rough edges; then grate thickly over it bread crumbs and a sprinkle of brown sugar. Put the ham into a dripping-pan with a pint of Madeira wine and a half-pint of its own drippings, which the dish you have dressed it in will usually afford, and baste it every few minutes until it is nicely browned and the wine thoroughly absorbed.

To Roast a Ham.

Take a new ham that has been salted for some weeks. If smoked, parboil it before roasting. While it is before the fire, baste it with white wine and sugar. When it is half done, remove the skin, stick it full of cloves, and let it roast as long again, basting it with fresh wine and sugar until thoroughly cooked.

Ham Toast.

Boil one pound of lean ham. Mince it very fine. Add the yolks of three eggs, one tablespoonful of butter, two tablespoonfuls of cream, and season well with cayenne pepper. Stir it over the fire until it begins to thicken, then spread it over thin slices of hot toast from which the crust has been pared.

To Broil Ham.

Cut very thin slices, and lay them in hot water for half an hour. Take them out and wipe them dry. Dip each slice into egg and bread crumbs, and broil them lightly over a clear fire.

6

To Cure Hams.

One hundred pounds of meat, six gallons of hot water, nine pounds of salt, three pounds of brown sugar, three ounces of saltpetre, dissolved alone. Do not put it on the meat until it is cold.

A Virginia Receipt for Bacon.

The pork must be well fattened on corn, and not cut out till the day after it is killed. Salt it well with fine salt and ground alum mixed, about a teaspoonful of saltpetre rubbed well on the hocks before the salt is applied. Lay it carefully in the tubs, with the skin down; let it lie four weeks. At the end of that time hang up the middlings, joints and chines; have the hams and shoulders covered with nicely-burnt hickory ashes, well sifted; let them lie two weeks, then hang them up with the hocks down. Keep a smoke, but no fire, to heat your meat. Old stumps are very good, or chips smothered with saw-dust. Be careful not to let one piece touch another in hanging.

Towards the spring, when the weather is warm and damp, put in just wood enough to keep alive, and a good deal of tobacco and red pepper. Do this at least once a day, it destroys the fly that deposits the egg for insects. It is best occasionally to have a smoke of that sort all the spring. Your meat-house must be dry, and have air-holes—auger holes bored high up in the gable ends, or a lattice door which you can lock, opening the close door in fine weather. Kill the hogs on the increase of the moon. By following these directions you are sure to have good bacon.

N. B.—The pork must not be salted in whisky barrels; molasses barrels are the best. The whisky is said to injure the bacon.

To Make Sausage Meat.

For a bushel of meat, chopped fine, add one teacupful of red pepper, one of black pepper, two teacupfuls of sage, one of sugar, one tablespoonful of saltpetre, all powdered, and salt enough to taste. Mix all together and try it, adding what seasoning it may require to suit your taste.

VIRGINIA SAUSAGE MEAT.

Pick the sausage meat to get out all the pieces of bone and strings. Wash it in luke-warm water and lay it on a table to drain. Let it stand all night. Take off some of the fat from the back bone to mix with the lean. If you use "leaf fat" when you fry your sausage, it will melt away to gravy and leave a little knot of lean, hard and dry, floating in a sea of melted grease. The fat must be taken off before the chines are salted, and washed, skinned, and put to drain with the lean. Next day chop it fine, picking out all the strings. When fine enough, season it with salt, sage, black and red pepper, to your taste. Pack it in a close vessel. If you wish to stuff them, you must have some nicely-cleaned chitterlings kept in salt and water ten days or a fortnight. Stuff them, hang them on sticks and dry them. A little smoke improves them; too much makes them bitter.

To SOUSE PIGS' FEET.

Let the feet be young and tender. Cover them with water, and boil them very slowly. When the bones are ready to fall out, take them from the fire and sprinkle a little salt over them. Set them away to cool, and when cold, remove all the grease from the top and the bones. Take them from the liquor, and add to it good strong vinegar—a pint of liquor to a pint of vinegar. Boil these together, with whole pepper, cloves and allspice. They require a great deal of salt. Taste them, and if there is not enough salt, add more. Throw the hot liquor over the feet and set them away till cold.

Hopping John.

One pint of lady peas to one quart of rice and one pound of bacon. Boil the peas and bacon together until soft; then add the rice, well washed. Stir it well, and let it boil until it boils up. Then pour off the water, leaving just enough to cover it well. Cover it and set it on a slow fire until thoroughly done. When you pour the water off, add a teaspoonful of whole black pepper.

POULTRY.

TURKEY.

THE turkey is a true son of the soil. *He* has never been asked for his naturalization papers! When Columbus launched his three caravels, he was an old inhabitant, and strutted and gobbled his unmolested way along the whole Atlantic seaboard. He has long since fled to the unsettled wilds and woody regions of the Far West, where the foot of man is seldom seen. In the Western States the wild turkey is still a familiar dish, but it is seldom seen in the cities of the Atlantic coast; here they are only to be obtained in the severe winter weather, when they are brought in a frozen condition many hundreds of miles. They are then very fine. The flesh is much the same as the domestic bird, but it is darker in color, more juicy, and has a slight game flavor. It is cooked in the same manner as the tame bird. Either wild or tame, it is universally admitted to be the finest fowl brought to table.

ROAST TURKEY.

The turkey must be young and plump. It should be roasted before a fire in a roaster and frequently basted. The body and craw should be stuffed with bread stuffing. The gravy must be made in a saucepan from the drippings in the roaster, carefully removing the fat. Some prefer the liver mashed with the

(85)

gravy. As many do not like the taste of liver, it is best, perhaps, to serve it on the dish and omit it in the gravy. The time,
required for cooking must depend upon the size of the bird,—
from two to three hours is generally required. Cranberry sauce
is commonly served with roast turkey.

BOILED TURKEY.

Turkey boiled is preferred by many persons; others think
that much of the fine flavor it possesses passes into the water.
In boiling a turkey it must be stuffed with a bread stuffing in
body and craw. Tie the legs and wings close to the body before
putting it on the fire. When the flesh begins to crack open
about the legs, it will be cooked enough. The sauces that accompany boiled turkey recommend this method of cooking it.
The first is oysters, stewed richly, and the second celery sauce,
made very much in the same manner.

BONED TURKEY.

The process of boning a turkey is very complicated and
difficult, and had better be left to professional skill. Although
the appearance may differ, the same result as regards flavor can
be obtained thus: Stuff the turkey inside and in the craw with
a rich force-meat. Take care to bind the legs and wings tightly
to the body, so as almost to imbed them in it, making the outside as nearly as possible a plain surface. Simmer it gently
till quite tender in as little water as will cook it, turning it
often. Have prepared a rich meat jelly, clear and well flavored.
Place the turkey, with the breast downwards, in a deep vessel,
and pour the melted jelly over it. Set it away to cool. The
vessel in which it cools will form a sort of mould, and should
be oval, to suit the shape of the bird. When quite cold, set the
vessel for an instant in hot water, to loosen the jelly; then turn
it out on the dish. As jelly looks better broken, place some of
the prettiest fragments over the top, with a sprig or two of
curled parsley. Boned turkey is always eaten cold.

Turkey, with Plum Pudding Stuffing.

Mix bread crumbs, butter, salt, pepper, and an egg well beaten; then throw in a teacupful of large raisins. Mix it well, but do not wet the dressing. Stuff the craw first, and sew it up with a large needle and coarse thread. Put the remainder into the body of the fowl. When the turkey is ready to serve, cut and remove the stitches carefully. In stuffing, leave room for the raisins to swell. If the turkey is to be eaten cold, scrape out the dressing and moisten it with a little gravy, heated thoroughly, and serve it alone hot.

Devilled Turkey.

Take a cooked leg of a turkey or fowl. Slash it all over to the bone. Salt and pepper it well, using both black and cayenne. Mix some made mustard with flour, and plaster it over the leg. Place it on the gridiron and broil it over a clear fire. Serve it hot.

Scalloped Turkey.

Cut up cold turkey into small pieces. Put a layer of bread crumbs into a buttered dish, moistened with a little milk; then lay in a layer of turkey, seasoned with salt and pepper, and a small piece of butter; then add another layer of crumbs, and so on till all is finished, adding any filling, gravy, or scraps left from the turkey. Then beat two eggs; add to them two table-spoonfuls of milk, one of butter, and a little salt. To this add cracker crumbs until it is thick enough to spread over the top of the turkey. Bake it half an hour, keeping it covered about twenty minutes; then remove the cover to let it brown.

Turkey in Jelly.

When the weather is very cold, a turkey may be prepared to last for several days, for lunch or for little suppers. Take a large tender turkey. Make a stuffing of bread crumbs, a little chopped pork fat, and an onion minced, with pepper and salt. Stuff the craw and the inside of the turkey as full as possible, and sew them up. Put it in a pot just large enough to hold it, and cover it with water. Let it simmer very slowly for several hours, keeping the lid of the pot on, and adding boiling water if the turkey should not continue covered. When the turkey appears thoroughly cooked, take it off the fire and put it away till cold. Pour the water in which it was boiled into a crock and set it away to cool. The next morning remove all the fat entirely from the top of this liquor, and put it on the fire in a kettle perfectly free from grease; then put in enough gelatin to stiffen it; the quantity must depend upon the quantity of liquid and also upon the strength of the liquor. If it should have jellied, it will not require so much gelatin. Taste the liquor, and if it requires salt, add it; then throw in a teaspoonful of sugar and a blade of mace, and the whites of two or three eggs to clear it. If the liquid is too light in color, add a little browned sugar. A little lemon juice may be added if approved of. Strain the jelly through a bag.

Cut the cold turkey in pieces of a convenient size. Take the breast bone out. Have ready some cold smoked tongue or ham, minced fine; mix enough of it with the stuffing to give it a savory flavor. Then place the pieces of turkey in a tall wide stone pot, as wide above as below. Put the stuffing at intervals between the pieces of turkey, and when all of it is in, pour the warm jelly over it and let it run well through the whole. Put the pot in a cold place, and take out the pieces of turkey when needed after the jelly has become hard. When it is served, a few capers will be an improvement, but they must not be put in the pot with the turkey, as they will interfere with its keeping.

CHICKENS.

Chickens should never be cooked the day they are killed; the flesh is then very stringy. They should be drawn as soon as possible, and the inside wiped with a dry cloth, but no water used. The livers, &c., should be put away by themselves. A little piece of charcoal laid inside will aid in preserving them. Chickens should be young and plump. Old ones should be boiled or fricasseed. For roasting, they should be stuffed with a bread stuffing both in the inside and in the craw; for boiling, only in the craw. In making chicken jelly, soup or gravy, immerse the claws, after they are cut off, in boiling water for a minute or two; the skin will come off like a glove. Throw them in the saucepan and let them cook with the rest. A rich gluten is found in the claw. Chickens are very good served cold in meat jelly, and make a handsome dish.

Philadelphia Chicken Salad.

For one pair of ordinary-sized chickens use one tablespoonful of mustard, if it is very strong, if not, half as much more. Mix it with water; then add the yolk of one raw egg, and pour in oil gradually, mixing it well together until half of the oil that is desired is used. Then mash the yolks of nine eggs, boiled hard, to a smooth pulp with a little vinegar, rejecting the eggs that will not mash and become mealy. Then beat in the yolks of two raw eggs, and continue with the oil, adding vinegar to taste. It must be beaten a long time, when it will become like a thick custard. One large bottle of oil will suffice for two pairs of chickens.

For salad, select tender chickens with plump breasts; or, if preferred, the breasts of turkeys. They may be either boiled or roasted. Cut them up in small pieces, and mix in celery, cut very small. The celery must be quite dry when added. Have the dressing made and the chicken prepared some hours before wanted. Sprinkle the chicken with a little vinegar, pepper and salt. When ready to serve, mix the chicken and celery well with the dressing, arrange it in dishes with young lettuce leaves, and spread a thick layer of the dressing on the top.

This dressing is intended either for lobster or crabs.

Another Chicken Salad.

Boil the chickens till perfectly well done. In preparing a great number for a large entertainment, a few are sometimes roasted. If turkey is used to mix with the chicken, it is always roasted. All the veins, sinews, fat, hard pieces and skin, must be carefully removed. Chop the whole up evenly in small pieces. Two or three hours before needed, place it in a large crock and pour enough of the dressing over it to moisten the whole. Half an hour before serving, place the chicken on large flat dishes, first putting a wreath of tender young lettuce leaves around the edge. Then place the lettuce leaves through the whole, at intervals, and handsomely upon the top. Then spread over it a thick layer of *Mayonnaise* dressing.

When the season will not admit of using lettuce, celery is substituted; some persons prefer always to have celery cut up with the chicken, the proportions about one-third celery, two-thirds chicken.

To Fricassee Chicken White.

Make a little white gravy with veal trimmings, mace, onion, salt and white pepper. When sufficiently done, strain the liquor from the meat and return it to the saucepan. Have the chicken ready cut up, and place it in this gravy. Stew it gently till the chicken is well cooked. Then take a gill of cream, the yolks of two eggs, and beat them well together. Thicken the gravy with flour and butter, well mixed. The last thing throw in the egg and cream, stirring it well, but do not let it boil after this, or the egg will curdle.

To Fricassee Chicken Brown.

Cut up the chicken. Fry the pieces a light brown. Put them in a stew-pan with sufficient gravy, already prepared. Thicken the gravy with butter and flour, mixed, and color it with sugar, browned. Season it with mace, and salt and pepper. If you like the flavor, add a little white wine.

To Fricassee Chickens.

Joint the chickens, and lay them in salt and water for one hour. Then put them on to boil in a small quantity of water, with mace, pepper and salt; add half a pint of cream or milk, thickened with butter and flour rolled together. Add chopped parsley just before serving.

Chicken and Tomatoes.

For four small chickens, take six large tomatoes and one or two onions, a slice of salt beef or pork, two or three large green peppers, the seeds and veins removed, a small bunch of fresh pot herbs, three cloves, a few pepper corns, half a tumbler of white wine and one of water, and a large piece of fat or butter. Put the whole in a stewpan and let it cook slowly. When nearly done, add rice, well washed and picked, in quantity sufficient to soak up the gravy. When the rice is well swelled and tender, remove the saucepan to a slow fire to simmer, covering it well with a cloth under the lid. When done, the rice should be dry and tender.

Boiled Chicken and Macaroni.

Boil the chicken in the usual way. Boil six ounces of macaroni for ten minutes, in half a pint of water, with a tablespoonful of butter. Strain it and put in two small onions, with three cloves stuck in each; then pour in half a pint of milk or cream, enough to cover the macaroni, and season it with salt and pepper.

Boil it very gently for half an hour, till the macaroni has soaked up all the milk or cream; pour over it cheese grated very fine, and then pour the whole, very hot, over the chicken, which may be served whole, or cut up as for a fricassee.

CHICKEN CURRY.

A dish for six or seven persons may be made thus: Take one large or two small fowls; cut them up in pieces large enough for serving; put them in salt and water until the ingredients are ready; take two tablespoonfuls of powdered ginger, one of fresh turmeric, a few cloves, some mace, cardamom seeds, cayenne and black pepper and salt. Put into a large mortar three or four onions of good size; pound them well with the spices until they form a paste. Brown the chicken in butter. While this is doing, place a saucepan with three pints of water on the fire. When it boils, throw in the paste, and when this has cooked a short time, put in the chicken and let it all stew together. Rice must be served in a separate dish to eat with it, the rice boiled dry and well. Curry may be made of lamb, veal, or any sweet poultry. Serve the above in a deep dish capable of containing a great deal of gravy.

If you wish your curry in the form of a soup, boil your meat in sufficient water and stir in the above paste, with a tablespoonful of flour mixed with it. A breast of mutton makes a very good curry. The meat should be cut in spoon-pieces for helping conveniently. Taste before serving, to see if it has salt and pepper enough. Eat it with rice, and if you like a little acid, add some drops of lime juice in your own plate. A very good curry may be made from the cold mutton or fowls left from yesterday's dinner.

CHICKEN CURRY.

Chickens to be roasted plain, jointed and cut up. Put two tablespoonfuls of curry powder in a pan, and let it brown in an oven a minute or two. Take two sliced onions, and brown them in about two tablespoonfuls of butter in the frying-pan. Remove the onions, when browned, and put them into the pan with the curry powder, salt, and four tablespoonfuls of cream; add the chicken. Let stew from five to ten minutes. Cold roast veal may be prepared in this way, but must be chopped.

CHICKEN PILAU.

Cut up a chicken as for a fricassee. Let it simmer slowly, with enough water only to cover it. Season it with pepper and salt, and a blade of mace. Have ready a large teacupful of rice, which has been well washed and left in water to soak. When the chicken is cooked enough, not till ready to fall apart, but allowing for further cooking, take it off the fire. Drain the rice, and put it in the pot with about a pint of the liquor in which the chicken was boiled. Salt it and let it boil till nearly done; then drain off the liquor if any remain, but not too dry. Put the chicken into the middle of the rice, heap the rice around it and let the whole stew gently in a corner of the fire.

A FLORIDA PILAU.

Take a fat chicken. Cut it up in small pieces. Then fry one onion, one clove of garlic, five tomatoes and a piece of pork altogether until brown. Then add a pint of rice, with water enough to cook it, and a little allspice, and let it boil gently. When the rice is thoroughly cooked, set the pot on one side of the fire to simmer gently till it is time to serve it.

TO MAKE A PILAU.

Boil a pair of fowls, and, when well cooked, reserve a part of the water in which to boil the rice, keeping the rest to add afterwards. When the rice is done, mix it with butter; lay one half in the bottom of a deep dish, lay the fowls upon it, and put the other half of the rice on top, adding the remainder of the liquor. Then spread over all the well-beaten yolks of two eggs, and bake it in a moderate oven.

PHILADELPHIA CROQUETTES.

Mince turkey or chicken as fine as it is possible; season with salt, pepper, the smallest dash of powdered mace, and a little onion, grated. Then make a sauce thus: Take a large tablespoonful of butter, two tablespoonfuls of flour, half a tumbler of cream and a little salt; mix these smoothly together and boil it, stirring all the time. Then pour the sauce over the mince and mix it thoroughly together. When it is cold and hard, take out a tablespoonful and shape it into a pyramid. Have ready the yolks of eggs beaten light in a plate. Roll your pyramid in the egg and then in bread or cracker crumbs, aiding with your fingers to shape it. Drop your croquette into boiling lard, which must be deep enough in the pan to cover it, and when it is brown, lift it out of the lard with a perforated skimmer and lay it upon a dish spread with soft paper, to absorb superfluous grease. If you wish your croquettes to be very superior in delicacy, use half sweetbread and half turkey or chicken; this makes them soft and creamy. The above quantity of sauce is enough for half a turkey. It is better for inexperienced cooks to use a brush for the egg, touching the outside very lightly with it. Too much egg will form a cake and fall off. Some prefer to mix the egg with the whole of the ingredients. Wire frying baskets are much used for croquettes.

CROQUETTES.

Boil a pair of chickens with a little salt, and skin them. Take out the bones and mince them as fine as possible. Work two tablespoonfuls of flour into a quarter of a pound of butter, and stir it into the minced chicken. Then add a pint of rich cream, half a grated nutmeg, pepper and salt to taste, a pinch of ground mace, a tablespoonful of chopped parsley, half a small onion, chopped very fine. Mix all these together and let it stew ten minutes. Take it off the fire; add the yolks of four eggs and stir it well. Spread the mixture on a dish to cool. Take out a spoonful, roll and shape it in flour. Take the yolks of four eggs, the juice of one lemon, and a little salt, a tablespoonful of cream. Mix all together and dip each croquette in it. Afterwards roll them in fine bread crumbs, made of stale bread grated and sifted. Fry them a light brown in boiling lard.

PRESSED CHICKEN.

Put a fowl into a porcelain-lined kettle with salt, a few cloves, and whole allspice, but no water. Put the kettle into another of boiling water, and let it remain two hours, or until the fowl is tender. Then remove the skin and bones, chop the dark and light meat together, but not very fine, and place them in a dish. Pour over it the strained liquor which remained in the kettle. Let it cool; then fold it in a cloth and press it with a heavy weight. To be sliced when cold.

FRIED CHICKEN.

Cut the chickens in pieces and season them with pepper, salt, and a dust of meal, and then fry them, after which lay them on a dish and cover over to keep warm. Then pour the grease out of the frying-pan and put into it a teacupful of cream, a blade of mace, a little salt and pepper, a saltspoonful of flour and a teaspoonful of butter mixed together. Let these simmer together a few minutes. Place the chicken in the dish in which it is to be served and pour the sauce over it.

CHICKEN PIE.

Cut one or two chickens in pieces of a convenient size for helping. Put them in a saucepan with water, but not enough to cover them. Add pepper and salt, and a blade of mace; if you like the flavor, add a piece of celery about two inches long. Let the chicken simmer slowly, frequently turning it in the water, that the upper pieces may go to the bottom, and let the saucepan be well covered, to keep in the steam. When the chicken is nearly cooked, take it out of the water. Skim the grease off the water; then make a thickening of flour, mixed well with butter, and stir it in. Let it thicken over the fire for a short time; then have a good paste prepared, line the baking dish with it, place the pieces of chicken within it, and then pour in the liquor from the saucepan. Several hard-boiled eggs, cut in half, are sometimes put in the dish with the meat. If the gravy is to be very thick and rich, stir the yolk of an egg, well beaten, into the liquor before putting it in the dish. Keep the giblets whole, and lay them in with the rest. Cover the dish with the paste, and bake it only long enough to bake the crust. If the gravy should dry up, and there is any remaining in the saucepan, add it by pouring it through a hole beneath a little ornamental tuft, made of crust, on the top of the pie.

Chicken Pie.

Take a tender young chicken; cut it into small pieces; put it into a small pan with a little salt, and cover it with water. Cover the pan and let the chicken cook till tender. Then make a rich pastry. Cut little squares of paste and put them in with the chicken; also a lump of butter, some pepper and a little rich cream. Then cover the whole with the pastry, and make a hole in the centre of the cover; also with a fork make holes in the top crust to prevent blistering. Chicken pie should always have a great deal of gravy; this must be made from the water in which the chicken was simmered. Take as much of it as will be necessary to fill the pie dish, and stir into it a small piece of butter and a very little flour, not more than a small teaspoonful. Add a blade of mace, and give it a quick boil in a saucepan; then pour it over the chicken when it is in the baking-dish.

To Make Chicken Pot Pie.

Make a paste of any degree of richness that you prefer. Cut it into long broad strips and line the pot with it, placing them like the staves of a barrel. Cut the chicken in pieces, salt and pepper it, and if onion is acceptable, put in about a quarter of an onion. Cut up two potatoes and add them. Make some large flat dumplings of rich paste and mix with the chicken. Then rub some flour and butter together; stir this in some hot water and make the mixture smooth. Pour it into the pot with the chicken, and if it is not enough to cover the chicken, add a little warm water. Then turn the tops of the crust lining the pot over the chicken, and make a lid of crust to go over the whole; a hole in the middle of this must be left for the gravy to bubble through. The crust must be thick. When the pie is done enough, serve it on a large dish, place the chicken in the middle, and arrange the pieces which lined the pot, and ought to be well browned, on the outside, putting the softer crust and dumplings inside.

Spring Chicken.

The young spring chickens are too delicate for roasting, and not mature enough for fricasseeing. They are better either broiled or fried. For broiling, split them down the back, and broil them before the fire in a folding wire broiler, turning them frequently; dust them with a little flour and baste them with butter. When they are cooked through, place them on a hot dish, rub more butter over them and serve them hot.

Chicken Pudding.

Beat ten eggs very light; add to them a quart of milk. Melt a quarter of a pound of butter; stir the butter into the milk with as much flour as will make a thin batter. Prepare four chickens; cut them up in large pieces, as in carving at table. Put them in a saucepan with as little water as will cook them, some salt, pepper and parsley. Let them simmer till tender. Then take the chicken from the water and place it in a deep baking-dish. Pour the batter over the whole and bake it.

To Roast a Fowl with Chestnuts.

Roast about two dozen chestnuts; shell them while hot and take off the skin. Chop them in pieces about the size of a grain of corn. Have ready two dozen boiled chestnuts. Shell, skin and pound them in a mortar, with the liver of the fowl and a small piece of the fat of boiled ham, a little pepper, and sufficient salt. Then add enough boiled chestnuts, whole, to make sufficient stuffing for the craw and inside of the fowl. Roast the fowl, and thicken the gravy with boiled chestnuts pounded to a paste. Throw in a few whole boiled chestnuts, and stew them up for a short time with the gravy, and when it is served, pour over the fowl some gravy and a few chestnuts.

GEESE AND DUCKS.

Roasting is the only mode in which a goose is cooked. It should be young; there is no food more distasteful than an old goose. If the weather is freezing, it is well to let it hang in the air two or three days. Singe the bird well. Stuff the inside and the craw with a rich stuffing, either of bread or boiled mashed potatoes, mixed with powdered sage and onions. More onions are used with a goose than with chicken or turkey. Baste it well, and if the breast shows signs of drying too much, cover it with a piece of paper skewered on.

Goose is usually eaten with apple sauce.

To Roast Ducks.

Ducks should be young and tender. They are stuffed with a bread stuffing and sometimes with mashed potatoes. Dried herbs and onion are used in both of these stuffings. Chestnuts are sometimes used to stuff ducks. They are also dressed with olives. The olive stones are taken out, and they are placed, with a little gravy, around the birds on the dish when served.

To Stew Ducks.

Half roast a duck; then carve it into pieces and put it in a stewpan, with a pint of beef jelly, a small onion minced, a little pepper and salt. Simmer it about fifteen minutes and skim it well; then add about a quart of green peas and a piece of butter rolled in flour. Cover the pan close, and let it stew a half hour longer. Serve it with sippets of toast.

GAME.

VENISON.

VENISON is either roasted or broiled. For roasting, the saddle is the choicest part. While before the fire it should be closely watched, and if it shows signs of becoming too crisp, it must be covered with white paper, stuck on with a skewer. Venison is always served very much underdone. For those who like it better done, a few slices may be cut at table and cooked in a chafing dish, with currant jelly and gravy.

Venison steaks must be broiled in the same manner as beef steaks. Small slices may be cooked with great advantage in a folding broiler, which must be frequently turned to keep in the juices.

The inferior parts of the deer are used for pasties. The legs are often dried and used like dried beef.

VENISON SAUSAGES.

Mince a portion of the fore quarter or neck of venison. Add to it one half of the quantity of pork, also minced. Season it with pepper and dried herbs. Make this up into little pats and fry them. The fat in them will be sufficient for frying.

VENISON PASTY.

Bone a neck and breast of venison. Cut the meat into pieces small enough to be "helped" easily. Boil the bones and trimmings in a saucepan, and season them with pepper and salt, a little mace, and an onion, cut up fine. Let the bones stew till all the juices are extracted. Strain off the liquor and put the pieces of meat into it, and let it all simmer slowly for twenty minutes, stirring into it a good lump of butter mixed with a little flour. Have prepared a rich paste; line the dish with it. Take the venison from the fire; stir into it a glass of red wine, and pour the whole into the baking dish. Cover the top with the paste and bake it till the crust is done.

A mutton pasty may be made in the same manner, but without the wine.

RABBITS.

RABBITS are commonly fricasseed like chicken, either in a white or brown sauce. Their flesh is in the best condition in mid-winter. This animal is cheap and plentiful, but is not in much repute for the table.

To STEW RABBITS.

Divide the rabbits into quarters. Lard them or not, as you please. Dust them with flour, and fry them with lard or butter. Then put them into an earthen pipkin with a quart of warm water, pepper, salt, and a blade of mace. Mix well with flour a piece of butter the size of a small egg; stir it smoothly into the liquor. Let it stew slowly for half an hour; then add a glassful of white wine, and serve them in the gravy.

BIRDS.

ROASTING is universally conceded to be the best method of cooking most game birds. The canvas-back duck, so renowned for the delicacy of its flesh, is always roasted. This bird is found nowhere but in America. On its return from the far north in the fall, its flesh is not palatable, but after feeding a little while on the wild celery which attracts them to the rivers where they abound, they soon become fat and juicy. Epicures have given the law as to the cooking of these birds, and have ordained that they shall be served while the flesh and gravy are still of a bright red. The time for roasting them varies from fifteen to thirty-five minutes. These ducks should not be drawn till they are about to be cooked, and very little water should be used in cleaning them.

Next to the canvas-back is the red-head, which in delicacy of flavor is not far inferior. The variety of wild ducks, however, is so great, and the method of cooking so similar, that it is unnecessary to give particular directions for each. The widgeon, mallard, teal, black duck, &c., are all roasted.

Pheasants, grouse and prairie hens are always roasted. This is also considered the best mode of cooking partridges, though a greater latitude is given in preparing them. In those localities in our country, principally in the Western States, where they are plentiful, it is common to break up and stew down half a dozen for making the sauce. They are sometimes boiled, and at large dinners often, thus cooked, take the place of turkey when out of season. Partridges keep longer than most birds.

Game will keep an indefinite time if frozen. It must, however, be cooked as soon as thawed. No bird is better for being kept longer than two or three days. Snipe, plover, rail and reed birds may be eaten on the day they are killed.

Game birds should be basted in their own juices and dredged with a very little flour. Larding interferes with the natural flavor of the bird, though it renders it more juicy. If this mode of preparing them is preferred, it is best not to use a larding needle, as is the practice with meats, but instead, to cut a very thin slice of bacon fat and skewer it delicately over the breast, apron-fashion, in which garb they must be served.

Snipe and woodcock are frequently roasted without drawing them. Though sanctioned by epicures, this is a disgusting practice, as articles of food offensive to man are often found in their stomachs.

It is difficult to give rules as regards time in cooking birds so much depends upon circumstances. About twenty minutes are required for partridges; for grouse and prairie hen, from thirty to thirty-five minutes; snipe, woodcook and plover, about fifteen.

The reed bird of Pennsylvania is the bobolink of New York and the rice bird of the south. Its flesh is very delicate, and is said to resemble closely that of the European ortolan. The small size of the bird renders them difficult to clean.

Birds are served with or without their heads, according to taste. Snipe and woodcock, however, must always be served with their heads on, as their long bills proclaim them, and are highly prized. Some of the smaller kind are served with their claws.

CANVAS-BACK DUCKS.

Canvas-back ducks must be roasted quickly before a brisk fire to keep the juices from flowing out. From fifteen to thirty-five minutes is the range allowed to suit different tastes. They are always eaten very much underdone, so that a rich, high-colored blood will follow the knife. They are never stuffed or dressed in any other manner. The breast is very large and full, and is usually the only part eaten.

Serve them hot, and let the plates be well warmed. Currant jelly is commonly eaten with them.

For those who like their food a little more cooked, a chafing dish will render a few slices of the breast more palatable. Currant jelly may be added if desired.

To Roast Wild Ducks.

Put an onion inside of each duck, with a little pepper, salt, and a tablespoonful of red wine. If the fire is good, twenty minutes will roast them. Serve them with onion sauce, or the following gravy : Boil the necks and gizzards with an onion till the liquor is about a pint; then add a blade of mace, a slice off the end of a lemon, half an anchovy, and pepper and salt. Boil it to half a pint. Color it with browned sugar. Strain it and serve it with the ducks.

Woodcock.

Woodcock, when prepared for connoisseurs, are roasted. with the entrails left in them,—the gizzard only is removed. When placed before the fire, lay a piece of toast beneath each bird to absorb the trail, and serve them upon this toast. They require from fifteen to twenty minutes to roast, and must be basted with butter. If drawn, the process is the same.

Woodcock are sometimes stewed in a pan, with very little water, dredged with flour, and basted well with butter. Their own juices soon flow out and make a good gravy.

A favorite way of cooking them is to split them down the back and broil them. Baste them with butter, and serve them on toast.

Snipe.

Snipe, like woodcock, should be roasted to be eaten in perfection. They are sometimes larded. If this is resorted to, it is best to cover the breast with a thin sheet of the fat of pork, skewered on. They are sometimes stuffed, but this is not the most approved manner. The stuffing absorbs too much of the juices of the bird.

Partridges.

Partridges are usually roasted in the same manner as grouse. They may be cooked whole, by putting them in a stewpan with a little butter and water, seasoned with salt and pepper. Cover the stewpan close, and turn them frequently, so as to keep them moist with the gravy. Thicken the gravy, and add a little browning, if you choose. Partridges may be split down the back and broiled over a clear fire. If this mode is preferred, when they are sufficiently cooked, place them on a hot dish and rub them over with butter, and serve them upon toast, hot.

To Dress Pheasants or Partridges in Jelly.

The day before the birds are cooked, boil some calves' feet till the bones fall out. Strain the liquor from them and set them to cool. The next day skim off all the fat with great care, finally wiping the top and the sides of the pan with a cloth. This will be found a stiff, hard jelly. Put the jelly on the fire in a bell-metal kettle. Beat the whites of three eggs and mix them with a wineglassful of pale, good vinegar, the juice of a lemon, a blade or two mace, a teaspoonful of whole white pepper, a teaspoonful of sugar, and enough salt to flavor it properly. Put these into the jelly and let it boil. When it begins to break away and clear, pass it through a flannel jelly strainer till clear; then pour a little in the bottom of a large bowl or mould. Place your birds (which must have been well roasted in the meantime) with their breasts downward in the bowl, and when the jelly begins to "set," pour in the rest of it. Let it stand all night. The next day loosen the jelly in the mould, by dipping it in hot water, and turn it out on the dish in which it is to be served.

To Roast Grouse.

These birds are usually allowed to hang some time when the weather is cold enough. After drawing and cleaning them, cut off the heads. Tie them across with pack thread, to keep them in shape. Suspend them by wires, or the usual hooks in a tin roaster, and roast them in front of the fire, basting them frequently with butter and water. Many persons bake them

in a pan, but it is universally acknowledged that baked meats
are inferior to roasted. Serve them with sippets of toast in
their own gravy, seasoned, or with bread sauce made of crumbs
saturated with the gravy

To Roast Reed Birds.

Roasting is the best methed of cooking these little birds.
This can easily be accomplished by suspending them from the
little wires usually found in roasters, or tin kitchens, as they
are sometimes called. They can be frequently turned and
easily basted. They take a very short time to cook, and must
be carefully watched. Baste them with butter and serve them
hot.

To Bake Reed Birds.

Select a number of large potatoes of the same size and shape.
Wash them well and pare them, taking the skin off as thin as
possible. Cut a deep slice off one end of each, and with a
knife or teaspoon scoop out a space in the inside of the potato
large enough for the bird. Drop a small piece of butter inside
of the bird, pepper and salt it, and then put it into the hollow
made in the potato. Place as a lid the piece cut off; then cut a
slice off the other end to enable it to stand. Repeat this with
the rest of the birds. Place the potatoes in a baking dish close
beside each other and put them in the oven to bake, with a
very little water at the bottom to prevent burning. Bake them
slowly, and serve them in the dish in which they were baked,
or they will lose their shape. Reed birds may also be boiled,
enveloped in a crust like a dumpling.

To Broil Reed Birds.

After the birds are picked and cleaned, keep them on ice till
ready to be cooked. Use very little water in cleaning them.
Season them with pepper and salt, and put them in a folding
wire broiler. Turn the broiler frequently, and baste them with

a little butter. When they are done, place them in a hot dish, with some small pieces of butter rubbed over them, and cover them. Serve them on toast and keep them covered.

To Stew Reed Birds.

After they have been properly prepared, put them in a stew-pan with a little water. Rub them well over with butter, and season them with pepper and salt. Cover the pan and let them simmer slowly. When done, serve them in their own gravy. Keep them hot in a covered dish.

PIGEONS.

Pigeons may be dressed in many ways. Their flavor depends a great deal upon their being drawn and cleaned as soon as killed.

For roasting, they may be stuffed as you do fowls, and cooked in a tin roaster before the fire. For baking, they may be prepared in the same manner, and baked in a pan in the oven, adding a little water and seasoning for the gravy, and basting them with a little butter.

To Broil Pigeons.

Split the pigeons open down the back. Season them with pepper and salt and let them lie for ten minutes; then baste them with flour and put them on the gridiron, turning them rapidly from side to side. When done, spread butter in lumps over them and serve them hot.

Pigeons in Jelly.

Pigeons in jelly make a very nice dish. Stew the birds whole, with pepper and salt, and a little mace. When done, put them in a stone pan till cold; then pour over them clear meat jelly, which you must have ready prepared, and which must be melted for this purpose. While melted, a little lemon juice may be added to it, or any flavor you like.

PIGEON DUMPLINGS.

Season the pigeons well with pepper and salt. Lay each pigeon in a piece of puff paste rolled half an inch thick. Tie each one in a cloth, and boil them gently two hours.

PIGEONS STEWED.

Pigeons may be stewed by laying them in a stewpan between layers of cabbage, cut as for slaw. Season them with salt and pepper. Thicken a little broth with flour and pour it over them. Cover the pan well, and let them simmer until the pigeons are tender.

Stewed without the cabbage, they should be done in the same manner, and served with mushrooms.

SQUABS IN OLIVES.

Clean them nicely and lay them in salt and water. Take a quarter of a pound of butter, a quarter of an onion, three tablespoonfuls of flour, and a little mace, cloves, and pepper and salt, and stew them together for half an hour. Then add the olives, stoned, and let all stew slowly for an hour longer.

LITTLE DISHES.

BROTHER JONATHAN.

Make a "mush" of Indian meal, adding enough wheat flour to prevent the pieces from breaking when sliced. Let the mush be made the day before it is to be used, and set it to cool in a deep pan, that the slices may be large enough. Turn out the cold mass and cut it into slices; and then with the top of a small teacup cut it out in circles like short cake. Place your little circles around a flat, round plate or dish, in a row. Then add another row on top of these, and so on till you form a low pyramid. Sprinkle each row freely, as you place it, with Parmesan or other rich, dry cheese, grated. Throw red pepper over the whole, and dot it with little pieces of butter and a little grated bread. Brown it in a quick oven, as you do macaroni, and serve it in the dish in which it is baked. The mush must be salted when boiled. Two or three yolks of eggs beaten and stirred into the mush while warm will add to the richness.

CHEESE BOXES.

Take two tumblerfuls of milk, a quarter of a pound of fresh, sweet butter, and a good quarter of a pound of wheat flour. Boil these till they make a thick, smooth cream. Cool it. Then mix the yolks of six beaten eggs and half a pound of grated cheese—Parmesan, or rich cheese old enough to grate. Then beat the whites of six eggs to a froth and mix them slowly

(111)

with the above mixture. Have prepared some little paper boxes, made of stiff paper, shaped according to your fancy. Grease them well with butter. Fill them with the mixture immediately and place them in the oven on tins. If allowed to stand too long in the oven they will fall; but they must remain in long enough to cook the ingredients well. Fill the boxes half full, as they rise a great deal. Serve them as soon as done. They should be of a light brown. Taste the mixture, and if salt is required, add it; and if you choose, a little cayenne pepper.

<h2 style="text-align:center">PANNIKINS.</h2>

Have ready some little earthen pans, such as are sold for toy milk pans, capable of holding one egg only, a little broader at the top than at the bottom. Heat them in the oven, and when quite hot take them out, and with a " paste brush" butter them thoroughly inside. Break an egg carefully into each pan. Set them in the oven till the white of the egg is hard enough to take the form of the pan. Turn them out on the dish in which they are to be served in a circle. On the top of each sprinkle a very little fresh parsley, chopped fine; or, if you prefer it, a little smoked tongue, grated. Have ready a sauce of bread crumbs, beaten up with a rich gravy, browned and seasoned; the sauce should be of the consistency of mashed turnip. Place this in the middle of the dish, the eggs enclosing it. A mince of veal, seasoned with a rich gravy, may be used; or, if you prefer it, richly stewed spinage instead of the bread sauce. Be careful not to cook the eggs too much; the yolks should be semi-liquid, and the whites only firm enough to keep in form. This is an ornamental dish.

<h2 style="text-align:center">LETTUCE CUPS.</h2>

Pound any cold fish that you may have in a mortar, being careful to remove the skin and bones. Make a *Mayonnaise* dressing; stir a portion of it in the fish. Have ready small, delicate heads of lettuce. Remove the outer leaves that are old and tough. Fill each lettuce head with the fish, and place them round a dish. Drop from a teaspoon into each head a little more of the dressing and serve them for lunch.

LAMB AND TOMATO SALAD.

Take equal proportions of lamb and tomatoes; cut cold roast lamb in small slices; scald, peal, and remove the seeds from the tomatoes. Put them together in a dish in alternate layers, sprinkling a thick *Mayonnaise* dressing over each layer. Let it remain in the refrigerator till served.

GIBLETS.

Take the giblets of turkeys, chickens, geese or ducks. Have them carefully cleaned. Put them in a saucepan with an onion, a little mace, salt and pepper. Cover them with water, and let them stew till tender. When they are about half done, add a sweetbread or some calves' brains. Mix some flour and butter to thicken the gravy, and stir it in. When the sweet-breads are cooked, add a little mushroom ketchup and serve it. This makes a very nice little dish when served in a puff paste shell.

A NICE LITTLE DISH OF BEEF.

Mince cold roast beef, fat and lean, with a little onion, very fine. Season them with pepper and salt and moisten them with gravy. Fill scallop shells half full with this, and the remaining half with potatoes, mashed smooth with cream. Put a little lump of butter on each and brown them in the oven.

CHICKEN AND RICE.

Chop some cold chicken into small pieces. Mix it with an equal quantity of cold boiled rice. Put it in a small baking dish, with pepper and salt to taste, and cover the top with an

8

egg beaten light. Moisten it with a little broth or chicken gravy and brown it in the oven. Mashed potatoes may be used instead of rice, or the remains of macaroni left from the day before.

COLD MUTTON.

Slice the mutton. Put the bones and trimmings into a stew-pan and boil them for gravy. Skim the grease off carefully. A short time before they are needed, put the slices into a wide saucepan, or chafing dish; the latter is the best. Pepper and salt to taste; a little mixed mustard, a wineglassful of currant jelly, and some pickles cut up, or capers. The gravy must be strained and used to cook it.

VEAL PATTY.

Three pounds of veal, one pound of fresh pork, two crackers, pounded fine, two eggs, one and a-half nutmegs, one teaspoonful of black pepper, half a spoonful of cayenne, two tablespoonfuls of salt. All must be minced very fine and well worked together. Put some crumbs and butter over the top. Set the dish in a pan of water, and bake it in a moderate oven for two hours. If it begins to burn or harden on the top, cover it with a dish or paper. Serve it cold, cut in slices.

MINCE FOR PATTIES.

Two ounces of ham, four ounces of chicken or veal, one egg, boiled hard, a little mace, cloves, salt and pepper. Mince all fine. Add four tablespoonfuls of hot, rich gravy, the same of cream, and one ounce of butter. This will be nicer if eaten hot. When you are ready to serve the patties, put the mince in the shells. If eaten cold, the shells can be filled at any time.

A Little Pasty.

This can be made of any kind of cold meat hashed and seasoned highly. Line a dish with pie-crust. Pour the meat in hot. Cover it with a crust and bake like oyster pie.

Tomato Toss-Up.

Peel and remove the seeds from six large tomatoes. Put them in a pan with a spoonful of melted butter, some pepper, salt, and a small onion, minced. Fry and stir the whole together, and add to it when nearly done cold meat or fowl, shredded. Let it simmer a short time, and serve it hot.

Risotto.

Pick and clean carefully a pound of the best rice. Boil it in enough water to cover it, adding a little salt. Do not stir it at all, but be careful that it does not burn. In twenty-five minutes it will be done. While the rice is cooking, boil six or eight well-made sausages for fifteen minutes. When the rice is done, place it in a well-buttered mould, laying the sausages in it at intervals so as not to touch each other. Put the mould into a hot oven and bake it for a few minutes. When ready for it, turn it out of the mould and serve it with a sauce made from strong broth or meat jelly, thickened with a little flour and browning. Use no butter or grease of any kind. Serve the sauce in a boat. If sausages are not liked, force-meat balls of any meat you prefer may be substituted.

Rice Pie.

Into one quart of nicely-boiled rice stir a large spoonful of butter, less than a pint of sweet milk, two eggs, and a little salt. Lay in a baking dish alternate layers of this mixture, and cold turkey and ham, cut quite fine. Cover the mixture and bake it for twenty minutes.

POTATO DUMPLINGS.

Boil and mash six large potatoes. Add a large piece of butter, salt, pepper, a little onion, and any herb you prefer. Make a rich paste. Roll it out as for apple dumplings. Fill the paste with the potato mixture, and boil it for twenty minutes. Serve it with bread crumbs browned in butter.

A good substitute for meat at dinner, or as a side dish.

SOAKED PASSOVER BREAD.

This delicate bread is made into many nice dishes for breakfast, dinner and tea, mixed with milk, butter, pepper and salt. It can be fried in butter like large hominy.

SIMPLE CROQUETTES.

Take cold fowl, or fresh meat of any kind. Add a little ham, fat or lean. Chop very fine, and add half as much stale bread, grated, salt, pepper, a dash of nutmeg, a teaspoonful of made mustard, a tablespoonful of ketchup, and a lump of butter. Knead all well together till it resembles sausage meat. Make them into balls, rolls or pyramids. Dip them in beaten egg. Roll them in sifted bread crumbs and fry them brown.

KIDNEYS (A NICE BREAKFAST DISH).

Boil and chop one dozen lamb kidneys very fine, and mix them into a smooth, rich paste with yolk of egg. Cut small squares of bread, taking off the crust. Cover them on both sides with the kidney paste, and fry them like doughnuts in plenty of boiling lard.

KIDNEYS.

Boil a beef kidney. Chop it very fine, and mix it with yolk of egg into a smooth, rich paste. Cut small squares of bread, removing the crust. Cover the pieces on both sides with the kidney paste, and fry them very quickly in plenty of boiling lard.

BEEF KIDNEY.

Take a fresh beef kidney, removing the fat, and let it soak in salt and water for two or three hours; then put it on the fire in cold water and let it stew for several hours, until perfectly tender. If the water smells strong, change it while cooking, as kidneys vary very much in this respect. Slice the meat off, leaving all the white part behind, as that is not fit to be used. Have ready a pan with a lump of butter in it the size of an egg. Let this brown; then add some browned flour and a cupful of hot water, and boil all into a smooth gravy. Chop the kidney fine. Add to it the gravy, with some pepper and salt, and let it stew slowly for a short time before serving.

FROGS.

The hind legs alone are eaten. They may be broiled or made into a white or brown fricassee, seasoned with mushrooms or tomato ketchup. The flesh is delicate, and resembles that of tender chicken.

SOUSED TRIPE.

After the tripe has been properly prepared by the butcher, put it on to boil in water for about ten or twelve hours. It must be sufficiently tender to mash with the fingers before it is soft enough. Then take it out and boil it in milk and water to whiten it. Set it away to cool, and then cut the tripe into small pieces. Put it into a porcelain-lined saucepan and cover it with vinegar. Throw in some pepper corns, some ground black pepper, cayenne, a little mace, and plenty of salt. Let it stew for a few minutes; then add some of the water in which it was boiled, or all if it is much reduced in bulk. Taste it to see if it is salt enough. Stir it well and turn it out into a stone pot. When it is cold, it will be jellied and firm.

FRIED TRIPE.

Prepare the tripe by rolling and tying it with wrapping cord. Boil it until it is so tender that a fork will easily turn around in it. Let it stand until the following day, and put it into a weak brine until it is wanted. Cut it into slices. Dip them in egg and cracker crumbs, and fry it in pieces like oysters.

SPICED TRIPE.

Roll and wrap the tripe tightly with cord. Boil it very tender, which will take eight or ten hours; then spread the rolls upon a flat surface. Let them stand until next day. Cut them into slices and put them in jars, adding three small red peppers, or cayenne and salt to taste, and a spoonful of celery seed. Some pieces of horseradish will preserve the vinegar and give it a pleasant flavor.

SCRAPPLE.

Take the faces of the porkers, with the odd bits of lean taken off in trimming the pork. Add a small portion of the liver, and boil them all together till the bones drop out. Pick out the bones and other useless parts and chop the meat fine. Have the liquor in which the meat was boiled strained and the fat removed from the top. Thicken this liquor with Indian meal, and boil it till it is a thick batter; then put in the chopped meat. Add powdered sage, salt and pepper. Boil all together for a few minutes and pour it hot into pans. For use, cut it in slices and fry it, or eat it cold.

SOUSED PIGS' FEET.

Boil, until ready to fall apart, a set of small pigs' feet. Put a little salt in the water Boil the water nearly all away. Take out the bones. Add one teaspoonful of allspice and a good deal of black pepper and salt, and a cup of vinegar. Stir well over the fire in the reduced water. Set it away to cool, and serve it cut in slices.

FRIED NOODLES

Beat two eggs, and add to them a tablespoonful of water and half a teaspoonful of salt. Mix in sufficient flour to make a stiff paste. Roll it into thin sheets. Dry and cut them. Boil them in water for twenty minutes. Have ready a pan containing butter and browned bread crumbs. Put the noodles into this. Mix all thoroughly and fry. Serve as a side dish.

FORCE-MEAT.

Beef or veal are the meats used for force-meat. They must be first cooked. Chickens or turkeys make excellent force-meat, but they are too expensive for this purpose. Mix with the meat sweetbreads or calves' brains. Fresh meat should always be mixed with a little ham, pork or tongue, to flavor them. Chop the meat very fine, season it with pepper, salt, a little mace, and an onion, which should be bruised into a paste in a mortar. Beat two or three eggs and stir them into the meat; then make them into balls, roll them in bread or cracker dust and fry them.

EGG TOAST.

Break six eggs into a dish and beat them very little, adding salt. Cut some slices of bread; dip them into cold water and then into the egg. Fry a few slices of salt pork; take out the pork and fry the slices of dipped bread in the fat until they are light brown on both sides. When all the bread has been fried, add the slices of pork to the remainder of the egg and fry them also.

ANCHOVY TOAST.

One quart of milk, the yolks of three eggs and four teaspoonfuls of anchovy paste. Make a soft custard of the milk and eggs. Take it from the fire and stir in the paste. Toast and butter on both sides some bread. Dip the buttered toast into the sauce. Place the toast in a covered dish and pour the rest of the sauce over it.

WELSH RABBIT.

Mix together some rich cheese and about the same weight of milk, a piece of butter, salt, cayenne pepper, and mixed mustard to your taste. Stew it all together quickly, and serve it with or without pieces of toast, as you fancy.

A RABBIT THAT IS NOT WELSH.

One teacupful of grated cheese, one teacupful of cracker dust, two eggs, beaten until quite light, one teacupful of boiled milk and one wineglassful of wine. Season with mustard, cayenne pepper, salt, and one tablespoonful of butter. Stir all smoothly together, and bake it immediately.

NEW ENGLAND BEAN PORRIDGE.

Make a soup of a roast beef bone. Boil it in a gallon of water for one hour. Then add a pint of beans, carefully washed and soaked, and let them boil for three hours. Season it with pepper and salt. Wet one cupful of Indian meal and add to it, and boil it for one hour longer. Then strain it through a colander. Care should be taken to add sufficient water from time to time, as it boils away.

DRIED BEEF. (FROM A GOOD HOUSEKEEPER.)

Dried beef should always be boiled for three or four hours before using it. It is best to select a piece about four pounds for present use. After boiling it, take it out of the hot water, dry it with a towel and hang it up in a dry cellar. It will be fit as soon as cold for chipping or cooking with cream. Some persons boil only the hard, dry ends of the beef when they can no longer chip it; but it is far better to boil the whole piece in the beginning.

DRIED BEEF DRESSED WITH CREAM.

Chip the beef very thin. If it is very dry and salt, let it simmer over the fire for a few minutes. If it is fresh and moist, it will only require scalding for a few moments. Throw out the water. Put the beef in a frying-pan with a teacupful of cream, and add a little pepper. Stew them well together and serve it hot. Some persons prefer a little milk and butter in place of the cream.

FRIZZLED BEEF.

Chip very thin as much dried beef as you require. If it is dry and hard, let it stand a few moments after it is cut in boiling water. Pour off the water and fry it in a little butter until it curls.

POTTED BEEF.

The coarser, tougher parts of beef, which are usually sold quite cheaply, may, by a little knowledge and care, be made palatable, and even delicious. Boil the meat until tender. Chop it fine, and pound it in a mortar until the fibres are well separated. Add salt, pepper, cloves, allspice or mace, and a little sugar. Pack it tightly in stone jars or bowls, and pour over it a thin layer of melted butter. It will keep for a long time. Slice it thin, and eat it cold with bread and butter.

BEEF BOLOGNA.

Fifteen pounds of beef, one and a-half pounds of pork fat, six tablespoonfuls of brown sugar, six tablespoonfuls of black pepper, six tablespoonfuls of salt, two tablespoonfuls of cloves, two tablespoonfuls of allspice, one tablespoonful of mace or nutmeg, and two tablespoonfuls of saltpetre. Chop all fine in a cutter, and put it in large skins or new muslin bags. Press it in the skins or bags firmly, and then under a board, for twenty-four hours, with a heavy weight on it. Keep it in pickle for nine days under the board weight; then drain it and smoke it three times. To be chipped and eaten like bologna sausage.

A Nice Little Relish Dressed in a Chafing Dish.

A cupful of tomatoes cut up fine, one tablespoonful of butter, pepper and salt to taste. Let it heat up well; then drop in slices of cold lamb, cold roast beef, veal or poultry. Let them simmer together a short time; then add a teaspoonful of mushroom ketchup.

Ragout.

Brown four tablespoonfuls of flour in a pot, and add a piece of butter the size of a walnut, with as much water as will make it of the consistence of cream. Stir it well. Cut into small pieces two pounds of cold lamb, mutton or beef, and put it into the pot with a pint and a half of water, half a teaspoonful of cayenne, the same of black pepper, and a little salt. Stir all these well in the pot; then add eighteen peeled tomatoes, four large carrots, cut into small pieces, and twelve potatoes. Boil the whole slowly for three hours, taking care that it does not burn.

Turnovers.

Mince very fine cold mutton, veal or beef, and season it highly. Make a nice crust as for meat pie. Cut it out with a small saucer. On one-half the round of paste heap some of the mince, and turn the other half neatly over it in a three-cornered shape. Brush the top with the yolk of an egg, lay small bits of macaroni crosswise on the egg, and fry them very quickly, like doughnuts, in boiling lard.

HAM AND POTATO.

Boil some potatoes; slice them quite thin, put them in a pan with a good-sized piece of butter, and let them heat thoroughly, but not fry. Boil four eggs hard and chop them fine; and chop fine about as much cold boiled ham as there is of potato. Put all into a china dish in layers, with a little salt, parsley, and chopped onion on each layer. Pour over the whole four large cupfuls of milk or cream. Cover the top with bread crumbs. Put on them small bits of butter, and bake it a light brown.

E G G S.

OMELET.

BEAT the whites and yolks, separately, of three eggs, to a
froth ; beat in with the yolks a tablespoonful of flour, a little
pepper and salt, and chopped parsley; then add the whites of
the eggs, and fry the whole in butter.

OMELET.

Beat the yolks and whites of one dozen eggs separately ; then
mix them together, add salt and pepper to taste, some parsley,
chopped fine, and if liked, a little shallot or onion, minced very
fine, or bruised in a mortar. When the whole is mixed together,
put half a pound of butter into a frying pan, and heat it over a
very warm fire; then pour in the mixture and fry it till done.
In order to prevent its sticking to the pan, loosen it with a knife.
This omelet should be about an inch thick, and should not be
turned in the pan.

WISCONSIN BREAKFAST EGGS.

Beat twelve eggs well, and add two tablespoonfuls of cream
and some salt. Have a lump of butter boiling in the frying
pan, and pour the mixture into it. As fast as the egg cooks on
the bottom, slip a knife under, tilting the pan a little, so as to
let the raw egg run towards the butter. When it forms a little,
cut it in pieces as you would a pie, so that the uncooked egg may

(125)

run over the edges, for it must be cooked only on one side. When done, add black pepper. Eggs go much farther in this way. This will fill a large dish.

OMELET.

Beat well four or five eggs; add a tablespoonful of cream or milk for each egg, making a batter; season it with pepper and salt. Boil some butter in a frying-pan and pour the batter in. Loosen the edges occasionally with a knife, and by tilting the pan from side to side, allow the middle to run toward the sides and become more thoroughly cooked. Omelets are seldom made without something to give a flavor. Chopped parsley is commonly used. The other articles usually chosen for this purpose are tender boiled ham, smoked tongue, oysters slightly roasted, onions boiled very soft, boiled celery, &c—all of these minced very fine, and stirred in with the egg before putting it in the pan. This is an economical omelet, as it requires but few eggs. But the most approved method is to use butter and eggs alone, adding any of the above articles to taste.

OYSTER OMELET.

Beat six eggs very light, and add to them a gill of cream; season with pepper and salt, and have ready one dozen fine oysters cut in half. Pour the beaten eggs into a pan of hot butter, drop the oysters in as evenly as possible, and fry it until the omelet is a light brown. Turn it over, roll it together, and serve it immediately.

STEAMED OMELET.

Beat two raw eggs with a little butter and cream—a teaspoonful of cream to two eggs; add pepper and salt to the taste. Put this into the dish in which it is to be served, and place it over boiling water in a steamer, stirring it until cooked sufficiently.

To Pickle Eggs.

Boil the eggs till they become perfectly hard, then remove the shells and lay them carefully in a large-mouthed jar; pour over them boiling vinegar, well seasoned with whole pepper, allspice, mace, ginger and a few cloves of garlic. When cold, fasten the mouth of the jar very close. In a month they will be fit for use.

To Fry Eggs as Round as Balls (A Receipt of 1794).

Having a deep frying pan and three pints of clarified butter, heat it as hot as for fritters, and stir it with a stick, till it runs round like a whirlpool; then break an egg into the middle, and turn it round with your stick till it become as hard as a poached egg. The whirling round of the butter will make it as round as a ball. Then take it up with a skimmer and put it into a dish before the fire. They will keep hot half an hour and yet be soft, so you may do as many as you please. You may poach them in boiling water in the same manner.

To Scramble Eggs.

Beat half a dozen eggs very light. Have prepared a small skillet, or a chafing dish, in which a large piece of butter is simmering. Add enough salt and pepper to season it; then pour in the eggs, and stir them with a spoon all the time, so that the whole may be equally done. Have a hot dish ready; turn the eggs quickly from the skillet, cover them and serve them hot.

OPEN AIR COOKING.

CLAM BAKE.

IT is scarcely necessary to say, even to the uninitiated, that a clam bake is exclusively a seashore festival. It can take place only close to the spot where the clams have a "pre-emption right."

According to the simple habits of those of our people who dwelt near the sea, a clam bake in former times was an easy and economical method of promoting social gatherings, giving a good excuse for a holiday, and holding out the inducement to old and young of a day's relaxation and enjoyment. When all was arranged by the promoters of the project, verbal invitations were informally given, and every "eligible" was sure to hear of it. When the day came, old coaches that had retired on unlimited furlough, old chaises that had afforded peaceful shelter to many a roosting hen, were drawn from their dusty shelter and furbished up for the old people. Youths and maidens, with sturdy fathers and mothers, trudged along on foot, or if the home was too distant, came in "large assortments well packed" in the most capacious hay wagon that could be found.

On reaching the shore, the fishermen,—for there was sure to be some among them,—who knew the habits of the bivalve, began their digging in the sands and gathered their store for the feast. Meanwhile some of the younger members prepared a large circle, slightly scooped, in the sand or turf, while others,

9

(129)

forming themselves into foraging parties, gathered brush, wreck-
wood and sea-weed for the fire. The clams were then placed,
edge downwards, in lines around the circle formed for them.
Sweet potatoes, in their skins, and Indian corn, in their gauzy
husks, were interspersed among them, and thin layers of sea-
weed, brush and light wood of every sort were strewn thickly
above all, and the fire was lighted. Then the cloth was laid,
all the appliances for which having been brought by the party.
At length when all was ready—for it took two or three hours
for all this—the fishermen, with long iron rakes, scattered the
burning embers, and the clams, steamed in their own juices,
and the potatoes and corn, cooked to a turn, were brought to
light. Then began the feasting,—clams were eaten from the
shell, little pats of butter enhanced the flavor of the sweet
potatoes and corn, and with mirth and laughter and good
humor there was nothing to desire.

If the neighborhood owned a fiddle, it was sure to be there,
a dance finishing the happy occasion; and when the parting
came, every one went home better and happier for their day's
pleasuring.

The above is a receipt for an old, well-tried and economical
clam bake.

A clam bake in the rock-bound regions of our coast varies
somewhat in the mode of cooking from those of the flat and
sandy shores described above. A large fire is built upon the
rock, or upon heavy slabs of stone, some hours in advance.
When the fire is burnt out, the embers are quickly cleared away,
and in great profusion clams are piled in heaps upon the hot
stone. Lobsters, crabs and oysters are flung in, with sweet
potatoes and ears of corn, and the whole, covered with a heavy
mass of sea-weed, steams and bakes till done.

Clam bakes vary according to the habits of those who partake
of them. They are sometimes made the means of gathering
gay and youthful parties at seashore watering-places, and are
only clam bakes in name, all the accompaniments of the luxurious picnic superseding the modest clam. For one of these

there are no limits in providing,—trained servants have charge
of the feast and serve it; the bake is inspected with curious eye,
though few clams are eaten—kid gloves, with three buttons,
having little affinity for clam shells! Nevertheless, the clam
bake has done its good work; it has furnished the rallying cry
for a very enjoyable day, and to many a new and pleasant
memory.

There are also clam bakes "charitable." Some good woman,
endowed with much energy and but little money, has a desire
to aid some noble charity. She organizes a clam bake to carry
out her plans. The whole neighborhood, far and near, is invited to take tickets. The supply of clams is abundant. They
cost nothing, and the men and lads who gather them work for
the good cause without pay.

This clam bake is, however, greatly enjoyed. Enough to
eat, a crowd of neighbors and friends to talk to, and much
inward satisfaction at having helped on the good work unite in
bringing about this result.

Clam bakes political are sometimes arranged by a few ardent
politicians, who, desirous of urging some public measure or ad-
vancing the interests of some candidate, invite the country
round to a clam bake, at which the celebrated Mr. So-and-So is
expected to speak. The neighborhood—that is, the masculine
portion—responds. Mr. So-and-So "addresses the people."
Several well-known individuals do the same. Clams are taken
at intervals, more speaking follows, thirst naturally ensues, and
there is a great absorption of what is supposed to be spruce
beer!

The clam bake commercial usually takes place at some
attractive spot near the sea, where picnics and pleasure parties
of all sorts may be accommodated for a fixed sum by an enter-
prising individual who thus gains his living. A large wooden
building, with a simple outfit for feasting, will here be found,
while swings from the limbs of great trees, nine-pins, croquet
&c., are amply provided for all.

The huge ring or oval for the "bake"—for in cases of this

kind it must be very large—is prepared early in the day, and great latitude is allowed in providing for it. Oysters, fish, and other comestibles, form a part of the supply. The whole of these arrangements are made by the proprietor; the feast is served by his attendants, and the visitors have nothing to do but enjoy themselves, the day being ended, if so desired, by music and dancing.

There are doubtless various sorts of clam bakes not alluded to above. Enough, however, has been said to enable the seeker after information to arrange the particular clam bake he may desire to embark in, the usual latitude being allowed, as in all "receipts," to "sweeten and spice to taste."

To Cook Trout, or any Fish without Scales, when Fishing.

On arriving at the stream in which you mean to fish, select a spot most favorable for your purpose,—one affording plenty of wood and bushes, stones for cooking purposes, and hollow trees or old stumps for a "cache." Build a large fire, as you will require a good supply of ashes and coals, and let it burn down well, to secure the requisite supply. While your fire is getting up, wash in the stream the flat stones to be used as plates and put them near the embers to heat. Scour the fish with sand and wash them well, to remove the slime. Open them, and allow as little water as possible to remain inside while washing them.

To roast them, select the fish that are under nine inches in length. Cut off their heads, score them lightly, and pepper and salt them inside and out. Cut one or more branches (sweet birch is best) and stick the fish upon the twigs, running the twig along the upper side of the back bone. Hold the branch before the fire; by watching the inside of the fish, it is easy to see when they are done.

To Bake or Steam Trout.

Prepare the fish as above, but do not remove the heads, which are highly approved when thus cooked. Season and wrap them well in a large sheet of thin, strong paper; then envelop each one in five or six folds of coarse straw paper. After saturating each fish, so encased, in the stream, that the straw paper may be thoroughly wet,—the fish being protected from the water by the buttered inside paper,—lay them side by side in a bed of hot ashes and coals hollowed out for the purpose. Cover them well with the hot embers, and allow a minute an inch for cooking; that is, to a fish ten inches long allow ten minutes. Remove them from the ashes by inserting a long forked stick beneath and drawing them out. Unroll them carefully on a flat hot stone. Open and butter them. Trout from nine to twelve inches long may be cooked in this manner.

There are other ways of cooking them on the stream, as frying them on flat stones, which have been made hot in the fire, or in the case of large trout, by "planking." The latter is by far the most approved method.

The angler will find that a loaf of bread from which a portion of the crumbs has been hollowed out, to receive the butter, is the easiest manner of carrying this necessary article. These, with papers of pepper and salt well wrapped in a napkin, may be easily hidden in the bushes, or in the hollow of an old log or stump.

In baking fish in the above style, some sportsmen do not remove the intestines; this custom is derived from the Indians, and is sanctioned by connoisseurs.

To Dress Crabs on the Shore.

When you reach the crabbing shore, make ready your gypsy kettle, which is a large iron pot swung over a blazing fire, by suspending it from a tripod of strong poles. Fill it with water and let it boil while you engage in the pleasant sport of catching crabs. This, in a well-chosen spot, such as the shores of the Chesapeake bay, you will soon find.

Plunge the crabs while alive into the boiling water. If any show signs of weakness, throw them away—they are unwholesome. Let the crabs boil till they are perfectly red, which will be in about fifteen or twenty minutes. Pour off the water and break open the shells—only as you want them. Take off the claws and lay them aside. Then force off the upper shell and set it aside for a dish. Remove the fingers which lie between the outer and inner shell and the sand bag, which is easily found. All the rest is good, especially the fat, which is usually of a reddish yellow and found in the cavity of the shell. Break the crab in half, and you will find the meat revealed like the kernel of a well-cracked shellbark. A pinch of salt is all you require to enjoy your crab ; some prefer it without.

If you prefer a more elaborate mode of cooking, the crabs may be "devilled" thus: Pick out all the bits of snowy and truly dainty meat into the red shell which you have preserved, season it with pepper, salt and vinegar, a bit of butter and a few bread crumbs, and bake it in the hot embers.

A crab soup or stew ranks with, though not so famous as, the New England fish chowder. It is made by adding to a quart of carefully-picked crabs a half gallon of boiling milk, to which is added a quarter of a pound of butter, mixed with a tablespoonful of flour, and a seasoning of chopped parsley, a single slice of onion, and pepper and salt. This can easily be prepared in your extempore kitchen.

If you have had the forethought to bring with you a bottle of salad dressing and some lettuce leaves, a crab salad can be magically prepared.

OPOSSUM.

The 'possum is never caught in the daytime. Choose a moonlight night; and when the dogs find the tree he is napping in, cut it down. When the tree is down, the dogs will soon have him.

If the occupant of the hollow limb should chance to be the "hostess" of that snug home, and not the "host," a pitiful nature will spare her for the sake of the little brown noses that, in all probability, will be seen peeping out of the fur-lined pouch which she carries about her. He will, also, prudently remember that the little noses, if spared, will in time furnish future roasts.

Opossums are in the best condition in the fall of the year, when the persimmons are ripe, upon which fruit they become very fat. Put them in a cage, and feed them for several days before killing.

Skin and draw the 'possum. Cut off the legs to the first joint and part of the tail. Stuff the head and body like a turkey and roast it before a brisk fire. Opossums are never eaten hot. The flesh is very sweet and luscious, resembling that of a young pig.

Idaho Method of Cooking a Deer's Head.

Dig a hole two feet square and one foot deep; build a fire in it and allow it to burn to embers. Remove about half of the remaining coals; throw in the hole a thin layer of green grass or leaves, on top of which put the "head" in the same condition as when taken from the animal. Cover it thoroughly with a layer of green leaves, and the embers and ashes previously taken from the hole. Allow the head to roast an hour and a half; then remove it and pull the skin from it. Season it with salt and pepper, and you have a most delicious dish.

Idaho Smothered Quail.

Cover the quail all over with hot ashes and embers. Let them remain thus fifteen minutes. Then take them out and remove the skin with feathers attached. Open them, and the entrails will fall out. Season them with pepper and salt and a little butter.

IDAHO METHOD OF BROILING GAME OR MEATS.

Sharpen at one end a stick about two feet long and an inch in diameter. Prepare the meat by shaping it into thin pieces; run the stick through the pieces and hold it over the fire. Season them when half done with pepper and salt, and hold them over the fire until cooked. Be careful to use only coals. If you place the meat near the burning wood it will be smoked.

IDAHO ROASTED ONIONS AND POTATOES.

Roll each onion and potato in a piece of wet brown paper, and cover them in hot ashes and coals. Those of a medium size will require about three-quarters of an hour to cook.

SPORTSMAN'S CAKE.

Indian meal is easily carried, and makes a very palatable addition to a dinner in the woods. Pour boiling water over the meal to scald it. Make the mixture stiff enough to shape. Add a little salt. When you have finished frying your meat or fish, make up little cakes of this dough and drop them into the hot pan and brown them—in the case of fish, in a little butter, and in the gravy when it is meat. If you have no frying apparatus, this dough can be baked on a board before the fire or upon hot stones. If you have no means of heating water, have your meal scalded before setting out, and carry it in a damp cloth.

A MICHIGAN RECEIPT FOR MAKING SHORTCAKE IN CAMP.

Take the top of your provision box, or one of the boards from the bottom of your boat (camp supposed to be on the shores of Lake Superior). As it will probably be rough, cover it with a napkin, then you have a good pasteboard. Get your Indian guide to find a smooth sapling, peel off the bark, scrape it smooth, and then you have your rolling-pin. Mix half a pound of butter in half a pound of flour; but as you have probably left your scales at home, measure three or four tablespoonfuls of butter and one quart of flour; add a small spoonful of salt. Wet it with the coldest water you can get, roll it out about one-third of an inch thick, and of a shape suitable to your cooking utensil. If you are so luxurious as to have a camp-stove or baker, you can cut the paste into cakes and bake them as you would in civilized life; but if you take things after the manner of the aborigines, you will pour the grease from the frying-pan in which the salt pork has been cooked, and put the sheet of paste into it, cooking it over some coals drawn from the fire. There is still another way. If you can find a smooth, flat stone, heat it thoroughly in the fire; then withdraw it, and having dusted it with flour, bake your cake upon it. Eaten with a good mug of tea, a thin slice of pork, brown and crisp, and a broiled trout, all seasoned with good appetite, nothing can be more delicious.

A MICHIGAN RECEIPT FOR COOKING BROOK TROUT IN CAMP.

Having cleaned the fish, find a slender, flexible branch of a tree (not pine or its congeners); fasten the fish by its head to the end of the branch. Stick the other end into the ground, at an angle that will allow the fish to hang in front of the fire, where it will get the most heat. Put a small piece of pork on its head, so that a little of the fat will run down on the fish. Place a piece of " hard-tack " under it, to catch the drippings. Keep it turning, so that both sides will cook alike. When sufficiently done, eat it with the hard-tack, and be very thankful for so good a meal.

The Indians cook them in this way, only omitting the first direction, and carrying it out at this place. Though sounding badly to ears polite, it is not at all disagreeable as they do it.

To Roast Oysters in Camp Along Shore in Maryland.

Having selected the largest and best of the oysters brought to shore, wash them by a dash or two of water and an old broom. Fill an iron pan with them, and set it on a bed of coals. Keep it there till the oysters show signs of opening their shells. Have ready another smaller pan, fresh and clean, upon another bed of coals, into which put a good-sized piece of butter, a little salt and pepper, and some vinegar. Then open the oysters with an oyster knife, drop them in the butter, and eat them when they are steaming hot.

Many persons prefer to open the oyster when the shell is well heated over the coals, and eat it from the shell. This was doubtless the primitive method followed on these shores by the "original possessors of the soil," the modern domestic implement having, in the natural course of things, superseded the "scalping" knife.

A Virginia Brunswick Stew.

Take two squirrels, well skinned and cleaned, and put them in a pot with two quarts of water, and a small slice of fat bacon, a quarter of a peck of tomatoes, six white potatoes, cut up fine, a quarter of a peck of okra, a quart of lima beans, two large onions, and one pod of green pepper, with seasoning to taste. Let it stew for four hours; then add six ears of corn, cut from the cob, and let it stew another hour. Be very careful that it does not burn. If it is too thick, add a little boiling water. If you have no squirrels, a pair of young chickens may be used. This is a well known Virginia dish for picnics and hunting-parties, the *artiste*, selected for his skill in making the stew, hanging a large pot over an open fire in the woods, and setting up his kitchen beside the hamper in which he has transported his requisites.

Eggs Roasted in the Sand.

Clear a space in the sand large enough for the purpose, and make a fire of brush, sticks or drift-wood. When the fire has burned out, and only the embers remain, scrape them aside, and also some of the surface sand. Have the eggs prepared with little holes made in the points by a pin or sharp-pointed pen-knife, to prevent bursting. Set each egg on the large end, in the hot sand, and cover them with leaves, and then with the hot sand and embers. They will take about eight minutes to roast. The velvety softness of roasted eggs can only be appreciated by those who have tried them.

Idaho Miners' Bread.

Take two quarts of self-raising flour, add a teaspoonful of salt and nearly one quart of water. Mix these together with a spoon, and when the batter is free from lumps, bake it in the fire-place, in a gold pan.* using a similar one for a cover. To be eaten at once.

* The " gold pans " referred to above are, it is presumed, those by which the miner literally makes his daily bread, viz., the pans in which he washes his " gold-dirt."

SEVEN RECEIPTS

FROM

AN ONEIDA SQUAW.

BAKED BEAR'S MEAT.

Rub the meat well with sage, pepper and salt. Put it in the oven, and keep it well basted. For eight pounds, it will take about two and a half hours to bake in a hot oven. Make a nice gravy, thickened with flour, but do not use all the grease, as it will be too much, and can be sold to the traders for hair oil!

BEAR'S MEAT.

Cut the meat into strips. Salt it a little, and then hang it in an open chimney to smoke a little. When you want to eat it, pound it in a mortar, moisten it with a little water, season it with pepper and salt, make it up in little cakes, and fry them in lard.

WOODCHUCK.

Stuff the chuck with bread, butter, pepper, salt, onions and dried herbs. Roast it for about two hours, basting it well. Make a nice gravy, as you would for roast pig.

MUD TURTLE.

Put the turtles alive in boiling water, and as soon as the shells will come off, pull them apart, and stew the meat with enough water to cover it. Put in pepper and salt and a lump of fat. Thicken it with flour mixed with water. Make some dumplings of two eggs, beaten, and two tablespoonfuls of thick sour cream, made stiff with flour. Drop the dumplings into the gravy before you thicken it, and then boil it fifteen minutes.

MUSKRATS.

Parboil the muskrats first; then cut them up, and put them on to stew with water and a little lard. Let them cook down until brown. Add pepper and salt, and thicken the gravy with a little flour, wet with cold water.

INDIAN BREAD.

Make a weak ley from wood ashes. Cover about five quarts of ripe yellow corn with the ley, and boil it about five minutes. Remove it from the fire, wash it well in fresh water, and put it to drain. Then pound it in a wooden mortar, and sift it. The coarser parts may be kept for hominy. Add to the fine corn a pint of white beans, that have been boiled quite soft and dry, and mix them together with sufficient boiling water to make a good dough. Then make them up in little cakes with the hand, and boil them slowly for two hours, moving them from time to time with a stick, to prevent the cakes running together.

HULLED CORN.

Boil ripe corn in weak ley until the hulls come off easily. Then wash it well, and put it in fresh water, and boil it till it is well swelled. Then wash it again, and boil it in water in which you have put a little salt for a short time. Then dish it. Add pepper and butter, and salt if needed.

VEGETABLES.

VEGETABLES, to be eaten in perfection, must be fresh. They should be well washed and examined before using, as snails and insects sometimes lodge in them.

Green vegetables should be put on in hot water. The time required will depend upon their freshness and size. About thirty or forty minutes will generally suffice.

Potatoes must be put on in cold water. New potatoes require a much shorter time than old ones. Old ones take from forty to fifty minutes. They should be boiled in their skins. In roasting or baking them, wash them well, and let them cook quickly. When potatoes become old, towards the spring, each one when taken from the fire should be put into a coarse cloth and wrung. This makes them very mealy.

Dried vegetables, such as peas, beans, okra, &c., should be soaked all night before using them. Beets require from two to three hours to boil, according to their age; turnips about an hour; cabbage an hour and a half; parsnips three quarters of an hour; carrots two to three hours; onions about an hour. Fresh vegetables need much less time to cook. Tomatoes can scarcely be too much cooked. The seeds of the tomatoes impart a slight bitterness, and they are more richly flavored without them. The okra is so tender and delicate a vegetable that it is unnecessary in cooking them to cut them up, in some cases not even in soup. By keeping them whole, the mucilage, so much prized, is not boiled out of them.

(143)

To Boil Potatoes.

Set them on the fire without peeling, with enough water to cover them, and let them boil quickly. Try them with a fork, and when soft, drain off the water, cover the pot with a cloth, and let them steam in the chimney corner. Serve them whole.

If you wish them mashed, pound them well, adding salt and butter, and, if liked, a little cream or milk. If you wish them browned on the top, mould them in a bowl, set it in the oven, on a tin dish, or in front of a hot fire, and let it brown. Slip the shape off the tin with a broad knife, when ready to serve.

In the spring, when potatoes begin to sprout, cut out the eyes, pare and boil them. When dinner is ready to be served, take them out of the pot, one by one, and wring them in a coarse cloth. They will be quite dry, and in appearance mealy and fine. A perforated tin, shaped like a syringe, is often used to press them through, and gives them a very fine appearance.

Stewed Potatoes.

Pare and boil the potatoes, and set them away to cool. Cut each potato, when cold, into six or eight pieces. Make a sauce of half a pint of milk, a piece of butter the size of an egg, and plenty of salt. Use pepper to your taste. Boil the sauce with a little dash of flour in it, and stew the potatoes in it for about a quarter of an hour. When ready to serve, sprinkle a little chopped fresh parsley over them. Care must be taken in boiling the potatoes not to cook them enough to make them lose their shape.

Potato Croquettes.

Mash the potatoes very smooth. Add a little milk or cream, some salt, and a well-beaten egg. Mix all well together, shape them into balls or pyramids, and fry them quickly in plenty of boiling lard.

Potato Marbles.

Potato marbles are shaped with the little instrument made for such purposes, and to be purchased at the kitchen furnishing establishments. It will save waste to use for the purpose the potatoes which are prepared for boiling and mashing. Cut one or two balls from each potato, throw them into salt and water, and let them remain all night. Parboil them; drop them into boiling lard, and fry them a light brown. They make an attractive dish, and are suitable to serve with fish.

Saratoga Potatoes.

Peel the potatoes, slice them with a cold slaw cutter, and throw them into iced water. Let them lie in it for several hours—even for a night; then wipe them dry. Have ready a skillet, with boiling lard quite deep in it. Throw the potatoes in, and they will speedily become brown. Lift them out with a skimmer full of holes, and lay them upon a dish on which are spread sheets of soft paper, to absorb the grease.

Potato Salad.

Boil some potatoes; and, when cold, slice them. Have ready a dressing of sweet oil, chopped fresh parsley, vinegar and pepper, in which an onion, peeled and scored, has been suffered to remain just long enough to give the dressing a flavor. Pour this over the potatoes, and stir them well together in the salad bowl. There must be a great deal of oil. If you like, add mustard.

Potato Balls.

Stir into some mashed potatoes the yolk of an egg; make them into balls, dust them with flour and roll them in egg and bread crumbs. Fry or brown them in an oven.

10

To Cook Sweet Potatoes.

Wash them well, scrape or pare them, and put them into boiling water. If large, cut them in two lengthwise. When boiled, pour off the water, set the pot on the stove, uncovered, to let the steam escape. Season as follows : For potatoes for six persons, put in a piece of butter the size of a hen's egg, a pinch of salt, a little pepper, a tablespoonful of sugar sprinkled over them, and half a cup of good, sweet cream. Cover tightly and let them stand on the stove for about five minutes before serving.

Sweet Potatoes Roasted.

To eat sweet potatoes in perfection they must be roasted, not steamed ; or, first boiled and then put in the oven to dry. The good old way, when we had wood fires only, and the potatoes were buried in the chimney corner in hot ashes and cinders, is the best. At present, where coal is used, we must be content with an oven. Wash the sweet potatoes and place them on a shelf of the range oven; watch them, and from time to time turn them, that they may cook evenly. When they are done, which can be told by squeezing them, take them from the oven and keep them in a hot place until ready to serve. To be eaten with butter, and as soon as possible after being taken from the oven. Be sure to serve them in their skins.

Fried Sweet Potatoes.

Pare the potatoes raw and cut them lengthwise in slices. Have a pot of boiling lard ready, into which drop the slices. When brown, put them into a colander and set it in a hot oven to drain. Serve them hot and eat them with butter. White potatoes are good cooked in the same way.

South Carolina Mode of Boiling Rice.

Wash the rice in cold water, pick it well, and let it lie in water till you are ready to use it. Then pour the water off, and sprinkle the rice into a saucepan of boiling water, already salted. Boil it steadily for twenty minutes; then take it off the fire and drain all the water from it. Place the saucepan, with the lid partly off, in a corner of the fire, where it is only moderately warm, to allow the rice to "soak" or dry. The moisture will pass off, and each grain of rice, swelled and burst open, will stand alone. When served, the grains will fall apart if shaken. This is the only proper method of preparing rice to be eaten as a vegetable. Its flavor is very different from the watery, paplike substance that is often served up as "boiled rice."

RICE CROQUETTES.

Boil about half a pound of rice in one quart of milk. When it is thick and stiff, take it off the fire; add two ounces of butter, the yolks of four eggs, and whatever flavoring is preferred. Set it away in a dish till it becomes cold enough to form into smooth round pats. Dip these into the yolk of egg, then into fine bread crumbs, and fry them in equal quantities of butter and lard.

TO STEW SALSIFY.

Scrape and wash well six or eight roots, and boil them until they are quite soft; then cut them in pieces half an inch long. Mix a piece of butter the size of an egg with flour very smoothly; add two or three tablespoonfuls of the water in which they were boiled, and stir it all into the saucepan with the salsify, seasoning it with salt and pepper. Stir it frequently and let it stew gently for half an hour. If you wish it very rich, omit the water; use more butter, and add half a teacupful of cream just before serving.

TO FRY SALSIFY.

Wash and scrape a dozen roots of salsify, cut them into small pieces and boil them until quite tender. Mash them thoroughly,

and season with salt, pepper, and a tablespoonful of melted
butter. Beat an egg quite light and stir lightly through it.
Mould it into cakes the size of an oyster, dredge them well
with flour and fry them in hot lard.

STEWED TURNIPS.

Cut the turnips into pieces the size of a walnut. Boil them
for about an hour, to make them quite tender, but not to lose
their shape. Make a sauce of cream, butter, flour, pepper and
salt, and stew them till the sauce is thoroughly cooked.

PARSNIP FRITTERS.

Boil two large parsnips; mash them well into a batter made
of one tablespoonful of flour, two tablespoonfuls of milk, and
one egg. Season it with salt and pepper. Drop a tablespoonful at a time in boiling lard and fry them a light brown.

TO STEW CELERY.

Scrape the celery, but use none of the green parts. Cut it
into lengths of about an inch and stew it slowly for an hour and
a half. Pour off the water, and make a gravy of stock, thickened with butter and flour. Add pepper and salt to taste, and
make it of a light brown color by adding some of the brown
coloring for made dishes. Let it simmer long enough to cook
the thickening. If you prefer the celery white, thicken it as
for stewed oysters.

FLORIDA TANNIA FRITTERS TO BE EATEN WITH MEAT.

Boil one large tannia till tender. Mash it fine, adding salt,
black pepper, a spoonful of lard, one egg beaten, a pint of flour
and half a cupful of water. Mix all well together, and fry
them a dark brown in lard like fritters.

BAKED PEPPERS.

Wash clean some large green peppers and take out the inside. Take cold poultry and ham, or bacon, and chop it fine with crumbs of stale bread soaked in cold water, a spoonful of butter, a hard-boiled egg, cut fine, pepper and salt. Stuff the peppers. Place them in a pan and bake them.

BAKED CUCUMBERS.

Pare the cucumbers, chop them fine, with a small onion, put them on with very little water, and let them stew for ten minutes. Prepare a rich dressing as for poultry. Pour off all the water from the cucumbers, add the dressing and one tablespoonful of butter, and bake in a deep dish.

FRIED CUCUMBERS.

Slice the cucumbers when the seeds are full grown, and before they turn yellow or ripen. Sprinkle salt on the slices, let them stand for an hour, and fry them as fish, with hot butter or lard.

STEWED CUCUMBERS.

Pare the cucumbers and cut them in thick slices. Put them with a small onion, also sliced, into a saucepan, with a little water, and stew them for fifteen minutes. Pour off the water. Stir in a little flour, butter, salt and pepper. Let it remain on the fire for two or three minutes, and serve. A little vinegar is sometimes used as seasoning.

TO BOIL ARTICHOKES.

Wring off the stalks, pull out the strings, and wash them well. Have prepared a large pot of boiling water, add a little salt, place the artichokes in it, tops downward, and boil them for an hour and a half. To know when they are boiled enough, a leaf or two may be pulled off; if they break off easily, they are done. Take them out of the water and lay them upside down to drain. Serve them hot in a covered dish with melted butter.

To Dress Artichokes.

Reserve the very large artichokes and boil them. Take out several of the inner rows of the scales, cut off the tender portions of these, and chop them fine, with a tablespoonful of fresh meat, a tablespoonful of ham or pork, and a tablespoonful of bread crumbs. Season the mixture with pepper and salt, moisten it with a little gravy, and add a piece of onion as large as a nutmeg, mashed to a pulp. Fill the middle of the artichokes with this stuffing, set them in a pan, with a little rich gravy or broth at the bottom, cover it well, and let them stew slowly for an hour.

Boiled Jerusalem Artichokes.

Wash and scrape the artichokes and parboil them in water; then add salt, and boil them in milk until quite soft. Season them with butter, black pepper, and a very little nutmeg.

Baked Jerusalem Artichokes.

Boil one pint of artichokes in water for fifteen minutes, and then in milk. Mash them smooth. Mix them in a dessert-spoonful of butter, half a pint of bread crumbs, pepper and salt. Bake them in shells, and serve in a small dish.

Green Peas.

Most persons make the mistake of using peas as a fresh vegetable after they are overgrown. They should invariably be eaten while fresh and young, should be placed in cold water as soon as shelled, and gathered as short a time as possible before cooking. They require about one hour to boil, and are much improved by adding two or three lumps of loaf sugar. When the peas are quite tender, drain them thoroughly. Season them with salt and pepper, and add a large piece of butter just before serving.

To Dress String Beans.

These beans must be young and tender. The sooner they are cooked after gathering the better. String them carefully and cut them in small pieces. Put them on the fire in cold water, with salt to season them, and let them boil until a fork can pass through them; then strain off the water. Return them to the dry saucepan, add a good lump of butter, a little pepper, and a tablespoonful of cream, and let them stew gently for an hour or two before serving. No vegetable, except perhaps tomatoes, is so much improved by long and slow cooking as string beans.

Lima Beans.

Only the fresh young ones should be used. Lay them in cold water for an hour and a half after they are shelled; then boil them until quite tender. Drain them well, and season them with a little pepper and salt. Add a piece of butter after the beans are in the dish ready for serving.

Asparagus.

Scrape the stalks until quite white, and cut them all of an equal length. Tie them up in small bundles, and put them into water that is boiling hard. If the asparagus is fresh and young, it will require about one hour to boil. When tender, drain it, remove the strings from the bundles, and serve it in a vegetable dish, in the bottom of which are placed slices of toast. Pour melted butter over the whole.

New England Squash.

This squash is now grown in the Middle States, and is known as the "fall marrow squash." They are easily kept in the winter in a dry cellar, as they do not freeze readily, owing, perhaps, to a gum-like substance that lies between the rind and pulp; but they do not keep very late in the season. They may be boiled or baked. To boil them, pare and cut them in small pieces, put them on the fire with only sufficient water to cover them, and keep the pot covered. When they are tender enough to mash, turn them into a colander, and stand it over another vessel which is hot until all the water drains off; then mash them with butter, salt and pepper, and serve them hot. When properly prepared, they are dry, mealy, and of a sweet and delicate flavor.

To bake them, a slow oven is necessary; the hot ovens belonging to the ordinary range scorch them. Prepare the vegetable as for boiling, and place the pieces in a pan in the oven, with only a spoonful of water to prevent burning; its own juices will soon be sufficient in a slow oven. When the pieces are soft, mash them with butter, pepper and salt. If they do not look dry enough, set them in the oven, and they will become dry and mealy like boiled chestnuts. This applies only to the marrow squash. The crook-necked squash, with others of its kind, has a fibre too coarse to allow it to become dry or mealy. It resembles more the common pumpkin.

Carrots.

Boil the carrots until perfectly soft, with one or two onions. Carrots require a long time to cook, and when they are soft, the onion will be nearly boiled away. When quite soft, cut them in small pieces, and put them in a saucepan with a little meat gravy or soup stock, and let them simmer slowly for an hour or longer, with pepper, salt, a little vinegar, and a pinch of sugar. If you have no gravy or stock, use butter, flour and water for the sauce, and color it with sugar browned.

To Prepare Beets.

They require several hours to boil. After they are thoroughly done, pare and cut them into slices. Flour them, and put them into a saucepan with a little vinegar and water, a lump of butter, some pepper and salt, and a spoonful of ketchup. Let them simmer slowly for some time. The vinegar may be omitted and added at table.

Beets boiled very well and chopped up as small as coffee grains, make a very fine salad when lettuce is not to be had. A *Mayonnaise* dressing must be used for this dish.

To Dress Spinage.

Pick and wash the spinage in three or four waters, to remove all grit. Cut off the stems that unite the leaves, and when thoroughly washed, chop it fine on a chopping board. Put it in the saucepan without any water, and set it in the corner of the fire to wilt. The juice of the spinage is quite sufficient to stew it in. Those who boil it in water, and then drain it, throw away a large proportion of the flavor of the vegetable, which, like "tea," is drawn into the water. After the juice has flowed out, put it in a hotter place, and let it stew thoroughly, adding a good deal of salt. Some persons take it out after it is well stewed, and bruise it in a stone mortar, but if it is chopped enough when raw, this will not be required. It is very difficult to cook spinage without finding the juice separate from the mass, leaving a green water round the bottom of the dish. By long drying in the saucepan, this may be obviated, but it is a surer plan to bind it by mixing about a tablespoonful of flour with a large lump of butter, which must be stirred into it a sufficient time before serving, to allow the flour to cook. Add black pepper just before taking it from the fire. Cream and milk are sometimes used in cooking spinage, but they only make it more watery.

To Stew Tomatoes.

Put ten or twelve large ripe tomatoes into a pan, and pour scalding water over them, to remove the skins. Peel and cut out all the hard green parts; then cut them in half horizontally and take the seeds out. Mince an onion fine, and add it, with pepper and salt to taste. Put them on to stew in a pipkin, and let them simmer for several hours—the longer the better. When they have stewed for about an hour, add a piece of butter the size of an egg, and four or five tablespoonfuls of bread crumbs. Some persons prefer to thicken them with flour, in which case the flour and butter must be mixed together. Bread, having more or less alkali in it, in some measure destroys the extreme acidity. This effect is also produced by the onion.

OKRA AND TOMATOES.

Stew for an hour a can of tomatoes, adding pepper and salt. Wash a quarter of a peck of young and tender okras, cut off the stems, throw them into the stewpan with the tomatoes, and let all stew gently until the okras are soft and begin to open. Then stir them well. By cooking the okra in the tomatoes without previous boiling, the mucilage and flavor are both preserved. A little onion may be added to the tomatoes when first put on, if preferred. This preparation may be baked with bread crumbs on the top.

RICE AND TOMATOES.

Boil one pint of rice, and mix in it, while hot, one large spoonful of butter, and pepper and salt to taste. Add one can of tomatoes and one teaspoonful of sugar. Bake it in a well-greased pan.

BAKED TOMATOES.

Skin the tomatoes by pouring boiling water over them, and cut them in half horizontally, which will make it easy to remove the seeds from each cell. Make a stuffing of bread crumbs and onion, mashed to a pulp, and a piece of butter, seasoning it with salt and pepper. Fill each of the seed cells with this stuffing, and bake them slowly in the oven. They may be prepared in this manner and fried.

Baked Tomatoes.

Prepare the tomatoes as for stewing, with an onion minced. Salt and pepper them. Place them in a baking dish in layers, with bread crumbs between, and little dots of butter. Put the dish in a slow oven and let it bake for an hour or longer. The bread crumbs must be very thick on the top. Serve in a silver macaroni dish, which will conceal the dish it has been baked in.

Sliced Baked Tomatoes.

Cut them in slices, without removing the skin, and put about three layers in a deep pie plate. Sprinkle on each layer, pepper, salt, sugar, and cracker or bread crumbs, with butter on the crumbs. Bake them slowly for three hours.

Fried Tomatoes.

Cut them in slices, flour them well, and fry them slowly in the fat from fried pork.

To Stew Mushrooms.

Wash and peel the mushrooms, sprinkle salt over them and let them stand for a short time. To a pint of mushrooms add a small teacupful of water, and stew them for nearly an hour. If the mushrooms do not give out much juice, add a little more water, to prevent them from drying. When stewed, add a lump of butter as large as an egg, a small teacupful of white wine and a little red and black pepper. Keep them well covered and let them stew for a few minutes. A little cream or milk will improve them. If you desire the flavor of the mushroom alone, omit the wine.

Scalloped Mushrooms.

Mushrooms are very fine scalloped like oysters. Lay them in a dish, season them with pepper and salt, strew bread crumbs over them and drop little pieces of butter among the crumbs. Bake them in a moderate oven.

To Broil Mushrooms.

Choose for this purpose the large mushrooms, pick, clean and peel them. Take off the stems, and boil them in a little cream or milk; place the mushrooms in a fine wire folding broiler, hold this before the fire and turn it frequently, removing them as they are done to a hot dish in the corner of the fire, and replacing them with others. Strain the cream and stems, add a little salt and pepper and a lump of butter to the cream, and pour it over the hot mushrooms, keeping the dish covered. When all are done, serve them in the dish they are in, hot.

Mushrooms.

If the true taste of the mushroom is desired, use nothing that has a decided flavor of its own in preparing them. Select the freshest mushrooms, those that are neither very large nor very small. Peel them and brush them off well, put them into a porcelain-lined saucepan with a little cream, salt and pepper; let them simmer a few minutes, and when you remove them stir in a little piece of butter; keep them covered all the time and serve them hot.

Tomato Salad.

Scald and skin the tomatoes. When cold, slice them, and pour over them the following dressing: Mash the yolks of two hard-boiled eggs, add one teaspoonful of dry mustard, the same of salt, the same of sugar, three teaspoonfuls of fine French mustard, six tablespoonfuls of salad oil, one teaspoonful of vinegar and a pinch of sugar. Beat all well together.

This is also a good dressing for cold boiled asparagus.

TOMATOES AND EGGS.

Peel the skins from a dozen large tomatoes, put four ounces of butter into a frying-pan, add a small onion, minced very fine, and pepper and salt to taste. Fry them, and from time to time chop them while frying. When the tomatoes are well cooked, break six eggs into the pan, stir the whole quickly, and serve them hot.

To DRESS EGG-PLANT.

Take one large or two or three smaller ones, according to the size of the family; quarter and boil them till soft enough to mash. Turn them into a colander, let them drain, and remove the skin. Then put them into a bowl or pan, add a large breakfast-cupful of bread crumbs soaked in milk or cream, a lump of butter the size of an egg, a saltspoonful of chopped fresh parsley, a parboiled onion, chopped fine, and pepper and salt according to taste. Mix all well together, put it into a baking-dish, cover the top with bread crumbs and bake it for about twenty minutes.

To FRY EGG-PLANT.

Cut the egg-plants into slices about a quarter of an inch thick; salt them, and let them lie on a dish a little raised on one side, that the juice may run off. Let them remain thus for an hour, then flour them, add pepper and more salt, and fry them brown on both sides. Egg-plant may also be cooked in the same manner as salsify.

Corn Pudding.

Grate one dozen ears of green corn ; add to a quart of corn a teacupful of cream or milk, a lump of butter about the size of an egg, and a teaspoonful of salt. Mix all well together, bake in a deep dish for an hour and a half. To be eaten as a vegetable, with butter, pepper and salt. If the corn is old, more cream will be required; if young and milky, less.

Corn Fritters.

Remove the silk carefully from twelve ears of corn, cut the grains down the centre of the row and scrape out all the pulp with the back of a knife, or use one of the little implements made for this purpose. When all the corn is off the cobs, add about two tablespoonfuls of flour, two eggs, well beaten, and pepper and salt to taste. Stir the whole well together. Drop as many tablespoonfuls in a frying-pan of hot lard as the pan will hold, each spoonful forming a cake; turn each cake when brown, and serve them hot. If the corn is large, it will require three eggs for twelve ears, and if very milky, a little extra flour. It should be thicker than pancake batter. A hot fire will cook them in five minutes. These fritters are thought to resemble fried oysters.

Succotash (an Indian Dish).

Boil a quarter of a peck of beans and a dozen ears of corn. When cooked, pour off the water, leaving only enough for gravy. Cut the corn from the cob, stir in a lump of fat, and season with pepper and salt. This is an Indian dish, and the above is the simple method in which the red man prepared it. The modern improvement is to mix butter and flour instead of the lump of fat, and to add tomato ketchup while it is stewing.

Corn Pie.

To one pint of raw corn, grated, add a cupful of cream or milk, butter the size of an egg, salt and pepper to taste. Line a pudding dish with paste as for oyster pie, heat the grated corn before pouring it in the dish, and bake it.

Sour Crout.

Cut twenty heads of cabbage as for cold slaw—this quantity requires one pint of salt. Have ready a pickle tub; pack the cabbage in it in good thick layers, a large panful in each layer; sprinkle the salt in between the layers. When all is packed, lay a cloth over the top, on that put a round board with a heavy stone on top. It will be ready for use in three weeks. After using any of it, wash off the board and the cloth before replacing them. When you cook this dish, boil a piece of nice pork with it; the pork should be put on first, and about three-quarters of an hour before it is done, put the sour crout into the same vessel and serve with it in the same dish. By boiling some vinegar on the range at the same time this is cooking, your will prevent any disagreeable odor.

Sour Crout.
TO BE USED ON THE DAY IT IS MADE.

Shave the cabbage as for cold slaw. Wash it through a colander and drain it well. Place it in a large, deep pan, and pour enough good cider vinegar over it to saturate the whole by frequent tossings. Let it steep from one to three hours, according to the degree of acid preferred. Lift the cabbage out of the vinegar, and put it on the fire in a stewpan with a lump of butter, lard or drippings. Pepper and salt it, and let it simmer slowly for several hours; a little water may be necessary, to prevent it from drying or burning. If you do not find it acid enough on tasting, add some vinegar. A small piece of the fat of salt pork is a good substitute for the butter, giving it a greater resemblance to genuine sour crout.

To Dress Cold Slaw.

Cut a hard cabbage very fine with a regular cabbage-cutter. Put it on the fire in a porcelain-lined saucepan with about a teacupful of vinegar. When warm, stir into it a piece of butter the size of an egg, a small teaspoonful of powdered mustard (more or less according to its strength), a saltspoonful of sugar and enough black pepper and salt to season it. Stir these well, and let it boil for a short time. Have ready two eggs well beaten, the whites and yolks separately. Take the vinegar from the fire and let it stand until it has ceased to boil; then stir in the yolks of the eggs, and, lastly, the whites. Let it stand in a cool corner of the range, stirring it well, that the eggs may thicken a little without simmering. Taste the liquid, and add more pepper, salt or mustard if required. The quantity of cabbage used must regulate the quantity of the dressing. The above will probably be enough for half a large head of cabbage. About ten or fifteen minutes before dinner, pour the warm dressing over the cabbage, stir and toss it well, and place it in the dish in which it is to be served. If the vinegar should be too strong, dilute it.

Cold Slaw.

Shave a firm white head of cabbage very fine, lay it in a dish and sprinkle it well with salt and pepper. For half a small head, boil a large teacupful of weakened vinegar with a bit of butter the size of a walnut. Have ready a well-beaten egg, and when the vinegar boils pour it over the egg, stirring it well. Put it back over the fire, and stir it briskly with a fork until as thick as custard; then pour it over the cabbage and mix them thoroughly. Do not serve it until quite cold.

Cauliflower.

Lay the cauliflower in cold water for one hour; then put it into boiling water and let it simmer until the stalk is quite tender.

A large one requires about two hours to cook it thoroughly. Drain it very carefully by putting it into a colander over a pot, which should stand on the stove, to prevent the cauliflower from cooling. Serve it with plenty of melted butter.

KALE CANNON.

Take equal quantities of boiled cabbage and potatoes; chop the cabbage fine and mash the potatoes. Boil with the cabbage one large onion, and mash it fine. Mix these well together, adding a lump of butter, salt and black pepper. Stew it slowly over a moderate fire, and serve it in a covered dish. The half of a large cabbage will be enough when mixed with the potato to fill a large dish. Good beef drippings may be used instead of butter. In cold weather this mixture will keep for several days.

CABBAGE.

Boil it for about half an hour; then drain it, and let it cool. Chop it and put it into a baking-dish with salt, pepper, some butter, and milk enough to moisten it well, and bake it for half an hour, or long enough to brown it lightly.

STUFFED CABBAGE.

Steam a cabbage till half done; then open every leaf separately until you come to the heart. Cut this out, and chop it fine with bread crumbs and minced ham, and season it with pepper, mustard and salt. Mix all well together, and put in the middle of the cabbage and between the leaves. Tie it up in a muslin cloth and boil it in salted water till tender; then pour over it a sauce made of milk, a little butter, flour and pepper. Serve it hot.

11

PILGRIM DUMPLINGS.   (A DISH USED BY OUR FOREFATHERS
IN THE PLACE OF POTATOES.)

Take a quart or more of corn meal; wet it with cold water
and add a little salt; make the batter stiff; mix it with the hands
thoroughly, and make it into balls about twice the size of an
egg; put them into a kettle of boiling water and boil them for
an hour.   Potatoes were often boiled with the dumplings.   The
modern way of making them is to mix one quart of meal with
a pint of sour milk and a teaspoonful of soda; to be covered
with a cloth and steamed for an hour.   They are eaten with
ham, pork or beef gravy.

TO DRESS MACARONI.

Wash and drain as much macaroni as will fill the dish.   Put
it on the fire in boiling water, and let it boil till it is soft
enough to pass a fork through it.   American macaroni takes
longer to boil than the Italian.   Strain it through a colander.
Dry the saucepan and replace the macaroni in it immediately;
then add milk or cream enough to nearly cover it, salt and red
pepper to your taste, and a piece of butter.   Have prepared
about half a pint of grated cheese.   When the macaroni has
become heated again in the milk, add the cheese.   Stir it well
and put it into a baking dish.   Strew grated cheese and then
bread crumbs over the top.   Set it in a quick oven to bake and
brown on the top.   Be careful not to leave it too long in the oven,
lest it become tough and leathery.   You may omit the baking
if you prefer.   In this case stew it a little longer, and just
before serving, place it in a dish and grate well-browned toast
over it, which gives it the appearance of being baked, without
the risk of drying or toughening it.   A little butter should be
dropped in spots over the top before baking.

BREAD.

The theories upon bread-making are so varied, and often so opposite, that it would be impossible to fix upon any one receipt as the best, among the numbers forwarded for this book. A few only that have been highly recommended will be added to our collection.

Every good housewife has her pet receipt, and every kitchen its oracle; experience must of course prevail over teaching. For the novice, then, who requires a little aid before her experience be bought, these few receipts are given. One injunction, however, must not be forgotten: let no inducement tempt her to use saleratus, or any other baking powder, in making bread. They rob the flour of all its sweet natural flavor, and render "the staff of life" a tasteless, unwholesome compound.

To Make Bread.

Pass four quarts of flour through a sieve; dissolve a table-spoonful of salt in a quart of milk-warm water, and add to it half a pint of baker's yeast. Make a hollow in the middle of the flour, and pour the yeast and water into it, leaving a wall of the dry flour around it after beating it well; then place the pan in a warm dry place in the kitchen, if it be winter. If the weather is warm, a cooler place must be selected. Cover it well and let stand all night; this must be done before bedtime. About eight or nine the next morning the dough will have

(163)

risen and covered nearly all the flour on the sides. Then knead in the flour till the dough is soft and easily kneaded. Take it out of the pan and knead it on the paste-board. Cut it into three or four pieces and knead each by itself. Lay each piece in a baking-pan. Set them in a warm place for one or two hours; they must rise nearly to the tops of the pans. Bake them for about half an hour. Keep the oven closed for ten or fifteen minutes before venturing to open the door. If an oven heated by wood is used, the bread will require nearly double the time.

Some persons add a tablespoonful of lard to their bread, others use milk. If milk is used, it must be scalded to prevent souring; about a quart will be enough for the above receipt.

Some persons add potatoes. If this is desired, boil three, and pass them through a sieve, after mashing them in the water to be used for mixing the bread.

Bread (Made Soft and Quickly).

Three quarts of flour; one tablespoonful of lard; one tablespoonful of salt; half a pint of yeast, and warm water enough to make a soft dough. Dissolve the lard and salt in the warm water; then add the yeast, then the flour gradually, stirring it with a spoon. Set it to rise in a warm place all night. In the morning take a part of the dough and mould it into biscuits for breakfast. Put the remainder into pans, letting it rise in the pans for half an hour before baking.

Bread Without a Sponge.

About seven o'clock in the evening put a pound and a half of flour into a deep pan, with a teacupful of yeast. Let it stand, without stirring, until about half-past ten; then add the rest of the flour, without stirring. In the morning work it thoroughly, and put it in pans to rise. When risen, bake it. A little salt is required, of course.

Yeast Without Hops.

This yeast is desirable, as it never tastes bitter, even in hot cakes.

Grate fine large potatoes, and add them when grated to one quart of boiling water. Let it boil for about five minutes; then remove it from the fire, and add to it one teacupful of brown sugar and one tablespoonful of salt. When it cools, add one teacupful of yeast.

Potato Yeast.

Boil and mash well twelve good-sized potatoes. Tie a handful of hops in a bag and boil them in a quart of water. Measure the hop tea when done, and pour it on the mashed potatoes. Measure the water in which the potatoes were boiled, and then from a kettle of boiling water make up what is lacking of a gallon of fluid. Add a cupful of brown sugar and half a cupful of salt. Let it stand till lukewarm, and add a cupful of good yeast. Set it to rise for twenty-four hours.

This yeast will ferment like beer.

Sponge Made of the Above.

Mash a hot boiled potato. Mix it with about two quarts of flour and two large kitchen-spoonfuls of the yeast. Beat it well, and set it to rise about one o'clock P. M. About seven, make up the bread with this sponge.

Yeast for Bread.

Take two quarts of very strong hop tea, six good-sized white potatoes, mashed through a sieve; add a half teacupful of flour, a half teacupful of salt, and one teacupful of sugar. Beat this mixture till it is quite smooth and let it boil up once. When cold, add a piece of leaven or some yeast to set it going, and bottle and cork it tight. Shake it well before using it. For bread, take two tablespoonfuls to one quart of flour.

BROWN BREAD.

One quart of Graham flour; one pint of Indian meal; one cupful of molasses; one teaspoonful of soda, and one of salt. Mix all together with one quart of cold water. Steam it in a pudding boiler for four hours. Turn it out on a baking plate, and bake it for one hour.

GRAHAM BREAD. (A SIMPLE AND VERY GOOD WAY.)

One quart of Graham flour; two tablespoonfuls of molasses; one teaspoonful of salt, and half a cupful of yeast. Mix them with warm water to a stiff batter, and when light, bake for about one hour.

GRAHAM BREAD.

One quart of Graham flour, salt, and one teaspoonful of soda, added dry to the flour; one tablespoonful of lard; one small cupful of molasses, and sour milk enough to make a soft dough or stiff batter. Stir it very quickly, and bake it slowly in deep pans.

NEW ENGLAND BROWN BREAD.

Two cupfuls of Indian meal; two cupfuls of rye meal; one cupful of wheat flour; one cupful of molasses; one and a half pints of sweet milk; one teaspoonful of soda; a pinch of salt. Boil it for four and a half hours without stopping. This bread is never baked.

LOWELL BROWN BREAD.

Three teacupfuls of Indian meal; two teacupfuls of rye meal; half a teacupful of molasses; one teaspoonful of salt, and one of soda. Mix in a little less than a quart of milk, and bake it for two hours.

Rye and Indian Bread.

One quart of Indian meal and half a cupful of molasses. Pour on enough boiling water to scald all the meal thoroughly. Set it away to cool, and when it becomes milk-warm, add one pint of rye flour, one cupful of yeast, and a little salt. Steam it for three hours, and bake for one hour.

Wisconsin Steamed Brown Bread.

Three cupfuls of sweet milk; one cupful of sour milk; three cupfuls of corn meal; one cupful of flour; half a cupful of molasses; a piece of butter the size of a small egg; one teaspoonful of saleratus, and a pinch of salt. Make it up into dough, and steam it three hours. Be mindful to cover the basin tightly within the steamer.

Graham Bread.

Three cupfuls of Graham flour; one cupful of white flour; one quart of water; two tablespoonfuls of yeast; two tablespoonfuls of molasses. Steam it three hours as above.

BREAKFAST CAKES.

GENERAL WASHINGTON'S BREAKFAST CAKE.

To one pound of flour, add one pint of milk, three eggs, one tablespoonful of butter and half a coffeecupful of yeast. Beat the butter very light, and set it to rise. When risen, shape it into little pats, and bake them in the oven.

POTATO BISCUIT.

Boil and mash six or seven potatoes. Stir in about half a pint of warm water and a large tablespoonful of melted lard. Add flour enough to make a thick batter, some salt and three tablespoonfuls of brewer's yeast. Set it to rise in a warm place till quite light—an hour or more. Make it into a stiff dough, and knead it a long time. Cut it into small cakes, put the cakes in the pans, and set them to rise on the warm hearth. Bake them in a quick oven for ten minutes. These cakes are very excellent, but those unaccustomed to make them will often fail. When potatoes are used in this way, they seem to require more flour for the second raising than ordinary dough. Cakes made of brewer's yeast will rise quickly or not at all.

GEMS.

Four cupfuls of flour, one cupful and a half of milk, and the same quantity of water. Mix and beat these thoroughly and

(169)

lightly for ten minutes. Heat the " gem pans " quite hot in the oven; then withdraw and butter them. Fill them about two-thirds full, and bake in a hot oven.

PACIFIC ROLLS.

One pint of milk, one and a half pints of flour, one egg, well beaten, and half a teaspoonful of salt. Stir the milk by degrees into the flour; then add the egg, and beat all thoroughly for a few minutes. Bake in a roll pan for half an hour, in a quick oven.

BREAKFAST ROLLS.

One cupful of hot milk, half a cupful of butter, three eggs, one cupful of home-made yeast, and flour enough to make a stiff dough. Set it to rise the night before.

RICE CAKES.

Boil one cupful of rice until quite tender. Add one pint of milk, one egg, and flour enough to bind all together. Salt it to taste, and bake on the griddle.

ROLLS.

One quart of milk, half a cupful of yeast, two tablespoonfuls of lard, two tablespoonfuls of sugar, and a little salt. Mix early in the morning, like batter, and at noon knead it like bread. Roll it out, cut it into rolls with a small saucer. It must rise for at least two hours.

PARKER HOUSE ROLLS.

Rub a piece of butter, the size of an egg, into two quarts of flour. Add one cupful of fresh yeast, one tablespoonful of sugar, one pint of cold boiled milk and a little salt. Let it rise all night, and knead it well the next morning. About two o'clock P. M. roll out the dough and cut it in circular pieces; then fold one side over, to come to the middle of the circle, and put a small piece of butter under the fold. Then fold the opposite side in like manner, the edges meeting in the middle, and put a piece of butter under that also. Bake the rolls in pans.

LAPLANDERS.

One pint of flour, one pint of milk, two eggs, a pinch of salt, one tablespoonful of melted butter. Mix the milk and flour together till there are no lumps, beat the yolks of the eggs and stir them in with the salt and butter. Beat the whites of the eggs very light and stir them in last, beating all well together, Have the pan very hot, then drop in a large spoonful for each biscuit.

MARYLAND BISCUITS.

Two quarts of sifted flour, two tablespoonfuls of lard, two tablespoonfuls of butter, a little water and salt. Make the dough as stiff as possible; work and knead it for half an hour or longer, until it is perfectly soft and pliable. Then beat it with the rolling pin for about an hour, or until the dough cracks loudly. Bake them in small cakes, the size of a milk biscuit. The success of this favorite tea biscuit depends entirely upon the long-continued pounding.

QUICK BISCUITS.

One quart of flour, a little salt, a tablespoonful of sugar, and three teaspoonfuls of yeast powder, mixed dry in the flour. Rub in a tablespoonful of lard, and mix with cold water, into dough. Roll this out, and cut it into biscuits, and bake them in a very quick oven. These biscuits are improved by using milk instead of water.

Fayal Biscuit.

Take a cupful of flour and one of milk, three eggs, a little sugar, a piece of butter the size of an egg, and two teaspoonfuls of baking powder. Bake them in cups or rings.

Tea Biscuit.

Sift two quarts of flour; stir into it a pint of boiling milk, in which you have broken up a small cup of butter. When this is smoothly mixed and cold, add half a cupful of yeast. Let it rise all day, then knead it again, and set it to rise once more in the pan. Make it up in small cakes, and bake them. These biscuits are said to "melt in the mouth."

Tea Cakes.

Nine tablespoonfuls of flour, three eggs, and one tablespoonful of butter creamed; make these into a batter, the consistency of batter puddings, and bake them in cups as quickly as possible.

Tea Rolls.

To one pint of flour add half a cake o yeast, a teaspoonful of lard dissolved in a teacupful of water, a pinch of salt, one egg and two lumps of loaf sugar. Mix all well and set it to rise for about six hours. Then work it into enough flour to bring it to the proper consistency, make it into rolls, put them in pans to rise again for fifteen minutes, and bake in an oven hot enough for plain bread.

Graham Gems.

Mix together two teacupfuls of sour milk, two tablespoonfuls of brown sugar, one large teaspoonful of saleratus and the same of salt. Make into a stiff batter with Graham flour. Have the gem irons quite hot, and bake for twenty minutes in a hot oven.

Graham Gems.

One egg, beaten light, one and a half cupfuls of sweet milk, and Graham flour enough to make a stiff batter. Bake twenty minutes in pans made very hot before the gems are put in.

Passover Bread for Breakfast and Tea.

Soak six passover biscuits all night. In the morning drain them through a colander, chop them fine and mix them with pepper, salt, butter and a very little milk. Make the mixture into a large cake and fry it well on both sides in butter.

Batter Bread—A Virginia Breakfast Cake.

Take six tablespoonfuls of flour and three of corn meal; add a little salt; beat up four eggs with sufficient milk to make the whole into a thin batter; put this into small tin moulds and bake them in a quick oven.

Buckwheat Cakes.

Remarks.—Buckwheat cakes being batter cakes, are always baked upon a griddle. If the griddle is of iron, it must be greased every time it is used with a piece of suet to prevent the cakes from sticking. Soap-stone griddles, now much used, prevent this necessity. By using one of these you avoid the taste of the grease, and the unpleasant smell of burning fat which is apt to penetrate beyond the kitchen. Caution the cook never to put the smallest particle of grease upon the soap-stone, as it will spoil it for future use. It is of great importance in preparing the batter to beat it for a long time, not only to make it smooth and without lumps, but also to render it light. Buckwheat cakes to be eaten in perfection should be served hot—*one* at a time. A pile, placed one over the other, as is so often seen, impairs their lightness. If they are well made and perfectly light, they will rise on the griddle and be filled with air holes. To make them thin like wafers is a mistake.

Buckwheat Cakes, No. 1.

Make a batter as thick as that for pancakes. Three quarts
of water, with meal enough to thicken it, will make cakes
enough for ten persons. Beat the batter well until there is not
a lump remaining. Add salt and about a teacupful of good
fresh yeast. The water must, in cold weather, be as warm as
the hand can bear; beat it again after the yeast has been put in.
Cover the crock with a towel and let it remain in a warm place.
If the weather is severe, not far from the fire. In eight or ten
hours it will be ready for use. The batter should run into its
proper size on the griddle without being spread by the ladle.
The batter, when risen, should be so light and spongy that the
cakes will rise quite thick. Thin buckwheat cakes made from
watery batter are seldom light. When the cake is turned on
the griddle, allow it to remain long enough to insure its being
thoroughly done through. They are usually buttered before
they are brought to the table, but this is a matter of taste.

Buckwheat cakes should be baked on a soap-stone griddle,
which does not require greasing.

Many persons add a little Indian meal to the buckwheat.
This, to lovers of the genuine buckwheat cake, is a heresy. In
this case there is not a decided flavor of either meal, and the
cake is a mongrel—not a buckwheat cake.

A smaller quantity of batter will require a shorter time to rise.
Much, of course, must depend upon the quality of the yeast.
Brewer's yeast requires less time than that which is made at home.

Buckwheat Cakes, No. 2.

One quart of buckwheat meal, one teaspoonful of salt,
two tablespoonfuls of wheat flour, and a teacupful and a half
of good yeast. Put the yeast in first and mix it with the flour,
then add a pint of fresh milk diluted with half a pint of warm
water; beat it long and well. If this batter is made at ten at
night, it will rise to the proper lightness by breakfast time the
next day. These cakes must be light, thick and spongy.

BUCKWHEAT CAKES, No. 3.

To one quart of warm water allow one pound and five ounces of buckwheat meal, one large tablespoonful of salt and two tablespoonfuls of brewer's yeast. Beat it well, and set it to rise in a warm place for about two and a half hours. If you wish them to rise earlier, put in more yeast. The time required for rising depends a great deal upon the quality of the yeast. Some persons add a tablespoonful of Indian meal, others a tablespoonful of molasses, to make the cakes brown well.

BUCKWHEAT CAKES, No. 4.

Mix with a quart of buckwheat meal a teaspoonful of salt, and if you like the flavor, add a handful of Indian meal. Pour a teacupful of baker's yeast into the centre of the meal; mix it gradually with cold water until it becomes a very smooth batter. It must be beaten long and well. Cover it and put it in a warm place to rise. When it is light enough to use, it will be covered with bubbles. Allow about a quart of water to a quart of meal. This, of course, varies according to the quality of the meal. To be baked on a griddle.

FLANNEL BREAD CAKE.

Half a pint of cream, the whites of two eggs, one tablespoonful of yeast. Beat all together, adding flour enough to make a thin batter. Bake it in square tins.

FLANNEL CAKES.

Beat the yolks of three eggs, and stir them into a quart of milk; add two tablespoonfuls of yeast—if the yeast is strong, one and a half tablespoonfuls will be enough. Thicken the eggs and milk with flour till the consistency is that of buckwheat or pancake batter; then add the yeast, and, lastly, the whites of the eggs, beaten light. This batter will take about three hours to rise. Bake the cakes on a griddle like buckwheat cakes, and butter them before serving.

To Make Flannel Cakes.

To one quart of milk, add four eggs; make a batter of the consistency of fritters, with flour and corn meal, in the proportion of one spoonful of meal to three of flour. Make the cakes up very early in the morning with a spoonful of yeast; set them to rise till breakfast-time, and then bake them on a griddle.

Another Receipt for Flannel Cakes.

One quart of flour, three eggs, a tablespoonful of butter, two of yeast and a quart of milk; beat them well together, and put the batter in a tin or stone vessel to rise. Bake the cakes on a griddle.

New England Breakfast Pancakes.

One pint of sour milk, soda sufficient to sweeten it, a little salt, one tablespoonful of molasses, and flour enough to make a stiff batter. Fry a teaspoonful at a time in hot lard.

Rye and Indian Griddle Cakes.

Half a pint of Indian meal, scalded soft with milk. When cool, stir into it half a pint of rye meal; add half a tablespoonful of molasses. The batter should be a little thicker than for buckwheat cakes. Make the cakes up just before baking.

Vanity Griddle Cakes.

To one quart of flour, add a teaspoonful of soda and a little salt. Mix it with sour milk or cream into a thin batter, and beat it briskly with a spoon for five or six minutes. Pour it on a hot griddle in very thin cakes and fry them quickly. Butter each cake as it is fried, and sprinkle powdered sugar over each. Serve only a few at a time, as needed, at table.

Soft Muffins.

Three eggs, one quart of milk, two ounces of butter, one teaspoonful of salt, two large tablespoonfuls of brewer's yeast or four of home-made, and enough of sifted flour to make a stiff batter. Warm the milk and butter together and add the salt. Beat the eggs very light, and stir them into the milk and butter; then stir in the yeast, and, lastly, enough flour to make a thick batter. Cover the mixture, and set it to rise for three hours in a warm place. When it is quite light, grease the baking iron and rings, set the rings on the iron, pour the batter into them and bake a light brown.

Griddle Muffins.

One quart of milk, four eggs, one tablespoonful of salt, one pound and ten ounces of flour. Beat all well together, and add three tablespoonfuls of brewer's yeast. Set it to rise for two or three hours before needed, and bake the muffins in rings.

Oven Muffins.

One quart of milk, four eggs, one tablespoonful of salt, two pounds of flour. Warm the milk, and beat all together well; add half a cupful of home-made yeast. Set it to rise for nine hours, and bake the muffins in rings in a quick oven for ten minutes.

Madison Muffins.

Three pints of flour, two eggs, a tablespoonful of lard, two spoonfuls of sugar in a cupful of yeast; make up the muffins

12

with warm milk, a little softer than for light bread. In the morning roll out the dough, cut it out like biscuit and bake them in an oven.

Flour Muffins.

One pint of flour, one pint of new milk, a small piece of butter, two eggs, whites and yolks beaten separately, and a little salt. Bake and serve them immediately, as they fall by standing.

Plain Muffins.

One quart of flour, salt, one teaspoonful of soda, added dry to the flour; mix in enough sour milk to make a soft batter. Pour it into well-buttered muffin rings and bake quickly.

Waffles.

One pound of butter, melted in a quart of milk, and ten eggs, beaten light. Thicken the milk and butter with sifted flour, and add the eggs and a little salt. It should be of the consistency of pound-cake batter. Add enough yeast to make it rise; the quantity must be regulated by the quality of the yeast. Set it to rise in a warm place. To be eaten in the evening, the waffles should be mixed early in the morning in winter, and in summer at midday. Bake them in waffle irons.

Waffles.

Three pints of milk, twelve eggs, the yolks and whites beaten separately, a quarter of a pound of butter warmed in the milk. Add flour enough to make the batter as thick as for pancakes, and a small teacup of yeast. The white of the eggs must be put in last. Beat it up well. Let it rise a little while, and bake in waffle irons well greased with butter.

Rice Waffles.

To one cup and a half of boiled rice, add two cups of flour. Mix it with milk. The batter must be rather thicker than pancake batter. Add a little salt. Then beat two eggs very light, and stir them in the last thing, giving it a good beating. Bake them in waffle irons.

Rice Cakes.

Pick and wash half a pint of rice, and boil it very soft; then drain it, and let it cool. Sift one and a half pints of flour over the pan of rice, and mix in a quarter of a pound of butter that has been warmed by the fire, and a saltspoonful of salt. Beat five eggs very light, and stir them gradually into a quart of milk. Beat the whole very hard, and bake in muffin rings or waffle irons. Serve very hot.

Rice Waffles.

These are made with a teacupful of rice, boiled to a jelly, and mixed with a pint of flour, a pint of new milk, three eggs well beaten, and a little butter. Mixed and raised as above.

Rice Griddle Cakes.

Take a large cupful of rice, boiled soft in milk, and while it is hot, stir in a little wheat flour, beating it till it is quite smooth and free from lumps. When cold, add two eggs and a little salt. Bake the cakes on a griddle.

Rice Pone.

One pint of nicely-boiled rice, three eggs, one pint of fresh milk, two ounces of butter, a small teacupful of corn meal, and a teaspoonful of salt. Beat the eggs as light as possible, add the milk and rice, melt the butter, and stir in with the corn meal and salt. Pour all into a baking-dish, and bake in a hot oven from a half to three-quarters of an hour.

RICE BREAD.

One pint of rice flour, three eggs, one dessertspoonful of butter. Set it to rise with yeast all night, or use sea foam. Mix it with fresh milk.

RICE MUFFINS.

One pint of soft-boiled rice, one teacupful of fresh milk, three well-beaten eggs, one tablespoonful of butter, and as much wheat flour as will make a batter thick enough for pound cake. Drop the muffins in a hot oven. They do not require turning. These muffins may also be made entirely of rice flour, and baked in small pans.

SOUTH CAROLINA RICE JOHNNY CAKE.

Equal proportions of fine hominy, rice and rice flour. The two former must be boiled and cold before the rice flour is added. Mix all with milk; then spread it on a board, and bake it before the fire. Split it open, and butter for the table.

RICE JOHNNY CAKE.

Half a pint of soft-boiled rice, with just enough flour to make the batter stick on the board; salt it and spread it on a board. Baste with cream, milk or butter, but cream is the best. Set it before a hot fire, and let it bake until nicely browned, then slip a thread under to disengage it from the board, and bake the other side, basting all the time.

Rice Puffs.

One pint of rice flour, one teaspoonful of salt, and one pint of boiling water. Beat light four eggs, and stir all well together. Put two or three spoonfuls of lard in a pan, make it boiling hot, and fry as you do fritters.

Virginia Quinimies.

One egg, one quart of sifted flour, two ounces of butter, one cupful of milk, one teaspoonful of salt. Knead and pound it well, roll it out and cut as for tea biscuits; then roll out each one separately as thin as paper, and bake them a very pale brown in a quick oven.

Feather Cake.

Two cupfuls of sugar, three cupfuls of flour, half a cupful of butter, two-thirds of a cupful of milk, two eggs, and two teaspoonfuls of baking powder. Bake it in tins.

Rye Flour Drop Cakes.

To one quart of milk add two tablespoonfuls of cream, a little salt and three eggs. Stir in rye flour to the consistency of pancakes, then give it a thorough beating with a large iron spoon, and afterwards add a little more flour to make it stiffer. Have ready a bowl of milk or water to wet the hand or spoon, that the dough may not stick; detach the little pieces from the large mass and drop them upon the oven hearth near the mouth, after the ashes have been swept away and the oven is a little cool. The cakes will quickly rise and crack open at the top. Bake them a light brown, and eat them hot with butter.

Brioche.

Put three ounces of butter into a pound of flour, put it into a pan and pour in a teacupful of milk, half a teacupful of home-made yeast. a saltspoonful of salt, and three eggs, beaten light.

Make this into a dough as soft as you can possibly knead it, and place the loaf in a well-buttered pan to rise. The milk should be warm when mixed, so as not to chill the yeast, and the pan must be close by, covered with a dish, as it takes four hours to rise, and if not covered, it becomes crusted hard. If the oven is hot enough it will bake in thirty minutes.

POPOVERS.

Two cupfuls of flour, two of milk, two eggs, a piece of butter the size of a walnut before melting it, and a little salt. Butter some large cups, fill them half full and bake in a quick oven.

BUTTERED BLANKETS.

Into one quart of wheat flour sprinkle a teaspoonful of salt; add a piece of lard the size of a walnut, and one egg; then add a teacupful of yeast, with one tablespoonful of sugar in it Make up the whole with lukewarm water into a soft dough; put it in a pan, cover, and set it in a warm place to rise. When well risen, work in a little more flour and make it into small rolls, put them into a hot, well-greased pan, so as not to touch each other. Set them to rise again for an hour and a half, then put them in the oven. When they have a nice brown crust, cover the pan over and let them remain in the stove for a few minutes longer; they will then be light and spongy. The above quantities will make about fifteen rolls.

"MOONSHINE."

Into one quart of flour rub two tablespoonfuls of butter, one tablespoonful of lard, and half a teaspoonful of salt; wet with cold water. When it becomes of the consistency of bread dough, beat it with a rolling-pin for fifteen or twenty minutes, holding and turning the lump of dough with the left hand, while beating with the pin. Roll it *very* thin, and cut it with a jag iron into long narrow strips. Bake them in a quick oven.

PREPARATIONS OF INDIAN CORN.

HOMINY.

HOMINY is made from Indian corn. It is nutritious and palatable. In many sections of the United States it forms an article of daily food. In the Southern States this is particularly the case. To many, a breakfast without hominy is no breakfast at all. As a diet for children it is in great repute; it is much liked by the little people, who through life remain constant to their early love.

The sweet, white, flint corn is always selected for this purpose. Formerly the process was very tedious; the grains after being shelled from the cob were steeped in ley and afterwards pounded, for the purpose of removing the thin skin or hull that encloses each grain. This was a process performed in every household. When the demand for hominy made its manufacture profitable, improvements were gradually introduced in preparing it, and it is now a large branch of industry. Machinery moved by steam performs all the work, and the hull is removed without the application of moisture.

This last result is particularly advantageous, as the hominy thus prepared does not spoil, and can be taken to any part of the world. This last recommendation has caused it to form one of the "regulation" stores of the United States Navy. For long cruises it is invaluable.

The first "pale faces" who landed on the American Continent learned from the "red man" how to make hominy, and this was the way he performed the operation:

The squaws, of course, gathered the corn and shelled it from the cob—they planted it also, no doubt. When the corn was ready, the red man cut down a tree, leaving the trunk standing of a convenient height. Then with fire he hollowed out the top surface and shaped it like a bowl. Into this the corn was thrown, and a ley made of wood ashes poured over it. After it had steeped long enough to loosen the skin, he beat it with a stone or heavy log, and his hominy was ready.

We have made some improvements since those primitive days, not only in hominy, but as regards "squaws!" It would be well if we could go further, and add also "in trees;" but we fear that trees in some parts of our land are still little regarded, and as lightly destroyed, as by the originators of the unpatented "hominy mill" described above!

Hominy is called by various names, according to the size of the grains in which it is prepared. These names, however, are differently applied in many of the States. When in whole grain, it is called "big hominy," sometimes "samp." In some localities "samp" is the half or quarter grains. The smaller kinds are called "grits."

Indian meal is the corn ground without any preparation, and is either white or yellow. The fine impalpable powder called "corn starch," and generally used for desserts, is made by a process not imparted to the public.

The white or sweet corn only is used for the table. The yellow is, however, very good when young and freshly gathered, if boiled and eaten from the cob with butter, pepper and salt. It is used chiefly for "feed" for horses, cattle, poultry, &c.

Few have the moral courage to eat corn off the cob in these days; but if there is any little act of impropriety done in a corner which ought to be condoned, it should be that of eating an ear of corn off the cob!

To Boil Large Hominy.

Take two quarts of hominy, wash it, and put it into a large iron kettle holding more than two gallons. Fill it eight or ten inches above the hominy with cold water. Let this boil for an hour; then pour off the water and fill the pot up to the same measure with boiling water. Let this boil from nine to ten hours. As the water disappears, fill up the pot with boiling water, but do not stir it nor let it stop boiling, and keep it well covered. When perfectly tender, uncover and move it where it will only simmer until the water is all absorbed; then pour it into a large earthen pan and mash it, or not, as desired. When served, each grain should stand alone, like popped corn. It is very tender and soft, with a creamy gravy. Season it while hot with plenty of butter and salt. Small white beans are sometimes boiled with the hominy.

To Boil Small Hominy.

Put a quart of hominy into two quarts of water, add a little salt, and let it boil slowly for an hour and a half. Stir it occasionally to prevent burning. Taste it, and if there is not enough salt, add more. When it is nearly done, pour in a pint of milk, and let it simmer until it is of a proper thickness.

To Boil Grits.

Wash well a pint of grits and boil it in two quarts of water, with a little salt, for twenty minutes, stirring it often. If any water remains, pour it off. Cover the pot, and place it in a corner of the fire to steam.

To Fry Hominy.

Take cold boiled hominy left from the day before, salt it and make it up into little " pats ;" if the hominy requires something to bind it together, use a little corn starch. Fry them in boiling butter or lard. They are excellent for breakfast.

BACHELOR'S PONE.

Melt a piece of butter the size of an egg in a pint of new milk. Beat very light the yolks of five eggs; stir them into the milk and thicken it with soft-boiled hominy and a little dash of wheat flour. The batter should be rather stiffer than for flour pudding. Add a little salt and heat all well together. Bake it in a shallow pan, well buttered. This pone is never cut with a knife, but always broken apart.

HOMINY WAFFLES.

Half a pint of cold boiled hominy, half a pint of rice flour and two tablespoonfuls of wheat flour. Stir these together with a pint of milk, a tablespoonful of butter and two eggs, well beaten. To be baked in waffle irons.

HOMINY CROQUETTES.

Break an egg into a pint of cold boiled hominy; add a tablespoonful of melted butter, the same quantity of flour, a teaspoonful of salt and a tablespoonful or more of cracker crumbs; stir these well together. Beat an egg, season it with salt and pepper, make up the hominy into little rolls or pyramids, roll them in the egg and then in the cracker crumbs, and fry them in deep boiling lard. These croquettes may be prepared, if for breakfast, the day before and kept on ice.

HOMINY BREAD.

Mix together a pint of hominy, boiled soft, one tablespoonful of butter, one pint of milk, and four eggs, beaten light. Thicken it with flour and bake it in a dish.

HOMINY CAKES.

Mash well together one pint of cold boiled hominy and two tablespoonfuls of wheat flour, and add two well-beaten eggs, two tablepoonfuls of milk and a teaspoonful of salt. Have ready in a frying-pan boiling lard about an inch deep, drop the hominy in by the spoonful, pat it down into an even cake, and when brown on one side, turn it carefully and brown the other side.

Hominy Cakes.

Boil a bowlful of hominy nearly all day, salting it while boiling. It must be put on the fire in boiling water. Before it gets cold, stir in it a piece of butter the size of an egg. When it is quite cold, add to it two beaten eggs. Drop this batter into a pan in little cakes and bake them.

Hominy Pancakes.

Put into one pint of boiled hominy while warm a tablespoonful of butter and three eggs, beaten light; then add a pint of sour milk and a teaspoonful of soda, and beat it all well together. As this is a batter cake, if it is not thick enough, add a little flour or corn starch to bind it. Bake the pancakes in a well-greased pan.

Hominy Drop Cakes.

Two cupfuls of hominy and one cupful of Indian meal, mixed with milk enough to make it the thickness of batter. Sour milk with a teaspoonful of saleratus in it is better than sweet milk. Add a little salt and stir in three eggs, well beaten. Butter a pan and drop the batter upon it in little cakes. Bake them for about fifteen minutes in a hot oven.

Browned Hominy.

Mash and season with salt and melted butter as much cold boiled hominy as required. Put pieces of lard and butter, mixed, into a small deep frying-pan, and as it melts over the fire, toss and turn it until the pan is hot and well greased ; then put in the hominy, cover the pan closely with a plate, and put it where it will not burn. When the hominy is thoroughly heated through, remove the cover and let it brown on the bottom and sides ; then turn the pan upside down on a hot platter and loosen the hominy from the pan.

To Warm Over Hominy.

Mash and season it with salt, wet it thoroughly with milk, and put it in the frying-pan, with a tablespoonful of butter to each quart of the hominy. Stir it with a fork all the time it is cooking, and serve it hot before it has had time to brown.

INDIAN CORN.

Sweet Corn as Prepared by the Indians.

Boil as many ears as you require of the sweet corn, such as is used for the table, and of the same degree of ripeness. It should not be boiled quite as long as for present use. Cut the grains from the cob, and spread them on large cloths in the sun, and let it dry thoroughly. Keep it in a dry room. When wanted for use, throw a few handfuls into a pot of boiling water, and boil till soft. This, in midwinter, will give a dish of corn as fine as if just plucked from the field.

It is excellent also in soups.

Mush.

Mix the corn meal with cold water and salt enough to season the whole, and stir it into a pot of boiling water. If it is not thick enough, add more meal. Stir it all the time, to prevent lumps. It will take about an hour to boil. To be served hot and eaten with cold milk.

FRIED MUSH.

Make a large potful of mush; turn it out into a deep pan. When cold, cut the mush in slices, sprinkle them with wheat flour, and fry them in butter, over a brisk fire. To be eaten at breakfast.

WEST INDIA MUSH.

One small cupful of Indian meal, moistened with cold water; when smooth, stir it in a pot of boiling water, to which add two ounces of butter, some orange peel, and a stick of cinnamon. Let it boil for one hour, flavor it with vanilla or peach water, and add sugar to taste.

VIRGINIA HOE CAKE.

Pour warm water on a quart of Indian meal; stir in a spoonful of lard or butter, and some salt. Make it quite stiff, and work it for ten minutes. Have a board the size of a barrel head. Wet it with water, spread on the dough with your hand, place it before a hot fire, and prop it aslant, so that it will bake slowly. When one side is nicely browned, run a thread between the cake and the board, and turn it so that the underside can brown. These cakes used to be baked in Virginia on a large iron hoe. Hence their name.

CORN ASH CAKE.

To one quart of sifted meal, add sufficient water to make a good dough, and salt to taste. Make it into a round cake about an inch thick. Bury it in the hot ashes, and let it remain for half an hour. Then wash it off in cold water, and eat it with butter milk.

GEORGIA ASH CAKE.

To one pint of sifted Indian meal, add half a teaspoonful of salt, and enough water to mix it very stiff. Mould it into a round ball with the hands. Draw out the hot ashes; put the ball upon the hot hearth, and pile the hot ashes on top. When baked through, uncover it, and dust the ashes from it. Those who object to ashes on the bread, wrap a cabbage leaf round the dough before putting it in the ashes, but it is sweeter baked without the leaf.

Corn Bread.

Indian meal requires more salt than other bread, and must be thoroughly mixed or beaten. If mixed over night, great care must be taken that it does not sour, which it does more easily than any other bread. If you find, in spite of all care, that it is acid, stir in a little soda, dissolved in boiling water (a small teaspoonful to each quart). Where milk is used, it should be baked immediately. Pans should be well greased before baking, as it sticks more than other flour. A quick oven is necessary.

Corn Bread.

Take ten ounces of sifted corn meal; add a teaspoonful of salt, then a tablespoonful of lard. Mix well, stirring it around and across the pan. Pour in slowly a pint of scalding water. Continue to beat it well; add one egg, then half a pint of milk and half a teaspoonful of soda. Beat it well, and put it in a hot skillet, with a little lard in it. Have fresh, live coals on the top of the skillet, and bake it quickly. The mixture is to be put in the skillet by large spoonfuls.

Mush Bread.

Boil one pint of corn meal until thick as mush. When quite cool, add one pint of new milk, a lump of butter the size of a partridge egg, and three eggs. Butter the pan, and bake it for one hour.

THIN CORN BREAD.

One pint of corn meal, over which pour one pint of boiling water. Mix well, and then add a teaspoonful of sugar, one of salt, and one of baking powder; pour this, spread thin, into pie plates, and bake to a crisp brown. Split and butter it while hot, cut it into sections as you do pie, and serve it for tea. You can use one egg beaten quite light instead of the baking powder, if you prefer, and add one tablespoonful of melted butter. This makes it richer.

INDIAN BREAD WITH BUTTERMILK.

To one quart of buttermilk, slighty warmed, add a teaspoonful of soda dissolved in water, two eggs, well beaten, a tablespoonful of melted butter or lard, and a little salt; stir in as much corn meal as will make a thick batter; beat it for a few minutes and bake it quickly in well-greased pans. It is liable to burn and requires watching.

ST. CHARLES CORN BREAD.

Beat two eggs very light. Mix with them a pint of sour milk or buttermilk, one pint of Indian meal, and a tablespoonful of melted butter. Add a teaspoonful of soda and a little salt. Beat the batter well and bake it in pans in a quick oven.

INDIAN MEAL PORRIDGE.

Boil a quart of fresh milk, mix a small teacupful of corn meal with a half-pint of cold water, allow it to settle, pour off the water and stir it into the boiled milk, stirring it well to keep it from being lumpy. Let it boil for a few minutes only; add salt to taste. To be eaten with milk, cream or sugar.

JOHNNY CAKE.

One quart of milk, two eggs, beaten quite light, one teaspoon-ful of soda, a piece of butter the size of an egg, a piece of lard the size of an egg, one tablespoonful of brown sugar, two table-spoonfuls of flour, and Indian meal enough to make a thick batter. Melt the butter, and beat all together for ten minutes. Put it in a pan, and bake it in a hot oven for three-quarters of an hour. Test with a broom splint, as you would cake.

MARYLAND PONE.

Three eggs, one pint of milk, one saltspoonful of soda, a piece of butter or lard the size of a walnut. Add Indian meal enough to make it as thick as porridge. Put it about an inch deep in the tin, and bake it in a quick oven.

INDIAN PONE.

Mix a quart of Indian meal with milk so as to make a thick batter, add a lump of butter the size of an egg and a little salt. Beat four or five eggs very light and mix them with the batter. Beat the whole thoroughly together and bake in a low pan or a Turk's-head, or in small pans. Serve it hot for breakfast.

VIRGINIA PONE.

Beat three eggs, and stir them into a quart of milk, with a little salt, a spoonful of melted butter and as much corn meal as will make a thin batter. Pour it into a baking dish and bake quickly.

COLD WATER PONE.

Make a very stiff batter of cold water, one quart of corn meal, and salt to taste; work it well with the hand; grease a pan and bake it for three-quarters of an hour.

Corn Meal Dodgers.

Into a pint of corn meal break two eggs; stir in milk suffi-cient to make a batter stiff enough to drop from the spoon, and add half a teaspoonful of salt. Drop this by the spoonful into a frying-pan of hot lard or beef drippings, flatten into cakes with the spoon, but do not let them touch each other; when brown on one side, turn them on the other. Serve them hot, split and buttered; adding, if you like, a sifting of brown sugar or some syrup.

Plain Dodgers.

Mix a quart of corn meal with enough boiling water to make a *very* stiff batter, and salt enough to season it. Drop this into hot lard, flatten into cakes about three-fourths of an inch thick, and fry them brown, first on one side then on the other. Split and butter them, and eat them while hot.

Carolina Corn Rolls.

Pour over a pint of meal sufficient boiling water to make a stiff dough; then add a tablespoonful of salt and let it stand until milk-warm. Work it well with the hands; then make it into rolls of an oblong shape and bake them from a half to three-quarters of an hour. An addition of a small lump of butter is an improvement. If rightly made, they will split open on top in baking.

Little Indian Cakes.

Put a tablespoonful of lard in a quart of meal and add two teaspoonfuls of salt. Pour boiling water on half the meal, stir it, add the rest, and as much cold water as will enable you to make it out in cakes of a convenient size. Bake them on the baking iron.

13

Maryland Corn Cake.

Mix a pint of meal with rich milk and a little salt, until thin enough to pour; add an egg, and bake on the griddle in thin cakes the size of a tea-plate. Butter and send them to the table hot.

Indian Cake.

Mix one egg with three tablespoonfuls of sugar, and add one cupful and a half of milk. To one cupful of flour and three-quarters of a cupful of Indian meal, add a teaspoonful of soda and one teaspoonful and a half of cream of tartar. Mix all together, heat the pan previously, and pour in the batter, baking gradually.

Corn Meal Muffins.

To one pint of sifted corn meal, add one teaspoonful of salt, one teacupful of boiled rice, cold, a light handful of flour and one egg. Dissolve a small teaspoonful of soda in a pint of sour or butter milk, and beat with a spoon to a thick batter the milk and other ingredients. If any more milk is required to make a batter, it is best to add warm water, as too much milk will be apt to make the muffins a little sour. Then add a tablespoonful of melted lard and pour the batter into rings well greased and hot. Bake it quickly. This will make exactly a dozen muffins.

Corn Muffins.

Warm three pints of milk; stir into it as much corn meal as will make it a thick batter; add two handfuls of wheat flour, two teaspoonfuls of salt, three eggs and a teacupful of yeast. Beat the whole well together, and let it rise for about six hours, then bake them like other muffins.

Indian Muffins.

To one quart of Indian meal allow three eggs, well beaten; warm a quarter of a pound of butter in a pint of milk, and stir it into the meal, with enough warm water to make it a batter; add the eggs and half a teacupful of yeast, with a little salt. Stir all well and set it to rise. Bake them in moulds or rings.

CORN RUSKS.

One pint of Indian meal, scalded with one quart of boiling milk, half a teacupful of melted lard or butter, a little salt and three eggs. Stiffen the batter with wheat flour, and put in enough yeast to make the dough rise. Set it to rise, and when light, roll it into little shapes, and bake them brown.

INDIAN MEAL WAFFLES.

Mix together half a pint of corn meal, one pint of flour, one teacupful of cold boiled hominy, one egg, half a pint of sour milk, a pint of sweet milk and soda enough to correct the acidity of the milk. Bake the waffles in irons over a hot fire. The secret of making good waffles is to have very thin batter, very tight irons, and a very hot fire.

INDIAN SLAPPERS.

Pour two quarts of boiling milk over a quart of Indian meal, and beat it till the lumps are all broken and smooth. Beat four eggs, add them to the milk, and stir them together well. Add enough salt to flavor them, and bake them on the griddle like buckwheat cakes.

INDIAN BATTER CAKES.

One quart of bolted Indian meal, one teacupful of flour, one quart of milk, one teaspoonful of salt, four spoonfuls of yeast and three eggs. Put the yeast and salt into the milk when quite warm; add the eggs, then stir in the flour and meal. Let it rise all night, and if it sours, add one teaspoonful of soda. Bake on a griddle.

INDIAN MEAL FLANNEL CAKES.

One pint of fine Indian meal, one pint of wheat flour, one teaspoonful of salt, and two gills of yeast. Mix the wheat and Indian meal together with as much tepid water as will make a thin batter; then add the salt and yeast, and let them rise over night.

CORN GRIDDLE CAKES.

Take a quart of rich milk, three eggs, a teaspoonful of salt, a spoonful of wheat flour, and as much corn meal as will make a very thin batter (the thinner the better). Bake on the griddle in small cakes; butter them, and send them hot to the table.

INDIAN CAKE.

One pint of sour milk, one cupful of Indian meal, two cupfuls of flour, one egg, a little sugar, one teaspoonful of salt, and one of soda. Mix all thoroughly, and bake for half an hour.

CORN CAKE.

One pint of milk, two cupfuls of Indian meal, two eggs, three tablespoonfuls of sugar, one teaspoonful of cream of tartar, half a teaspoonful of soda, and half a teaspoonful of salt. Bake it in two pans in a quick oven, for half an hour.

BOILED INDIAN PUDDING.

One pint of sour milk, two cupfuls of Indian meal, one cupful of flour, a lump of butter half the size of an egg, one teaspoonful of salt, one dessertspoonful of soda. (Use any fruit you like; raspberry is the best.) Take a three quart pan with a light cover; grease it; pour in a little batter, then fruit; another layer of batter, and so on until all is in. Have ready a pot of boiling water, and set the pan in the water. Boil it two hours, and be careful not to let the water boil over into the pan of batter.

BAKED INDIAN PUDDING.

Scald a pint of Indian meal with a pint of boiling water, and then add a pint of boiling milk. Stir in one cupful of butter, two tablespoonfuls of wheat flour, four spoonfuls of molasses, four spoonfuls of sugar, five eggs, well beaten, one wineglassful of brandy, a little salt and nutmeg. Bake it one hour.

INDIAN MEAL PUDDING.

To one teacupful of meal, mixed with warm water, add one quarter of a pound of melted butter, four eggs, beaten light, sugar to taste, and one spoonful of molasses. Season with peach or rose water. Add ground cinnamon, orange peel and a few currants. Bake it in a shallow earthen dish, as it must be not more than an inch in depth. This quantity will make two dishes. Bake it for one hour.

BAKED INDIAN PUDDING.

Boil a quart of milk; stir in three gills of Indian meal and nearly half a pint of molasses, and let it cool. Butter a deep earthen pan; put in a quarter of a pound of chopped suet and a tablespoonful of salt. Turn in the pudding, stirring it well, and bake it for five hours. Add a little ginger, if liked. (This is an old receipt for an old-time New England pudding. When baked in a brick oven, it was left in over night.)

BAKED INDIAN PUDDING.

Boil one quart of milk; add six tablespoonfuls of Indian meal, moistened with a little milk. When it thickens, pour it into a deep dish, adding one cup of molasses and one teaspoonful of salt. Before you put it into the oven, add one pint more of cold milk, but do not stir it. Bake it three or four hours.

Indian Meal Fritters.

One pint of white Indian meal, salt and one spoonful of sugar. Stir in enough boiling water to moisten it. Make it up in flat cakes and fry them in a very little boiling lard. To be split and buttered when served.

Hasty Pudding (Though Not Made in Haste).

Let the water boil ; salt it, and stir in Indian meal, a little at a time. When the meal is all in, set it on the top of the stove, and let it boil slowly for three or four hours. When taken out, it should be so soft that it will in a few minutes settle down smoothly in the dish. When perfectly cold, turn it out on the moulding-board, and dredge with wheaten flour till you can roll it out. Cut it into cakes a little less than half an inch thick, with a biscuit cutter, and fry them in drippings.

Indian Meal Pound Cake.

Sift a pint of fine yellow Indian meal and half a pint of wheat flour, and mix them well together. Mix together a nutmeg and a tablespoonful of powdered cinnamon. Stir till very light, with half a pound of white sugar and half a pound of fresh butter, adding the spice, with a glass of white wine and a glass of brandy. Having beaten eight eggs as light as possible, stir them into the butter and sugar, a little at a time, alternately with the meal. Give the whole a hard stirring at the last. Put it into a well-buttered tin pan, and bake it about two hours. This cake (like everything else in which Indian meal is an ingredient) should be eaten quite fresh.

PASTRY.

In this country it is usual to call all preparations of pastry with an under and upper crust "pies." In England everything of the pastry kind is a "tart," unless used for meats. Pies may be made from paste of any degree of richness, according to inclination. A rich puff paste in which the flour and butter are almost in equal proportions is the most choice and elegant. Paste is often made with equal proportions of butter and lard, and for some purposes with a portion of soda mixed with the flour.

To make good pastry is a nice and delicate operation. Flour varies very much in its capacity to absorb water, and it requires experience and judgment in mixing puff paste to know the proper quantity. Too little will make the dough tough and hard to roll out; too much will thin it and prevent the flakiness so desirable. All paste should be handled as little as possible. Good butter is essential. In localities where freshly-made butter is not always to be had, the butter must be well worked in two or three fresh waters. Butter for puff paste should always be cold and hard. In summer, ice water must be used. Flour should be of the best quality, and should be dusted, when needed, through a hair sieve during every stage of the process. A cool room should be selected for making paste, and a marble slab is preferable to any paste-board. The oven ought to be ready when the paste is begun, as it will not be so light if left standing. Nice discrimination is required in regulating an

(199)

oven and having it in proper baking order. Puff paste requires a quick oven. Paste less rich, and filled with fruit, will bake better in a more moderate one.

In making pies of green currants, gooseberries, rhubarb, &c., where it is necessary to thicken the juice, a teaspoonful of corn starch will be found a great improvement. When the lower crust is filled, strew the corn evenly over it, wet the edge of the lower crust with a little water, and when the top crust is put on, pinch the edges together. This will prevent the juice from running over, and when cold, a jelly will be formed.

All dried fruits for pies should be soaked in cold water for a night before using them. A large pan filled with dried peaches will be found in the morning with all the water absorbed and the peaches swelled to their original size.

To Make Puff Paste.

Sift one pound of flour through a hair sieve; divide a pound of good fresh butter into four equal parts; then weigh a quarter of a pound more of flour to dust with, which must be kept apart. Rub one of the quarters of butter into the pound of flour, then mix it with as little very cold water as will moisten the paste and make it easy to work it. Roll this dough out on the paste-board three times, each time adding to the rolled out sheet a quarter of the pound of butter, dotting it over in spots, and then dusting it with the sieve from the reserved flour. When this is done, set the lump of dough on one side of the board; cut off from it enough for one pie; roll this out very thin, dust it with flour, fold it up and roll it out again, and then roll it the proper thickness for your crust. The rolling out thin and dusting is to make it flaky. Use the hand as little as possible in making paste.

Shells for Tarts or Patties.

Tarts are made by filling shells with preserved fruits, after the crust is cold. Cranberries are excellent for this purpose.

For extra occasions it is well to buy the shells, which are always to be procured in our large cities. If they must be made at home, make a fine puff paste, cut out rings with a large cup or glass, then with a wineglass cut the middles out of some of these circles; this will leave a ring; place two or three of these rings, one on top of the other, upon a circle, and you will have a border of paste. Put them in the oven immediately, on baking tins, and if the paste is light you will have fine shells, which may be used either for preserves or for oyster or meat patties.

MINCE MEAT FOR PIES.

Three pounds of suet, shredded and chopped fine, four pounds of raisins, stoned and chopped fine, four pounds of currants, carefully washed, picked and dried by rubbing on a towel, fifty pippin apples, chopped fine, a fresh neat's tongue, boiled and chopped fine, cloves, mace and nutmeg—half an ounce of each—a pound and a half of sugar, one pint of brandy, one pint of white wine, the juice of one orange and of one lemon, and a quarter of a pound of citron. Stir all together, and put it away in a stone pot.

When the pies are made, stir up the whole of the mince meat, take from it as much as you will require for the baking, in a bowl, taste it, and if not flavored enough, add a little wine and the juice of an orange. When the pie is filled, before putting on the top crust, lay a few slices of citron on the surface.

TO MAKE MINCE PIES.

Add to a pound of fresh beef two pounds of suet, a pound and a quarter of currants, the same of raisins, stoned, three quarters of a pound of sugar, half an ounce of cloves and mace, mixed, one nutmeg, a quarter of a pint of rose water, and the same quantity of wine, the rind of two lemons, a quarter of a pound of candied orange peel, cut very fine, and two teaspoonfuls of salt. Moisten the whole with cider.

MINCE PIES.

One quart bowl of beef or fresh tongue, boiled tender and chopped fine; half a bowl of finely-chopped beef suet; two bowls of seeded raisins; two bowls of chopped apples; two bowls of currants, washed and dried; half a pound of citron, cut in fine slices, and two bowls of light brown sugar. Mix with a pint of brandy, one nutmeg, grated, one fourth of a teaspoonful of ground cloves, and a teaspoonful of ground cinnamon. This is enough for several bakings. When you wish to use it, add as much sweet cider as will make a good syrup for the pies, and if not sweet enough, add more sugar.

APPLE AND OTHER FRUIT PIES.

Make a crust of the degree of thickness preferred. Stew the apples and sweeten them to taste. If pippins are used, which are the finest apples in the world, sugar only will be required. If the apples used are not highly flavored, a little lemon rind stewed with them and some of the juice will improve them. A dash of nutmeg is often excellent in apple pie.

Some persons like the apples sliced very thin and put into the crust uncooked, with sugar sprinkled over them.

Pies made of fresh peaches are excellent, either stewed or put in the crust raw. Dried peach pie in winter is very good; the peaches must be soaked all night, stewed the next day and sweetened. Lemon rind, cooked with the peaches, improves them, and when cold, a little of the lemon juice and some nutmeg may be added.

Cherry pies are made of the fresh fruit, put into the crust either stewed or raw. Plums and gages are usually stewed first.

Almost all dried fruits may be used for pies, always taking care to observe that they require a night's soaking.

IMITATION APPLE PIE.

One cupful of bread crumbs, one cupful of sugar, one cupful of hot water, and enough tartaric acid or lemon juice to make it a little sour.

Pan Dowdy.

Line the sides of a deep baking-pan with a common pie crust. Fill it with apples, pared, cored and quartered, a teaspoonful of powdered cinnamon, two cupfuls of sugar, a cupful of cider, and a little water. Cover it with rather a thick crust. Bake it slowly four hours; then break in the crust and mix it well with the apples. To be eaten with cream.

Pumpkin Pie without Eggs.

Put two quarts of milk into a pan and set it over a kettle of boiling water. When scalding hot, thicken it with five tablespoonfuls of corn starch, wet with a little cold milk. Stir it a few minutes; then add two cupfuls of sugar, one large teaspoonful of cinnamon, one tablespoonful of ginger, a little salt, and a little nutmeg. Add one pint of pumpkin, which has been stewed and put through a colander. This will make four or five pies. Bake with bottom crust only.

Connecticut Pumpkin Pies.

Line the pie plates with light crust and put them away in a cool place. Pare and remove the seeds of a good pumpkin or winter squash; cut it in pieces and stew it quickly and carefully. Strain it while hot through a colander or hair sieve. Allow a pint of strained pumpkin to a quart of milk, four eggs, two cupfuls of powdered sugar, a small teaspoonful of salt, and flavoring to your taste; use either ginger, mace and cinnamon, or the grated peel of a lemon. Stir the flavoring well into the pumpkin, and having the milk heated to the boiling point in a pitcher placed in a kettle of boiling water, pour it gradually into the pumpkin. Return the mixture to the pitcher in the kettle, have the eggs and sugar well beaten, and put a small portion of the hot pumpkin in and beat it. Add more until the eggs are cooked. Put it again into the pitcher, stir and pour it into the pie plates, and bake it immediately.

Missionary Puddings.

Beat to a cream one pound of sugar and three-quarters of a pound of butter, and add a little brandy and rose water. Boil one quart of milk with three slices of stale baker's bread. Mix the above well together, and divide it into two parts, in separate pans, for the two kinds of pudding.

Take ten eggs, the yolks for the lemon and the whites for the cocoanut. Beat the eggs separately. Add the yolks to the portion intended for the lemon, and the whites to that for the cocoanut. Add the juice and grated rind of two lemons, or a lemon and an orange, to the yellow, and a grated cocoanut to the white. Bake them in a single crust with puffed edges.

An Old New England Thanksgiving Pudding.

Six apples, stewed and strained; six ounces of sugar; six ounces of butter; six eggs; the juice of two lemons, and the peel of one, grated, and a little rose water for flavor.

Line patty-pans, or a deep pie plate, with paste, and pour in the custard. To be baked without any top crust.

Lemon Pudding.

Mix together the juice of two lemons and the grated rind of one, two cupfuls of white sugar, one cupful of milk, two table-spoonfuls of corn starch and the yolks of six eggs. Bake it in a rich puff paste, without a top crust. Then beat to a stiff froth the whites of the eggs, with eight tablespoonfuls of fine sugar, adding a few drops of lemon juice. Heap this up lightly on each pudding, and brown slightly in the oven, leaving the door open. This will make two large puddings.

Orange Pudding.

The grated rind, pulp and juice of two oranges, the beaten yolks of two eggs, and one cupful of milk. Sweeten with sugar, and add a tablespoonful of flour. Mix this together; it will make one pudding. Line a deep pie plate with paste, and fill it with the mixture. After it is baked, frost it with the whites of two eggs, a tablespoonful of sugar and some orange juice. A similar pudding may be made of lemons. Bake it for one hour.

APPLE PUDDING.

Pare, core and stew six large apples. When cold, add three well-beaten eggs, the rind and juice of a lemon, add sugar to your taste. Bake it in a single crust.

COCOANUT PUDDING.

Cut up and wash one nut; grate as much as will make half a pound. Beat the yolks of six eggs very light; beat in half a pound of powdered loaf sugar, then the grated cocoanut. Stir in a glassful of wine and a small quantity of butter. This quantity will make two puddings. A teaspoonful of flour beaten in is an improvement. To be baked in a crust.

SWEET POTATO PUDDING.

One pound of sugar and one pound of butter beaten to a cream, and two pounds of sweet potato, boiled and mashed fine. Beat the potatoes by degrees into the butter and sugar, add five eggs, beaten light, one wineglassful of wine, one of brandy, one of rose water, two teaspoonfuls of spice and half a pint of cream. Have the puff paste ready; place a layer of it in the baking plate, taking care to have the edges double, that they may rise and look puffy. Fill the plate with the mixture, using no upper crust, and bake it in a quick oven. The above quantity will fill seven pudding plates.

PINE APPLE PUDDING.

Grate one large pine apple. Beat together half a pound of butter and half a pound of sugar, six eggs, the whites and yolks beaten separately, one glass of brandy, one tablespoonful of rose water and a little nutmeg, grated. Mix the ingredients together with the juice and pulp of the pine apple, adding a little grated bread, and bake it for about ten minutes in a crust.

Yam Pudding.

Boil a yam till thoroughly cooked, and, when cool, grate it. Mix a pound of the grated yam with half a pound of butter and half a pound of sugar, previously beaten together, a wineglassful of wine, one of rose water, and a little nutmeg. Beat six eggs very light, and stir them in. If the mixture is not sufficiently liquid, add a little cream. Bake in a crust of puff paste, without covers.

Squash Pudding.

For puddings, a commoner squash may be used than the "fall marrow," such as the crook-necked squash. Boil the squash, cutting it in pieces without paring it; as it must be passed through a sieve, the rind will remain. To every cupful of the squash when strained, allow one egg, a pinch of salt and half a cupful of sugar. Add to the whole nutmeg or the rind of a lemon grated, or both, if liked, and a glass of wine. Beat the eggs well, stir them into the mixture, and, with milk or cream, dilute it to the consistency of a thick batter. It does not become much firmer by baking, and must therefore not be made too thin. Some squashes are very watery, others dry. Make a lower crust of puff paste, with double or treble edges, and use soup plates for baking dishes, to avoid running over.

A commoner pudding may be made by leaving out the wine, nutmeg and lemon, substituting a teaspoonful of powdered ginger, with the same quantity of egg and sugar.

Pickering Squash Pudding.

Three pints of sifted squash, one quart of boiled milk, one pound of butter, one and a quarter pounds of sifted sugar, one nutmeg, four tablespoonfuls of rose water and seven biscuits, pounded. Scald the biscuit with the milk, and beat the whites and yolks of the eggs separately. Beat the butter and sugar to a cream, and add the eggs by degrees. Bake this mixture in a lower crust of puff paste, making the edge thick, so as to be rich and flaky.

MADISON APPLE PIE.

Line a deep pie dish with rich puff paste; slice the apples, previously pared and cored, into the pie dish, heaping it quite full. Bake it until the apples are done and the pie brown. Then take off the upper crust, lay it upside down upon a napkin, and season the pie by stirring into it cream and sugar, flavored with rose, cinnamon, or allspice, according to taste. Replace the upper crust, and serve it hot.

PUDDINGS.

ACCORDING to American usage, puddings are of three kinds. First, those that are boiled in water; second, those that are baked in pudding pans; and lastly, those that are made of some delicate composition and are baked in deep pie plates in a lower crust of puff paste, thick at the edges. "Pumpkin pies" are an exception to this rule.

In making boiled puddings, but few general directions are necessary. A bag of thick linen is best. Cut a circle about the size of a large saucer or teaplate. Sew "easily" round it a deep strip of the linen, hem this at the top and put a string in the hem, or sew the string on a little below the hem. Make it large, as it is easy to boil a small pudding in a large bag.

For boiled puddings, the bag should always be dipped in scalding water and squeezed, and floured inside. A pudding of flour should be tied tight; of bread, loose. Batter puddings should be strained through a sieve after they are mixed.

A pudding bag should always be kept in a place where it can contract no odors.

When a pudding is taken out of the pot, immerse it for an instant in a deep vessel of cold water. This will prevent its sticking to the bag.

Boiled puddings, made of crust with fruit rolled in them, should be wrapped in a cloth, like dumplings, and the ends carefully pinched together to prevent any water getting into the fruit. All boiled pudding are served with sauce.

14   (209)

For baked puddings, common white china, such as is made for the plated dishes so much used at present, is the best.

In the use of spices it should be remembered that allspice and cloves are seldom suitable for anything but meats. Nutmeg, cinnamon, and occasionally ginger, are the proper spices to combine with sugar. Lemon rind, if used, is best when rubbed off the rind on hard lumps of sugar. Some baked puddings are eaten with sauce.

CHRISTMAS PLUM PUDDING.

Beat separately the yolks of twelve eggs and the whites of six. Prepare a pound of raisins, stoned; a pound of currants, well washed and picked, dried and rubbed on a towel; a pound of beef suet, chopped and shredded; one pound of flour, sifted; half a pound of loaf sugar, pulverized; a quarter of a pound of citron, cut in small pieces; half a nutmeg, grated; one teaspoonful of powdered ginger, half a pint of cream, one wineglassful of brandy, and one glass of rose water. Mix the flour with the fruit, stir in the eggs, add the cream, spices, citron and suet, then the sugar, brandy and rose water. Beat it well all the time it is being mixed, and tie it tight in a pudding bag, well dusted with flour. Let it boil for six hours, turning it in the pot from time to time, that the fruit may not settle on one side or the bag burn. When it is taken up, plunge it for an instant into cold water to prevent sticking.

This pudding is very rich. A much plainer one may be made by reducing the quantity of fruit and eggs, and substituting milk for cream. To be eaten with wine sauce. This pudding is excellent warmed the next day.

Plum puddings may be made of any size, boiled for three or four hours and then hung up in a dry, airy place to keep until wanted. This is convenient for those who require one unexpectedly. It is also a good way to prepare a pudding to send to a distant place. Always be careful to mention how many hours longer it will require to be boiled.

Plum Pudding.

Take eight eggs, one pound of flour, three-quarters of a pound of butter, three-quarters of a pound of sugar; beat them well together, then add half a pint of new milk, and stir in a bowl a pound of seeded raisins. Dip the cloth in boiling water, dust it well with flour; put in the batter, tying it loosely, to allow it room to swell, and boil it without ceasing for four hours. The water must be boiling when it is put in.

Poor Man's Plum Pudding.

One cupful of molasses, one cupful of milk, half a cupful of butter, two eggs, one pound of raisins, not stoned, and chopped fine, spice, nutmeg and cinnamon according to taste, one teaspoonful of soda, flour enough to make a batter as for pound cake, and a little salt. Boil for four hours in a bag.

Long Branch Pudding.

Two cupfuls of flour, half a cupful of molasses, half a cupful of brown sugar, two eggs, half a tumblerful of water, a quarter of a cupful of butter, a small teaspoonful of soda, a teaspoonful of ground cinnamon and cloves mixed. Beat it well, and lastly stir in a quart of fruit, either blackberries, whortleberries, raspberries or cherries. If the latter are used, omit the spice. Boil it for two hours in a pudding bag, and serve it hot, with wine sauce.

Governor Hancock's Favorite Pudding.

Soak the crumbs of a small loaf of baker's bread, in a pint of milk; add salt, a tablespoonful of sugar, a piece of butter melted, and three beaten eggs. Cut up as many fresh leaves of tansy as will cover the palm of the hand, and stir them into the pudding. Make a rich, hot sauce, and flavor it with the grated rind and juice of one lemon. The pudding should be steamed or boiled for two hours.

Rolled Pudding.

Make a good paste with a pound and a half of flour and three quarters of a pound of butter. When it is rolled out, make it as nearly square as possible; afterwards shape it with a knife. If fruit is used, it should be very free from juice; if fresh fruits —such as blackberries, peaches or raspberries—they should be put in fresh and sweetened a little. Spread the fruit over the paste, which must be made thick, and roll the paste up in a long roll. Fasten it well at the seam and ends, tie it up in a cloth, and boil it like a dumpling.

The odds and ends of preserve jars may be used for this purpose. To make it very nice, preserved fruits should be used. Serve it with pudding sauce.

Centennial Pudding.

Pour a quart of boiling milk over a short pint of grated bread crumbs, and let it stand for an hour. Then beat it till it is smooth, and add sugar enough to make it quite sweet. Beat the yolks of five eggs, and stir into it, flavoring the whole with extract of vanilla. Bake it in a round baking dish, in a quick oven, but not hot enough to brown it. Set it away, and when cool, spread over the top some jelly or jam. Have the whites of the eggs beaten, with sugar, as for icing, and spread it thickly on the top of the jelly. Set it in the oven to harden. This may be eaten with or without cream, as a sauce. Serve cold.

Sponge Cake Pudding.

Slice into a well-buttered tart dish three small sponge cakes, and place on them two ounces of candied orange or lemon peel, cut in strips; whisk thoroughly six eggs, and stir into them a pint and a quarter of boiling new milk, in which three ounces of sugar have been dissolved. Grate in the rind of a small lemon, and when all is partly cooled, add half a wineglassful of brandy. While still warm, pour the mixture on the cakes, and let it remain for one hour; then strain an ounce and a half of clarified butter over the top, sift or strew pounded sugar thickly on that, and bake the pudding for half an hour in a moderate oven.

GINGER CAKE PUDDING.

Mix with one quart of sifted flour three teaspoonfuls of any good baking powder; add two cupfuls of brown sugar, two of molasses, one cupful of milk, half a cupful of powdered ginger, two teaspoonfuls of ground cinnamon, one of cloves and one of mace, both powdered fine, and five eggs. Beat the yolks and the sugar well together separately first, and mix the molasses well with the flour, adding a cupful of melted butter. Lastly beat the whites of the eggs to a stiff froth, add it to the other ingredients, and bake the pudding in a slow oven.

RUBICAM PUDDING.

Boil half a vanilla bean in a small cupful of water, till all the flavor is extracted; strain it into a quart of milk. Boil the milk, and when it is cold, add to it the yolks of ten eggs beaten light; sweeten it to taste, and add a wineglassful of brandy, then put in the whites of the eggs. Have prepared a quarter of a pound of large stoned raisins; butter a bowl, and stick the raisins, spread open, all over the sides and bottom of the bowl. Then pour the mixture of eggs, &c., into the bowl, and spread over the top stale sponge cake or bread, cut in slices and buttered on both sides, and sprinkled lightly with cinnamon. Set the bowl in a deep pan of boiling water, in the oven. Let it remain long enough to thicken, but not long enough to risk curdling the eggs. Turn it out when cold, and serve.

TIPPECANOE PUDDING.

Mix six tablespoonfuls of rice flour with a sufficient quantity of cold milk to make a smooth paste. Boil a quart of milk, and as soon as it begins to boil, thicken it with the rice and milk and let it cook for a little while; then take it from the fire, add sugar enough to make it very sweet, and flavor it with vanilla or peach water. Put it into the baking dish in which it is to be served, beat the whites of two eggs with powdered sugar till very light; pour this upon the top of the pudding and bake it for about ten minutes, or until it begins to brown. To be eaten cold with cream. It is extremely difficult to boil the rice and milk properly without scorching, unless a water bath is used. If there is no farina boiler at hand, set the vessel with the milk and rice in it in a large deep pan of boiling water and stir it all the while.

Hot Farina Pudding.

Melt two ounces of butter and mix it with three tablespoonfuls of farina ; then stir in a pint and a half of boiling milk and cook it till it is a thick "mush." When cool, add to it the yolks of five eggs, beaten light, five tablespoonfuls of powdered sugar, the grated rind of a lemon, and lastly, the whites of five eggs beaten to a froth, beating all well together. Butter a dish, sprinkle it lightly with flour, and pour in the mixture. Place the dish in a pan of boiling water, put it in a moderate oven, and let it bake for one hour. To be served in the dish in which it is baked with wine sauce.

Cold Farina Pudding.

Melt two ounces of butter with three tablespoonfuls of farina ; then boil one and a half pints of milk, and add to it the butter and farina ; cook it to a thick mush, let it cool, then add five tablespoonfuls of white sugar and the rind of one lemon. Beat separately five eggs, adding the whites to the mixture; last of all place it in a pan, set it in boiling water, and bake it for one hour. To be eaten with cream.

TAPIOCA PUDDING.

Boil a coffee-cupful of tapioca in a quart of water until perfectly clear. Pare and core eight sour apples, put them in a baking dish, lay slices of lemon with them and sweeten them well. Sweeten the tapioca with powdered sugar, and flavor it with vanilla; then pour it over the apples, put it in the oven and let it bake slowly till the apples are well cooked. Eat it cold with cream.

TO MAKE ALMOND PUDDING.

Half a pound of almonds, with a few small bitter ones finely pounded in a mortar (after having been put in warm water until the skin peels off); then add half a pound of loaf sugar, a quarter of a pound of butter, well creamed, the yolks of five and the whites of two eggs. Beat all together until perfectly light, then put it into the dish, which must be covered with a rich paste. Just before putting the dish into the oven, froth the whites of two eggs and grate a little sugar into them; this, nicely put on with a feather, improves the appearance of the pudding. Half an hour in a moderate oven will be sufficient to bake the pudding.

NEW JERSEY RICE PUDDING.

Pick and wash two tablespoonfuls of rice. Sweeten with sifted sugar two quarts of new milk, and grate a little nutmeg into it. Stir the rice in the milk and set it in a pudding dish on the back of the range. Let it simmer very slowly, stirring it occasionally to prevent its sticking to the bottom. When the whole is cooked to a rich cream, set the dish in the oven and bake it until it is a light brown. Simple as this pudding appears, it is most delicious when properly made and cooked. The rice, before putting it in to bake, should be quite dissolved by the long cooking. It should be very sweet, and the pudding dish should not be too shallow for the quantity of milk, as the surface exposed would cause too much evaporation. If the milk should have dried up too much before it is ready for baking, add a little more.

A Kansas Poor Man's Pudding in Grasshopper Times.

Two quarts of milk, one cupful of rice, uncooked, half a cupful of sugar, butter the size of a walnut, two teaspoonfuls of salt and spice to taste. Bake for three hours, stirring several times during the first hour.

Baked Matzo Pudding for Passover.

Soak six matzoth (Passover cakes) in cold water; when soft, squeeze the water from them in a cloth, add one pound of stoned raisins, three-quarters of a pound of brown sugar, two ounces of sweet almonds, chopped fine, two ounces of grated apple, two ounces of chopped suet or melted marrow, one teaspoonful of cinnamon, the rind of half a lemon, grated, one ounce of candied citron, cut fine, two eggs, well beaten, and a wineglassful of rum. Heat all together for twenty minutes, put into well-greased dishes and bake in a moderate oven two hours. Serve it sprinkled with white sugar and ornamented with blanched almonds.

Cinderella Puffs.

Sift eight tablespoonfuls of flour; beat eight eggs very light, the whites and yolks separately. Stir the flour into the yolks, then the whites; then add a quart of milk and a little salt. Beat all together, and bake in little cups or pans for half an hour.

Transparent Pudding.

Warm half a pound of fresh butter, but do not allow it to melt; mix with it a half pound of sifted sugar. Beat it very light, and add half a nutmeg, grated. Beat eight eggs as light

as possible, and stir them into the butter gradually.   Flavor it
with vanilla, peach or rose water.   Stir the whole very hard.
Butter a deep dish and bake it for half an hour.   To be eaten
cold.

GOLDEN PUDDING.

Boil half a pint of rice in water.   When cooked, add one
quart of milk and let it boil up once.   Pour it into a pudding-
pan, add the yolks of three eggs, well beaten, the juice and
grated rind of three oranges and of one lemon, and half a pint
of sugar.   Bake it, and put on the top when cool the whites
of the eggs, beaten stiff with white sugar; then brown it in the
oven for a few minutes.

SQUASH PUDDING.   (BAKED WITHOUT CRUST.)

To four cupfuls of warmed milk add three of crushed
crackers, two of boiled squash, one of sugar, a little salt, and
spice to taste, ginger or nutmeg, lemon and rose water.   Add
two beaten eggs, and mix all well together.   Bake it in a deep
buttered pan for about two hours in a moderate oven.   It is
very good without the eggs, adding instead another cupful of
squash and cracker.   To be eaten hot, spread with butter.

RHODE ISLAND SLUMP.

Pare and quarter twelve large sour apples.   Line the sides
of the kettle with crust made from raised dough, or of soda and
cream of tartar, allowing enough to fold over the top.   Put the
apples in the kettle, and add three cupfuls of molasses and a
little grated nutmeg and cinnamon.   Fold the crust from the
sides over the apples for the top crust, and cook it for half an
hour over a moderate fire.

TO MAKE CREAM PUFFS.

Beat well together two tablespoonfuls of flour, two eggs, and
half a pint of cream; stir in two ounces of melted butter, and

mix all well together, adding a little salt and nutmeg. Fill small moulds or cups half full of this batter, and bake them for a quarter of an hour in a quick oven, taking care to brown them on both sides. When they are cold, cut open one side and fill them with custard, chocolate cream, or any fruit jam. To be eaten cold and sprinkled with sugar.

Sweet Potato Pone.

Add to two quarts of grated sweet potatoes half a pound of brown sugar, the same quantity of butter, one pint of molasses, one and a half pints of water, the grated rind of two oranges, and a little of the juice; one dessertspoonful of salt, ginger to taste, and a small piece of citron. Mix all well together, and bake slowly in a bread pan.

Florida Potato Pone.

Grate five large sweet potatoes, add a pound of butter, or butter and lard mixed, a little salt, and sugar to taste, grated orange peel, cinnamon and nutmeg. Boil these ingredients in two quarts of water. Turn the whole into a well-buttered dish, and bake it from two to three hours.

Gooseberry Pudding.

Take one pint of stewed gooseberries with all their juice. Beat a quarter of a pound of sugar with two ounces of fresh butter. Beat three eggs till light, and add them to the butter and sugar; then stir in two ounces of grated bread. Butter a baking dish and pour the mixture in it, and bake it in a quick oven for a short time. Serve it with powdered sugar on the top.

Cottage Potato Pudding.

Peel, boil and mash two pounds of white potatoes. Beat them into a batter with a short pint of milk, two ounces of brown sugar, and two or three well-beaten eggs. Bake it for three-quarters of an hour. Three ounces of raisins or currants may be added.

FRIAR'S OMELET.

Stew twelve large apples to a pulp, stir in a quarter of a pound of butter, and add sugar enough to make it quite sweet, the quantity must depend upon the acidity of the apple. When the apples are cold, add four eggs, well beaten, and a little grated nutmeg. Butter well the bottom and sides of a baking dish, and strew thickly the bread crumbs all over it, so that they may stick on the butter. Put in the apple mixture, and spread bread crumbs thickly on the top, with a few little pieces of butter. Bake it in a moderate oven.

BAG PUDDING.

Take a piece of bread dough as large as a small loaf of bread and knead into it a small cupful of sugar, one small cupful of butter, or suet chopped fine, and one cupful of raisins. Let it rise for one hour. Tie it loosely in a floured pudding bag, and boil it for an hour and a half. Serve it with wine sauce.

PARSONAGE PUDDING.

One cupful of suet, chopped fine, one cupful of raisins, stoned, one of milk, one of molasses, two of flour, one teaspoonful of saleratus, and spice to taste. Boil or steam it for four hours, and serve it with hot sauce.

SUET PUDDING.

Four cupfuls of flour, two of chopped suet, three of milk, one of molasses, one of currants, one of raisins, three eggs, a teaspoonful of fine salt, two of cinnamon, two of cloves, and two of saleratus. Mix together the flour and suet with the spices. Beat the eggs very light, and add them alternately with the milk and molasses; dissolve the saleratus and put it in last, beating all well afterwards. Put the mixture into a mould or bag, steam it for three and a half hours, then put it, in the mould, into a cool oven to dry. Serve with wine sauce.

BERRY PUDDING.

Fill a pudding dish nearly full with berries and sugar, in layers. Put some bread crumbs in a bowl, soften them with milk, and add salt and sugar. Then spread this, like a paste, over the berries, about half an inch thick, and put bits of butter over it. Bake it, until the berries are cooked and the top is brown, about three-quarters of an hour. Blackberries, raspberries, strawberries or whortleberries can be used for this pudding.

BLACKBERRY PUDDING.

Make into a batter four tablespoonfuls of flour, half a pint of new milk, the yolks of four eggs, a quarter of a pound of butter, three-quarters of a pound of brown sugar, and wine and nutmeg according to taste. Butter a baking dish, pour into it the batter, and drop the berries in a few at a time. Bake in a slow oven, a little more quickly than cake.

NEW YORK PUDDING.

Take one quart of milk, four well-beaten eggs and a piece of butter the size of an egg. Stir in sifted flour until it is as thick as for batter pudding. Add half a pound of stoned raisins and half a teacupful of yeast. Put it in a deep pan, tie a cloth over the top tightly and set the pan in a pot of boiling water. The water should come up as far as the pudding, but not to the top of the pan, lest the water should boil over into the pudding. Boil it for about two hours and a half. When taken out, pass a knife round the edge of the top to loosen it, and turn it out whole. Serve with wine sauce.

Ginger Cake Pudding.

Take one quart of sifted flour and mix with it three tea-spoonfuls of yeast powder, two cupfuls of brown sugar, two cupfuls of molasses, one of milk, half a cupful of powdered ginger, two teaspoonfuls of cinnamon, one of cloves and the same of mace, pounded, and five eggs. Beat the yolks and the sugar well together; add the molasses and one cup of melted butter, well mixed, in the flour. Lastly, add the whites of the eggs, beaten to a stiff froth, and bake it in a deep pan.

Eve's Pudding.

Pare and core six large, juicy apples, and chop them fine, with six ounces of bread crumbs, six ounces of currants, well washed and picked, and three ounces of sugar. Then add six eggs, beaten well. Boil it in a mould for three hours, and serve it with any sweet pudding sauce preferred.

Baked Rice Pudding.

One quart of milk, three tablespoonfuls of uncooked rice. Make the milk very sweet, and grate in it sufficient nutmeg to flavor it. It must bake for four or five hours in a slow oven. Have ready another quart of milk, and as the pudding wastes by the long cooking, add more milk to it. This, though simple, is a delicious pudding, the rice and milk becoming of a rich, creamy consistence from the long cooking. To be eaten cold.

Spider Apple Pie.

Make a good dough of rye, wheat or Graham flour, and prepare it as for biscuit. Prepare the apples as for common apple pies, and put the apples in a heap in the spider, after well greasing it. Be careful that no apples touch the side of the spider. Roll out the crust as thick as the hand, and place it on top of the apples, pressing it down between the apples and the side of the spider. No under crust.

Dried Peach Pudding.

Mix together one pound of dried peaches, three-quarters of a pound of beef suet, shredded very fine, a teacupful of brown sugar, half a nutmeg, a little salt, four tablespoonfuls of cream, the same of flour, and a wineglassful of brandy. Tie up the mixture in a cloth and let it boil slowly for three hours. Serve with wine sauce.

A Bread and Butter Pudding.

Cut a loaf of bread into thin slices, butter and sprinkle a few currants on them, putting a layer of currants and a layer of bread and butter alternately, till you have put all in; beat up six eggs with a pint of milk, a little salt, and grated nutmeg; sweeten it to your taste, and add a little rose water. Pour these ingredients over the bread and butter and bake it for half an hour.

Boiled French Pudding.

One cupful of chopped raisins, one of suet, one of molasses, one and a half cupfuls of milk, one teaspoonful of soda, one heaped spoonful of cream of tartar, flour enough to make a batter as stiff as for brown bread.

Brighton Pudding.

One cupful of molasses, one of milk, half a cupful of suet, chopped fine, one teaspoonful of cream of tartar, one teaspoonful of saleratus, one teaspoonful of cinnamon, one teacupful of raisins, and flour to make a thick batter. Boil for three hours.

Cracker Pudding.

Butter a pudding dish and put into it as many split crackers as it will hold. Put a few raisins or currants, between the layers, and pour in enough cold milk to cover them. Let it stand for half an hour, and then bake it slowly for one hour. Serve with hot sauce.

Virginia Pudding.

Mix together one pint of milk, three tablespoonfuls of flour, one of sugar, two of melted butter, and five eggs, reserving the whites of three for the frosting. Bake it in a moderate oven; when done, add the frosting, made of the whites of three eggs and half a pound of sugar.

Boiled Flour Pudding.

Beat the yolks and whites of six eggs separately, making them as light as possible; stir gradually a quart of milk into seven tablespoonfuls of flour, beat it well, and then add the yolks of the eggs, still beating it, then the whites; add a little salt. Scald the pudding bag and dust it inside with flour; pour the batter into the bag, and tie it rather tight, to prevent the water getting in, but leave a little room for swelling. Plunge the bag into a pot of boiling water and let it boil for an hour and a half. Serve it with hot wine sauce, or cold sauce of beaten sugar and butter.

Plain Boiled Bread Pudding.

Pour one quart of boiling milk over two thick slices of bread, and beat it until perfectly smooth. Beat up well six eggs and add them; also three spoonfuls of flour. Then dip a cloth in boiling water, flour it, pour in the pudding, tie it tightly, and boil for one hour. Serve with a sauce of butter and sugar, beaten very smoothly and well mixed with one glass of wine. Grate nutmeg over the sauce. It must be quite stiff and cold.

Cottage Flour Pudding.

One cupful of sugar, two tablespoonfuls of melted butter, one egg, one pint of flour, one cupful of sweet milk, one teaspoonful of soda and two teaspoonfuls of cream of tartar. Bake for about half an hour in a moderately quick oven. Sauce for the same: One cupful of sugar rubbed to a cream, one beaten egg and one teacupful of hot water. Set the dish in a pan of boiling water upon the stove until it foams.

A Sweet Corn Pudding.

Twelve ears of sweet corn, grated, half a pint of cream, three spoonfuls of sugar, one egg, a little salt. Bake for one hour.

Palo Alto Pudding.

Mix well together one cupful of sour milk, one of molasses, one of raisins, three of flour, one teaspoonful of saleratus and a piece of butter the size of an egg. Boil it in a mould or bag for two hours.

Rye Pudding.

Beat together one and a half teacupfuls of rye meal, half a cupful of flour, one pint of milk, two eggs, whites and yolks, and a little salt. Pour the mixture into a bag, steam it for an hour and a half, and serve it with hot wine sauce.

Snow Pudding.

Put half a package of gelatin in half a pint of cold water, and let it stand for one hour; then add one pint of boiling water, half a pint of sugar and the juice of two lemons; strain all into a dish and let it stand all night; beat the whites of two eggs to a stiff froth and beat it well into the mixture. Pour it into a mould, and when served, pour over it a custard made of the yolks of four eggs and flavored with vanilla.

DUMPLINGS, FRITTERS, ETC.

APPLE DUMPLINGS.

MAKE a paste of about two pounds of flour to three quarters of a pound of butter, or butter and lard mixed, adding a little salt. Pare and core as many fine, large apples as the number of dumplings to be made will require, allowing one apple for each dumpling. Pippin apples have the richest flavor for cooking. Keep the apples whole, or quarter them, as is most convenient. Roll out the dough in a sheet thicker than for pies; place each apple in a piece of the proper size, and pinch the dough together, to close the seams. Shape it with the hand, making it perfectly round. Tie each one up in a little dumpling cloth. They will require about an hour to boil.

MOLASSES DUMPLINGS.

Take some light buscuit dough, not sweet; roll it in thick cakes, and boil them twenty minutes in equal quantities of molasses and water. Care must be taken to have the liquid boiling when the cakes are put in, and also not to allow one to rest on another, or they will be heavy. These cakes may be made with five or six ounces of butter to a pound of flour, with three or four spoonfuls of baking powder. Make up the dough with water and a little salt.

15

(225)

RICE APPLE DUMPLINGS.

Pare and core the apples; wash and pick the rice, and boil it soft. Tie each apple up in a linen cloth, and surround it with rice. Tie up the cloth, leaving a little room for the rice to swell. Boil them slowly for an hour and a quarter.

BAKED APPLE DUMPLINGS.

Make the paste in the usual manner. Pare and core the apples; fill the cavity of the core with sugar, cinnamon and lemon peel. Wrap each one in paste of the usual thickness; put them to bake in a dish or pan, with a little sugar and water at the bottom. Let them bake in a moderate oven, and serve them with wine sauce.

POTATO CRUST FOR DUMPLINGS.

To two quarts of flour, allow fourteen white potatoes. Boil, peel and mash the potatoes fine. Sift the flour into the potatoes gradually, mixing them well together with the hand. Add enough water to make a stiff dough, and a little salt. Roll it out on the paste-board as thick as you require it, and use it as you would paste made with shortening for apple, peach or any fruit dumplings. Dumplings should each be tied in a little cloth for boiling.

PANCAKES.

Beat eight eggs very light; stir them into a quart of new milk. Sift into this, gradually, a pound of flour, making it very smooth. If the batter is too thick to run easily, add a little more milk, and a little salt, if necessary. Fry the cakes in hot lard. They should be the size of a saucer. When one side is browned, turn them, and fry them on the other. To be served with cinnamon and nutmeg and sugar, which must be added at table.

CREAM PANCAKES.

Take a pint of cream and eight eggs, whites and yolks, a whole nutmeg, grated very fine, and a little salt; then melt half a pound of butter, and stir it in before frying. It must be made as thick, with about three spoonfuls of flour, as ordinary batter, and fried in butter. Before serving, strew sugar over them, and garnish the dish with preserved orange peel.

FRITTERS.

Beat the yolks of six eggs well; stir them into a quart of milk, and add by degrees three quarters of a pound of sifted flour, and enough salt to flavor them. Beat the batter very well; have it prepared some time before they are cooked, and from time to time give it a little beating, doing the same while the frying is going on. Pour the batter, by means of a cup or ladle, into a pan of boiling butter or lard. To be served very hot, and eaten with butter, sugar and nutmeg, or powdered cinnamon. They are sometimes served with a hard sauce of sugar, butter and a little wine, beaten till stiff, with nutmeg grated on it.

These fritters may be made with apples. Let them be of a soft and tender pulp; mince them on a chopping-board very fine, and stir a few tablespoonfuls into the batter just as they are about to be baked.

CLAM FRITTERS.

Stew the clams, until they are quite soft, in their own liquor. When they are done, take them out and place them on a chopping-board, remove all the hard parts and chop the remainder until it is a fine mince. Have already prepared a batter made of eggs, milk and flour, and stir the minced clams into it; the proportion being one-third clams to two-thirds batter. The quantity of batter must be regulated by the size of the family, and to be the same as that for an ordinary fritter made simply of batter. In this there is a wide range, some persons using more eggs to the same quantity of milk and flour than others. Some use water instead of milk. Four eggs, a quart of milk, and about three-quarters of a pound of flour, will make a very good batter for the above. After the clams are stirred in, the whole must be seasoned to taste, with salt, if necessary, and black pepper. These fritters are excellent for breakfast, and must be served hot. Oysters may be substituted for clams, if preferred.

FRITTERS.

A pound of flour, light weight, and the yolks of three eggs, well beaten. Stir the flour into water until it makes a rather thick batter, and beat it well; add a little salt. If, after beating it, it is too thick, add a little more water; beat the yolks well with the batter, and add the last thing the whites of the eggs, beaten to a froth. Fry them in boiling butter or lard, pouring the butter into the pan with a ladle, and make them the size you prefer.

BREAD FRITTERS.

Cut a loaf bread in slices of about half an inch thick; lay them on a flat dish, in a little milk and wine mixed together; let it remain a little while, but not long enough to cause the bread to fall apart; drain the pieces on a sieve; beat four eggs very light and stir into them four tablespoonfuls of wine. Have ready some boiling butter in a frying-pan, dip the bread into the eggs and wine, and fry them a light brown. When they are served, powder thickly over them some pulverized sugar.

PASSOVER FRITTERS.

Soak the passover biscuit in cold water all night; beat very light from four to six eggs, according to the quantity of biscuit used; mash the biscuit well, sweeten it to taste—it should be sweeter than pudding; add a little powdered cinnamon and some raisins; stiffen the batter, if too thin, with pounded biscuit, and drop it from a spoon into boiling butter or fat, and fry them.

BELL FRITTERS.

Put a piece of butter the size of an egg into a pint of water, let it boil a few moments, then thicken it very smoothly with a pint of flour; let it remaina short time on the fire, stirring it all the time, that it may not stick to the pan, then pour it into a wooden bowl, and mix with it six eggs, beaten very light. The whole should be well beaten together. Put some butter in the frying-pan deep enough to fry them well, drop the batter into it when it is boiling, and fry them of a light amber color.

RICE FRITTERS.

Boil, till very tender, two teacupfuls of rice; when it is cool, put in a dredging box full of flour, beat three eggs very light, and add them, with a little salt, to the rice and flour. Beat them all well together. Fry the fritters in lard or batter, and serve them hot.

WHITE PUDDINGS.

Take beef suet, chopped fine, add double the quantity of flour, make into puddings almost the size of your two fists, tie up in bags and boil six hours. Put them aside till you are ready to use them, and then put them on a tin plate and bake them brown in the oven. Eat them hot with buckwheat cakes.

DESSERTS.

KENTUCKY BOILED CUSTARD.

Put one gallon of fresh sweet milk into a porcelain kettle; set it on the fire to boil; meanwhile break ten eggs, put the yolks into a bowl, beat them hard, adding one tablespoonful of white sugar to every egg. When the milk comes to a boil, add a ladleful at a time, stirring hard, to the eggs and sugar. When about half the milk has been added, turn all into the rest of the milk in the kettle and let it come to a boil all together; then pour off through a fine wire sieve and set it away to cool. If desired, add a few drops of essence of lemon or vanilla, and beat the whites to a stiff froth; then add a few spoonfuls of fine white sugar to the froth, beating it hard. Pour the white over the cold custard in a glass bowl.

SNOW CUSTARD.

Dissolve half a box of gelatin in a pint of water, and squeeze the juice of four oranges into it. Soak the rinds of two of the oranges in the water, add two cupfuls of sugar and the whites of four eggs. Whip all well together till it forms a snow. Make a custard of the yolks of the eggs. Soak some macaroons in wine, put them in the bottom of a glass dish or bowl, pour in the custard, and heap the beaten snow on the top. Keep it in a cool place till served.

(231)

PHILADELPHIA CUSTARDS.

Mix in one quart of milk the yolks of eight eggs, well beaten. Sweeten it to taste, and flavor it with vanilla or peach leaves, boiled in a little milk.

Pour this mixture into cups, and put them into the oven in a pan of water. Watch them closely, and try them with a knife to see when they are done, which will be when they are a little firm. Do not cook them too long. Custards should be very sweet. Grate nutmeg over them when cold.

CHOCOLATE CUSTARD.

Dissolve slowly by the side of the fire an ounce and a half of the best chocolate, in rather more than a wineglassful of water, and boil it until perfectly smooth. Mix with it a pint of milk, well flavored with lemon peel or vanilla, add two ounces of fine sugar, and when the whole boils, stir into it five eggs, well beaten and strained. Put the custard into a jar or jug, set it in a pan of boiling water, and stir it, without ceasing, until it is thick. Do not put it into glasses or a dish till quite cold. This, as well as other custards, is better still when made with the yolks only of the eggs, more of which must then be used.

APPLE CUSTARD.

Pare, cut up and stew two pounds of apples. When done, stir in one tablespoonful of butter, half a pound of sugar, six eggs, and the rind of one lemon; then bake it for half an hour. Serve it cold, with sweet cream.

APPLE CREAM.

Boil twelve apples in water till soft. Mash them through a hair sieve, and add half a pound of powdered sugar. Whip the whites of two eggs, add them to the apples, and beat all together till very stiff.

Swatara Cream.

Beat together the yolks of four eggs, three tablespoonfuls of powdered sugar, and the rind and juice of a large lemon. The rind must be lightly grated, so as to avoid the tough white skin below. Whisk the whites of the eggs with a teaspoonful of powdered sugar until stiff. Have ready a pot of boiling water, and place in it the vessel in which the yolks have been beaten. Let it cook gently, so as not to curdle the egg, stirring it all the time. When it begins to thicken, stir in the whites of the eggs, and when thoroughly mixed, set it aside to cool. Serve it in custard cups or punch glasses. This is a simple but very delicate preparation. It is nourishing for convalescents and grateful to the palate.

Continental Cream.

Four eggs; one quart of milk; five ounces of sugar; two tablespoonfuls of vanilla; half a box or one ounce of Cox's gelatin, put to soak two hours before you are ready to use it. Beat the yolks of the eggs light, put the milk into a farina boiler, and when it boils, cool it a little and pour it gradually into the eggs; add the sugar, and return all to the boiler. Stir it all the time until it nearly boils; add the gelatin, and let it all simmer until it becomes as thick as a boiled custard. Put the vanilla into it, and remove it from the fire. When it is cool, beat the whites of the eggs to a stiff froth and add the custard to them gradually. Put it into a jelly mould. Serve it cold, with cream.

Mississippi Cream.

Beat well together six eggs and six tablespoonfuls of powdered loaf sugar, and add three pints of rich milk; stir it well with the eggs and sugar. Add a vanilla bean or a few peach leaves to flavor it. Put the mixture into a bell-metal kettle and place it on the fire. Stir it all the while, and never allow it to boil. After it is perfectly cold, sprinkle powdered sugar over the top of the custard. Pour it into a china bowl, and scorch the sugar with a hot iron.

Chocolate Cream.

Boil and sweeten two quarts of milk; scrape three quarters of a pound of good chocolate, and mix it smoothly in the milk. Then boil it in a "water bath," stirring it all the time, until the chocolate is sufficiently cooked. Cool it sufficiently to enable you to add the eggs without risk of curdling them. Then add the yolks of four eggs, well beaten. Stir the whole together, return it to the boiler, and let it cook gently, stirring all the time, till it becomes as thick as a rich custard.

Sago Cream.

Boil a teacupful of sago to a jelly in water, and add to it one quart of rich milk; when it boils, take it from the fire, to avoid the risk of curdling the egg. When it has ceased to boil, stir in the yolks of eight eggs, well beaten; sweeten it, and flavor it to taste with lemon, vanilla or nutmeg; return it to the fire, to thicken, stirring it all the time, that it may be smooth.

Almond Cream.

Pound together, until as smooth as flour, three quarters of a pound of blanched almonds and the same quantity of loaf sugar. Then add the whites of two eggs, mixed well with one quart of cream. Heat the mixture over a slow fire until it thickens, stirring all the time. Season with rose water and peach water.

Orange Cream.

Boil the peel of one orange in a pint of water and half a pound of sugar, and add the well-strained juice of three oranges. If the oranges are very large, two will be sufficient. Set it aside to cool for a short time. Then beat five eggs very light, stir them into the syrup, and put the bowl containing the whole on the fire, inside of a kettle of boiling water. Stir it all the time, and when it begins to thicken, take it off, and pour it into the dish or bowl in which it is to be served. Grate a little fresh orange peel lightly over the top.

SPANISH CREAM.

Soak half a box of gelatin in half a pint of milk for one hour. Beat the yolks of six eggs, with sugar to your taste, and when one quart of milk is just ready to boil, stir in the eggs and gelatin, which must be well mixed before the milk is poured upon it; then return it to the kettle, and let it thicken as for custard. Beat the whites to a stiff froth and pour it on the custard, stirring briskly. Season to taste with vanilla, and pour into moulds.

LEMON CREAM.

Beat the yolks of five eggs very light, and mix with them one pint of water, half a pound of sifted sugar, the peel of four large lemons and the juice of two. Stir all together, and heat over a slow fire until quite thick.

MERINGUE.

Beat the yolks of five eggs with a quarter of a pound of sifted sugar, and flavor with the grated rind of a lemon or orange, or with vanilla. Put a pint of cream into a bowl, and set it in boiling water. When the cream begins to boil, take it from the fire, and stir in the eggs and sugar. Return it to the fire, and stir it until it becomes a thick cream. Then pour it into a dish, and let it cool. Then beat the whites of five eggs very stiff, with sugar; put this on the cream, and set in the oven for a few minutes to dry.

Sponge cake in the bottom of the dish is an improvement.

Orange Jelly.

To one quart of orange juice add half an ounce of gelatin, melted in a very little water. Sweeten it according to taste; pour it through a sieve into the mould, and set it on ice until it stiffens. Rub one or two large lumps of sugar on the oranges, to heighten the color and flavor.

Cocoanut Marmalade.

One pound of grated cocoanut, one pound of powdered white sugar, and half a pint of cold water. Beat the whites of two eggs, and keep the shells to clarify the sugar. Make a syrup of the sugar; clarify it with the whites of the eggs till clear; then add the cocoanut, which must cook till transparent. Remove it from the fire, and when it ceases to boil, throw in the yolks of the eggs, which must heat only (not boil) over the fire till it becomes like a thick custard; boiling the yolks of the eggs makes them curdle. When it is cooling, add a little rose or peach water. Grate nutmeg on the top, and serve this like custard, in small cups.

Rice Meringue.

To one quart of milk add half a cupful of rice, and let it simmer for three hours, or until the rice is quite smooth. Beat the yolks of four eggs, sweeten to your taste, and add the grated rind of one lemon and a little nutmeg. Mix in the rice a small piece of butter. Beat the whites to a stiff froth, and add to it slowly the juice of the lemon and five tablespoonfuls of sugar. Pour the pudding into a buttered dish, drop the meringue lightly on the top, and bake it a light brown in a slow oven. Serve it cold.

Apple Citron.

Coddle some very green apples, rub them through a sieve, and to one pint of the pulp add three-quarters of a pound of

fine sugar. Squeeze the juice from two lemons, and boil the
peel well. When it is soft, take away the white inner lining of
the skin, cut the yellow rind into little slips, add them and the
juice to the apple, and boil it over a slow fire for one hour,
stirring it frequently to prevent burning.

WINE JELLY.

Into a large pitcher pour one paper of Cox's gelatin; add to
this the juice and rinds of three lemons and one pint of cold
water. Let this stand for one hour. In the meantime, boil a
few sticks of cinnamon in half a pint of water, strain the cinnamon water into the pitcher, add one quart of boiling water,
one and a quarter pounds of sugar and half a pint of wine.
Stir a few minutes, and strain through a sieve into moulds or
dishes.

FLOATING ISLAND.

Make one quart of soft custard of six yolks of eggs, one
quart of milk and eight tablespoonfuls of white sugar; flavor it
with one teaspoonful of vanilla extract. Beat the whites to a
stiff froth, and whip in six tablespoonfuls of fine sugar, half a
tumblerful of raspberry jam and the same of currant jelly.
Drop the whip delicately over the custard in a deep glass bowl,
pile it lightly in the centre, and drop over it here and there bits
of currant jelly or candied cherries.

FLOATING ISLAND.

Take the juice of two lemons, the whites of two eggs, three
tablespoonfuls of currant jelly, and a large cupful of white
sugar, and beat all to a stiff froth. Put it into a glass dish,
and pour in cream enough to float it.

APPLE FLOAT.

Coddle six or eight fine, large apples, and when cold, peel and core them. Rub the pulp through a sieve, then beat it up with powdered sugar to your taste. Beat the whites of five eggs with a little orange-flower water and rose water till it is a firm froth; then mix it with the apple by degrees, and beat all well together until stiff enough to float on cream or boiled custard.

AMBROSIA.

This is made of sugar, oranges and grated cocoanut. The latter comes in packages nicely prepared, but the fresh fruit is better, if in season. Peel and "fig" the oranges; open each fig with a knife, lengthwise, and push out the pulp, rejecting the thin skin and seeds. Arrange the pieces regularly around the dish, sprinkling the cocoanut and sugar alternately till your dish is full.

AMBROSIA.

Pare, seed and cut into small pieces two dozen oranges; have ready a box of grated cocoanut; place a layer of the cut oranges in a large glass or china bowl; sprinkle the oranges with pulverized sugar, then put in a layer of cocoanut and sprinkle it also with sugar, and so on, placing alternately the orange and sugar, cocoanut and sugar, until the bowl is full. Cover the bowl with a plate until it is to be served, to prevent the cocoanut from becoming discolored. Let it stand for ten or twelve hours before serving it.

CRIMSLECH FOR PASSOVER.

Soak six matzos (Passover cakes), squeeze them in a cloth to drain them, put them in a bowl, add one quart of matzo meal, one nutmeg, grated, a dessertspoonful of ground cinnamon, three pounds of raisins, stoned, four ounces of almonds, chopped, the grated rinds of two lemons, one pound of sugar, and half a pint of Jamaica rum. Mix all well together, then beat up sixteen eggs, yolks and whites together, add half a pound of melted suet, stir the whole mixture with the hand, which will make a thick paste. Make it up in little forms about the size of a croquette, keeping the hand well dusted with the ground meal to prevent the paste from adhering; grease a pan and bake them in a moderate oven for an hour and a half, turning them over occasionally and basting them that they may be uniformly browned.

Queen Esther's Toast for Purim.

Cut a loaf of bread in half-inch slices, beat light six eggs, dip each slice into the milk and then into the egg, sprinkle them with cinnamon and sugar, fry them in butter, and serve them hot, with a hot sauce of clarified sugar and cinnamon.

Haman's Ears for Purim Night.

Beat six eggs very light, and stir into them as much flour as will make a stiff paste. Then roll it out as thin as for a wafer, cut it in small shapes and boil them in butter.

Kichlers for Purim Night.

Make a batter as for pound cake, adding rather more flour, making the cakes thick enough to drop into boiling butter by the spoonful. Both the above to be eaten with clarified sugar made into a syrup and flavored with cinnamon and rose water.

Marmalada. (A Substitute for Custard in Passover.)

Blanch a pound of almonds, pound them in a mortar and add a quart of water. Put them on the fire with a pound of loaf sugar, and stir in the yolks of twenty eggs, beaten light. Be careful not to let the eggs curdle.

Apple Stephon.

Mix one pound of suet, chopped fine, and two pounds of flour with cold water into a mellow paste. Roll it well, and lay it in a deep earthenware baking-pan, which must first be well greased with suet. Then peel eight baking apples, core and cut them in slices. Mix together one pound of brown sugar, one-quarter of a pound of dried currants, one ounce of candied citron, a little ground cinnamon and cloves, the rind of a lemon, chopped fine, and the juice of one lemon, and put all in alternate layers in a baking-pan; close the paste over the top as you do an apple-dumpling, sprinkling brown sugar over the paste. Bake it in a moderate oven for four or five hours, basting it every few minutes with the syrup which appears round the edges. When done, turn it out on a flat dish as you would a mould of jelly and serve.

A Cocoanut Cake for Dessert.

Make a batter of one coffeecupful of flour, one teaspoonful of cream of tartar, one coffeecupful of sugar, a piece of butter the size of an egg, three eggs, and half a teaspoonful of soda dissolved in a wineglassful of water or milk. Bake this in thin cakes, as for jelly cake, in a quick oven. Then make a cream of one pint of milk, two eggs, one cupful of sugar and half a cupful of flour. Beat the flour, sugar and eggs together, and when the milk boils, stir them smoothly into it. Let it simmer gently for a little while and then become cool; then add half of a grated cocoanut, and flavor with vanilla. Spread the first layer of the cake with currant jelly, the second with the cream, and then put on the third, and cover it thick with icing. Before the icing is dry, grate the other half of the cocoanut and sprinkle it over the top.

Cream Pie.

Half a pint of milk, one egg, one heaped teaspoonful of corn starch, wet with cold milk and mixed smoothly, sugar and vanilla to the taste. Boil the milk, and pour it gradually into the bowl with the above ingredients. Put it back into the boiler and let it remain until it thickens, stirring it well all the time; then put it away to cool.

Sponge cake to be used with the above, which should be baked in jelly cake pans. One cupful of white sugar, one cupful of flour, four eggs, whites and yolks beaten separately, a small teaspoonful of cream of tartar mixed into the flour dry, half a teaspoonful of soda dissolved in rich milk or cream, two tablespoonfuls of butter. Mix the butter and sugar together, add the soda, and then the flour. After baking this, spread the cream custard between the layers as for jelly cake.

TINTED FROTH.

Beat to a stiff froth the whites of three or four eggs; add the syrup of damsons, or any highly-colored jelly or preserves. Serve it with custard, whips, floating island, trifle, or any other cold dessert.

OMELET SOUFFLE.

Beat the yolks and whites of six eggs separately till very light; then mix them together, and add six tablespoonfuls of finely-powdered sugar and a little peel, grated from the surface of a fresh lemon. Put a quarter of a pound of butter in a pan, and when melted, pour in the eggs and stir them. When they have absorbed the butter, turn them out on a plate or dish previously buttered. Set it in a quick oven, and when it has risen and browned a little, serve it. This omelet falls so quickly, that it is well not to put it in the oven until a few minutes before serving. It should be taken directly from the oven to the table. A silver plate or dish is the best thing to bake it in, as it cannot be transferred from the dish in which it is baked.

TO MAKE A SWEET OMELET.

Add to the yolks of four eggs a quarter of a pound of sugar, beaten very fine, and two tablespoonfuls of cream; beat all

16

well together, and thicken it with flour. Beat the whites separately until perfectly light, and then add the rest of the ingredients. Fry it nicely, and season it with lemon juice, or any other sauce.

Chocolate Corn Starch.

Boil one quart of milk and sweeten it well; then add the eighth of a pound of grated chocolate and boil it about five minutes. Stir in two tablespoonfuls of corn starch, mixed well and smoothly in milk, and let it boil till it is well thickened. Flavor it with vanilla. This should be cooked in a farina boiler. If you have none, make a water bath by using a large vessel of water to set your saucepan in; otherwise the milk is liable to scorch. Eat it cold, with cream.

Charlotte Russe.

One pint of good cream, the whites of three eggs, a quarter of a box of gelatin, one teaspoonful of vanilla extract, and two tablespoonfuls of wine.

Dissolve the gelatin in as little water as possible. Beat the cream to a stiff froth, and sweeten it. Beat the eggs light, and add them to the cream; then slowly add the dissolved gelatin, beating it rapidly while pouring it in, and add vanilla and wine. Line a glass dish with macaroons soaked in wine, and put it in a cool place to congeal.

Florida Charlotte Russe.

Beat to a froth one quart of sweet, rich cream, and flavor it with vanilla. Have ready an ounce of American isinglass or gelatin, well dissolved in tepid water. Scald a pint of sweet milk, and stir the gelatin in it till quite dissolved. Be careful not to leave it too long on the fire, as the boiling may curdle the milk. Strain this, to get rid of the dregs of the gelatin, and add a pound of sugar, powdered fine. Let this cool, but not stiffen; then add the cream gradually, stirring it gently to mix it well. Then pour the mixture into the moulds, which should be lined with sponge cake, cut in slices, or ladyfingers, laid evenly so as to unite. A sponge cake, baked in a fluted pan, with the centre cut out when cold, makes a good form. It is not necessary to have cake at the bottom of the mould.

CHARLOTTE RUSSE.

Whip a quart of cream to a froth, and drain it through a sieve. Melt one pint of unclarified calves'-feet jelly or gelatin, sweeten and flavor it with vanilla, and pour it into the froth of the cream, beating it all the time to mix it thoroughly. Have the moulds, the sides of which must be perfectly straight, well greased inside with butter, to prevent sticking; then place all round the sides and bottom of the mould slices of sponge cake, or ladyfingers close together, to form a wall. Pour in the mixture and set it away on the ice till needed. It must then be carefully slipped from the mould, to keep it in shape. Turn it out of the mould on the dish in which it is to be served.

TIPSY CHARLOTTE.

Put into a teacupful of cold water one-quarter of a box of Cox's gelatin. Let it stand for about two hours. Heat, until it is almost boiling, a pint of milk and pour it into the soaked gelatin. Add half a teacupful of sugar, and stir all over the fire till dissolved; then remove it from the fire and flavor it with vanilla. When cool, add half a teacupful of sugar and a teacupful of sweet cream, and beat the whole to a froth.

Take a large stale sponge cake. Cut off the top in one slice. Remove the middle of the cake, leaving the sides and bottom half an inch thick. Sprinkle over the whole of the inside a glass of sherry or Madeira wine. Fill it with the whipped mixture, replace the top, and set it in a cool place.

APPLE CHARLOTTE.

Boil four large apples, beat them to a pulp, and sweeten them, adding one egg and the grated peel of a lemon. Butter a baking dish, and line it with bread crumbs. Put the apples in the dish, cover it thickly with bread crumbs, dotting it over with little lumps of butter, and bake it a light brown.

CALVES'-FEET JELLY.

Boil one set of unskinned calves'-feet in three quarts of water until the meat drops from the bones. Strain the liquor off through a sieve, and set it away to cool until the next day; then carefully remove all the fat from the top, wiping the inside edges of the pan it is in finally with a cloth, so as to remove every particle of fat, which prevents the jelly from clearing. Then put the hardened liquor into a bell-metal or porcelain kettle, with half a pound of loaf sugar, the juice of two lemons, and the whites of five eggs, beaten light; stir it and set it over a brisk fire. Examine it with a spoon from time to time, to see when the particles begin to separate. When it looks quite clear, take it off the fire, pass it through a hair sieve into a flannel bag, and let it drip into a large vessel. If it has been boiled enough, and you have followed the directions about grease, it will be clear as amber. Gelatin has almost superseded the use of calves'-feet for jelly at the present time, but it is not so pure and well flavored as the feet. The old method of straining before the fire has given place to a regular straining apparatus, which may be bought at any house-furnishing establishment in large cities. It is not only an easier method, but more economical, as there is not so much waste.

SIMPLE LEMON JELLY.

One ounce of Cooper's isinglass, one pound of loaf sugar, three lemons, pulp, juice and grated rind. Pour one quart of boiling water on the isinglass, add the other ingredients, mix and strain; then add a glassful of wine, and pour it to cool in mould.

ICE CREAMS, Etc.

It is scarcely necessary, in the year 1876, to give elaborate receipts for making ice cream or water ice. Patent freezers and machinery worked by steam manufacture it now in such immense quantities, with such magical celerity, and so cheaply, that few persons care to take the trouble or go to the expense of making it at home. No town, village or cross-road settlement throughout the land is without its " Ice Cream Saloon," and this grateful luxury, so well adapted to our summer climate, may be found excellent and cheap everywhere.

For the benefit of the few who, in isolated situations, or for any especial reason, may desire to make ice cream for their own use, we will give a few general directions, and append a few receipts.

Good ice cream must be made of undiluted cream. In localities where cream is scarce, milk, thickened with arrow-root or corn starch, is used, or the milk is thickened like custard, with the yolks of eggs. In the latter case, a thin custard is made and frozen.

To make the best ice cream, use the richest undiluted cream and the best sugar. Make the cream very sweet, as freezing has the effect of diminishing the sweetness. About three-quarters of a pound of sugar to one quart of cream is the general rule.

If it is to be flavored with vanilla, use the vanilla bean. Cut it into small pieces, and boil it in half a teacupful of water till

the bean is exhausted; then strain the water from it into the
sweetened cream, and mix it well. It is not easy to specify the
quantity of vanilla bean, as they vary in size and in strength.
One bean may suffice for two or three quarts. It is best always
to flavor the cream according to taste.

When the vanilla bean is not to be obtained, the extract may
be used. When the cream is sweetened, put it into the freezer,
surrounded by broken ice and coarse salt; then add the flavoring. Be careful not to allow the salt to come up to the open
top of the can, for fear it should get into the cream. After the
cream has been in long enough to become completely chilled,
the can must be rapidly turned to and fro, the handle on the
top of the can being formed for that purpose. From time to
time remove the top, and beat and stir the cream vigorously
with a long wooden paddle, and as it begins to freeze on the
bottom and sides, scrape it off and continue the beating. Pursue
this course, turning and beating, until the whole mass becomes
thick. Cream, while freezing, if constantly beaten, will increase
more than one-third in bulk. When not beating, keep the can
covered. When it has become quite thick, and no longer easy
to be moved by the paddle, cover the can securely, to keep out
the salt, and pile the top with broken ice. The ice cream is now
ready for use.

This is the old-fashioned mode, and those who do not possess
a patent freezer, will be able to make ice cream of any sort, by
what is now considered a rather tedious process. The patented
apparatus for freezing are a great improvement, saving both
time and labor. By internal machinery and mechanical appliances, they beat, stir and scrape, and, in short, perform the whole
operation of freezing the cream properly, it being necessary only
to attend to a few simple directions, which accompany the
machines. All this, too, is done in a marvellously short time.

STRAWBERRY ICE CREAM

must be flavored with the juice of ripe fruit. Mash the strawberries through a coarse sieve, and when the juice is all pressed

out, strain it again through a finer sieve. Have the cream, properly sweetened, in the freezing can, and then pour in the juice, stirring it well. One quart of strawberries to two quarts of cream is about the proportion. Taste the cream after the juice of the fruit is added, and if not sweet enough, stir in more sugar. From three-quarters of a pound to a pound is the proportion of sugar.

PINE APPLE ICE CREAM

is made in the same manner. To extract the juice the pine apple must be grated. Cut the pine apple in quarters, from the crown downward, do not pare it, but keep the skin on. This gives a crust, as it were, to grate from, and to hold it by, and also insures the whole of the juice being obtained, as there is no waste in paring. Add the juice to the sweetened cream, and freeze it as above. One pine apple for about three quarts of cream, is usually found enough. It may be graduated to taste. Pine apples may be grated and added in the pulp to the cream, if desired.

RASPBERRY ICE CREAM

is made in the same manner as strawberry.

PEACH ICE CREAM.

Peaches, when used for flavoring ice cream, are mashed into a pulp and sweetened with a portion of the sugar, and are then stirred into the cream in the can. Great care must be taken to use none but the ripest fruit; a hard, acid or unripe lump is a great blemish. The fruit must be added according to taste.

LEMON ICE CREAM.

Grate the rinds into a bowl, and put a tablespoonful or two of water upon the pulp; stir and mash it well; then strain it into the cream; then squeeze the lemons, and add a portion of the sugar to the juice, and stir it into the cream. The rind flavor, and also the quantity of lemon juice, must be graduated by taste; one lemon is generally thought sufficient for one quart of cream.

Ice Cream Made of Milk.

When cream is not to be obtained, thicken good, rich milk with arrow-root or corn starch, the latter being the best. To each quart of milk, allow a tablespoonful of the flour. Mix it into a smooth paste, in a little milk; then stir it into half a pint of boiling milk. Set this on the fire, and let the flour cook a little while. When done, dilute it with cold milk, stirring it until smooth, and pass it through a sieve to get rid of any lumps remaining. Some persons boil the whole of the milk with the flour, but as boiled milk has a peculiar flavor, it is better to boil only a small portion of it.

Water Ice.

In making water ice, much is left to the taste of the person making it. Sweeten as many quarts of water as will be required, always remembering that freezing diminishes the strength of sugar; from one-half to a pound of sugar for a quart of water is the usual proportion. Taste the water after the flavoring is added; if not sweet enough, add more sugar. Water requires more sugar than cream or milk preparations.

Orange Water Ice

may be made of any degree of richness; it may be half orange juice and half water. The juice of six oranges to a quart of water, however, is generally thought sufficient. The rinds of the orange should be grated and steeped in a little water, and the water strained and added to the juice in the proportion most agreeable to taste. A lemon or two and their rinds are commonly added to the oranges, and is a great improvement, as orange juice, when squeezed, is rather vapid.

Lemon Water Ice

must be made as above ; as the fruit is very acid, it will perhaps
require more sugar.

For Strawberry, Raspberry and Pineapple Water Ice.

The fruit must be mashed through a coarse sieve and afterwards through a fine one, the pineapple being first grated.
Add the juice of the fruit to the sweetened water in the can,
stirring it well. Strawberries and raspberries will require at
least one quart of the fruit to two of water, or more if desired
very rich. It is best always to flavor and sweeten to taste.
One large pineapple will flavor about two quarts of water.

Water ices must be treated exactly as ice cream, the same
beating and stirring being required.

Frozen Punch

must be made of the best liquors, and, as it requires much
longer to freeze than cream or water ice, must be begun many
hours before needed.

It is usual at large and elegant dinners to serve the frozen
punch in small tumblers composed of ice. These are usually
made at the confectioner's by means of hot irons and chisels,
as they are troublesome, and require greater skill than can
always be commanded at home. The ice tumblers, with a
small doiley, beneath are served upon plates.

Raw oysters on these ceremonial occasions are frequently
served either in blocks of ice shaped for the purpose, or upon
plates made of ice. (See Oysters.) Celery and olives also are
served in similar vessels.

In preparing these luxurious articles, great attention must be
paid to securing perfectly clear and handsome blocks of ice,
and much room is allowed for the exercise of taste in fashion-
ing them.

RACAHOUT ICE CREAM.

Rub the racahout smooth in a little cold water; stir it into about half of the cream and boil it, taking care to stir it constantly to prevent burning; then stir it into the remainder of the cream. Sweeten it to taste. If the racahout is fine, a heaped tablespoonful will be sufficient to thicken a quart of cream. Put it into a freezer and beat and stir it like any other ice cream. This is not only a very excellent ice, but it is very nourishing for weak constitutions.

ORANGE WATER ICE.

Take thirty oranges with fresh rinds, squeeze them, and soak the rinds in cold water for half an hour. Pour enough of this water into the juice, to give the degree of rind flavor that is preferred, and add sufficient water to make the liquid of the strength desired. This must depend upon taste. Some persons like a strong "fruity" flavor, others do not. If the oranges are very sweet, the juice of a lemon or two will be found an improvement. Thirty oranges will make from five to seven quarts of water ice, according to the quantity of water used to dilute the juice. The preparation must be very sweet to make it palatable, and allowance must be made in putting in the sugar for the loss of sweetness in the process of freezing.

LEMON WATER ICE.

To two quarts of water add four pounds of sugar and the juice of twelve lemons and the whites of twelve eggs, beaten light. Soak the rinds of the lemons in water for an hour or two while the sugar is dissolving. The whites of the eggs must not be added till the cream begins to freeze.

CHAMPAGNE WATER ICE.

Rasp six lemons on a piece of sugar, and squeeze the lemon juice into a basin; add sugar enough to make it very sweet, and

bottle of champagne. Dilute it with water, but be careful
ot to make it too weak. Put it in a freezer and freeze it like
:e cream, beating and stirring it in the same manner, to make
smooth.

Concord Frozen Punch.

Squeeze the juice of six lemons into three quarts of water; to
ich quart of water add three-quarters of a pound of sugar;
eat the whites of four eggs very light, and stir them into the
:monade; then add a wineglassful of the best brandy and a
ineglassful of the best Jamaica rum to each quart of water.
'reeze it exactly in the same manner as ice cream.

Frozen Punch.

To one gallon of water add a pint of wine, half a pint of
'rench brandy, one pint of old rum, the rind of four lemons
ibbed on the sugar, and the juice of two. Sweeten it well, as
loses in freezing. If you find it weak, add more brandy.

CAKES.

A POINT of great importance in making good cake is to understand the management of an oven. Cake will not rise if the oven is too slow. On the other hand, if it is too hot it burns on the outside before the interior is heated. A large fruit cake requires a very slow, steady fire. Small cakes baked on tins or pans do not need so hot a fire as large cakes. Where a great deal of molasses and sugar form the ingredients, a more moderate fire than for pound or sponge cake is necessary. A good way to test the oven is to drop a little flour on the bottom of it. If it browns the oven will be hot enough.

Large cakes should be baked in earthen pans; metal pans heat too quickly, and are apt to burn the cake. It is well always to have a paper at the bottom of a pan. While baking, if it is doing too fast on top, spread a paper over it.

Raisins must always be stoned and currants well washed and picked. Currants require many waters, and in rinsing, a stream should run upon them through a colander. When washed, place a towel on a waiter and spread them on it, rubbing them to and fro; remove them to another towel, and you will find numberless little stems adhering to the linen. Finally, lay them on dishes to dry and pick them over carefully, to remove the stones invariably found among them.

In using baking powders, mix them with the flour. These powders should be made use of with discretion, as they are apt to impart an alkaline flavor or neutralize that of some of the ingredients.

(253)

Flour should be dry and sifted through a hair sieve.

The yolks and whites of eggs must be beaten separately.

It is a mistake to suppose that butter need not be of the best quality for cakes. If it is not good, baking will develop its inferiority.

It is best not to move cakes after they are once in the oven. Also be careful in opening the oven door not to allow a stream of cold air to flow in.

In testing a cake to see if it is baked enough, run a broom splint or skewer through it. If it is not done enough, some of the dough will adhere; if done, the splint will come out clean.

Cakes that are fried must be plunged into deep vessels of boiling lard. Try the lard first with a small piece of dough. Drop the cakes in; as they brown on the under side, turn them over with a skimmer. Let them be laid on paper in the bottom of a dish when taken from the hot lard, that the grease may be absorbed.

In giving plum, and others of the richer cakes, we have selected many of the most choice and expensive receipts. To make them less so, the butter and eggs must be diminished and the flour increased. It is very easy to simplify a really good receipt by this means.

POUND CAKE.

MRS. WASHINGTON'S RECEIPT, TAKEN FROM A MS. BOOK OF ONE OF HER COTEMPORARIES.

Take forty eggs; divide the whites from the yolks, and beat them to a froth. Then work four pounds of butter to a cream. Put the whites of eggs to it, a spoonful at a time, till it is well work^d; then put four pounds of sugar, finely pounded, to it in the same manner; then put in the yolks of the eggs and five pounds of flour and five of fruit. Two hours will bake it. Add to it half an ounce of nutmeg, half a pint of wine and some French brandy.

BLACK FRUIT CAKE.

One pound of flour, one pound of butter, one pound of sugar, ten eggs, two pounds of raisins, stoned and chopped fine; two pounds of currants; one pound of citron, cut thin; one glass of wine; two glasses of brandy; one nutmeg, grated; two teaspoonfuls of cinnamon, one teaspoonful of mace, one teaspoonful of cloves, mixed together. Beat the butter and sugar to a cream, then stir in one-fourth of the flour. Whisk the eggs very thick and add them very gradually, then the remainder of the flour, half at a time. After mixing well, add the wine, brandy and spice, then mix all the fruit together and add one-third at a time, and beat well. First butter and then line the pan with white paper; put in the mixture and smooth it with a knife; bake it in a moderate oven about four hours, watching it to see that it does not burn.

CONTINENTAL FRUIT CAKE.

One pound of butter, one pound of sugar, one and a half pounds of flour, one teacupful of cream, one wineglassful of brandy, one wineglassful of wine, one nutmeg, one teaspoonful of mace, one teaspoonful of cloves, two of cinnamon, a saltspoonful of salt, eight eggs, three-quarters of a pound of stoned raisins, the same of currants, well washed and picked, half a pound of citron, cut in small pieces, and two teaspoonfuls of yeast powder, which must be mixed with the flour. Beat the yolks of the eggs with the butter and sugar, the whites to be beaten separately. Then beat all well together, and bake it, with paper round the pan and on top, in a steady, quick oven, but not too hot. It will require about an hour.

HOCUS POCUS POUND CAKE.

One pound of butter and one pound of powdered sugar beaten to a light cream; add a wineglassful of brandy and half a wineglassful of rose water and a grated nutmeg. Separate the white from the yolks of twelve eggs; beat in each yolk separately with the butter and sugar; beat the whites until they are thick and stiff; add them to the batter and sugar alternately with one pound of sifted flour. The hocus pocus is one teaspoonful of azumea, or baking powder, sprinkled over the batter and well beaten in. Bake in cake pans.

PERFECTION SPONGE CAKE.

Fourteen eggs, one pound of sifted flour, two small, juicy, thin-skinned lemons, one and a half pounds of white sugar. Separate the yolks and whites, putting the yolks into the vessel in which the cake is to be be beaten. Put aside four whites for the icing; beat the eggs well, first separately, then together. Meanwhile add to the sugar, in a saucepan, three wineglassfuls of water, and let it dissolve before placing it on a hot fire, and stir it to keep it from burning. When boiling hot, pour it upon the beaten eggs, beating hard all the time, and pouring slowly till it is entirely cold; add the strained juice and grated rind of the lemons. Beat a little while longer to make the batter very light; stir in slowly the sifted flour, being careful not to beat it. This will make a large panful. Put the four omitted whites on a meat dish, add one pound of pulverized sugar; beat all very light with a knife, and add two tablespoonfuls of rose water. Beat it a few minutes longer, and spread on the under side of the cake, turning it while warm with a knife dipped in cold water; the heat of the kitchen will dry the icing, which should be laid on twice to make it thick. Score it into squares when nearly dry with a damp knife. An oven hot enough to bake bread with a tender, soft crust, will be of the proper heat. It will take half an hour to bake.

JELLY CAKE.

To make cakes that are baked in separate layers it is necessary to have the round flat tins made for this purpose. They are called jelly cake tins, and are usually the size of a dinner plate.

Make a pound cake batter, or that made for White Mountain cake. Bake it on the tins in very thin cakes—about half an inch thick. When baked, set them to cool on a flat table, so as not to warp. When cold, spread on the lower one currant, plum or any other fruit jelly you may have ; the acid fruits are best. Place a layer of cake on the top of this, and repeat the process. More than three or four cakes for one "jelly cake" will not look or cut well. The top may be finished with icing or sifted sugar.

Cream Sponge Cake.

One cupful of sugar, half a cupful of cream, three eggs, one cupful of flour and half a teaspoonful of soda. Beat very light, and bake slowly.

Mrs. Madison's Whim.

One pound and a half of sugar, one pound and three-quarters of flour, three-quarters of a pound of butter, six eggs, one pint of milk, raisins and currants, a pound of each, twelve cloves and half a nutmeg. Flavor with wine, brandy and rose water. Beat it well and bake it in a large pan.

Republican Cake.

One pound of flour, three-quarters of a pound of sugar, brown or white, half a pound of butter, six eggs, one teacupful of cream, a teaspoonful of saleratus. Beat together very thoroughly and bake in a moderate oven.

Rhode Island Cake.

One cupful of sugar, one cupful of milk, half a cupful of butter, two eggs, two teaspoonfuls of cream of tartar sifted

17

into one quart of flour; another half cupful of milk, with a teaspoonful of soda thoroughly dissolved in it; put the butter in last. Beat it very hard and bake it quickly.

WHITE MOUNTAIN CAKE.

Half a cupful of butter, three spoonfuls of baking powder, two cupfuls of sugar, three and a quarter cupfuls of sifted flour, five eggs, well beaten with the butter and sugar to a cream, one cupful of milk. Bake it in layers. Take the whites of four eggs, beaten to a stiff froth, with one pound of fine sugar; flavor it with vanilla or almonds, and put the icing between the layers of the cake and on the top.

LADY CAKE.

Two and a half cupfuls of flour, the whites of six eggs, two cupfuls of sugar, three-fourths of a cupful of butter, three-fourths of a cupful of sour cream or milk, one teaspoonful of cream of tartar mixed in dry flour, half a teaspoonful of soda dissolved in the cream, and one tablespoonful of the essence of almonds. Bake it in shallow pans.

CHEESE CAKE.

Mix a pound of dry cottage cheese (curd) with milk until smooth; make it quite sweet with powdered sugar, and add four eggs, well beaten. Put the mixture into a crust of light dough, and bake it in a quick oven. A tablespoonful of corn starch, well mixed in milk, is an improvement.

CHEESE CAKE.

Boil one quart of milk; as soon as it begins to boil, throw in the juice of four or five lemons; take it off the fire, strain it free from the whey, and add four eggs, well beaten, and half a pound of butter. Sweeten it to the taste; throw in a few currants, a little dash of flour to bind it together, and a little rose water and nutmeg.

Lemon Cheese Cake.

The yolks of eight eggs, beaten very light; three-quarters of a pound of sugar, half a pound of butter, well creamed; the juice of three lemons, and the peel of two grated. Bake these ingredients in small tin pans, with a puff paste at the bottom.

Almond Cheese Cake.

Blanch half a pound of sweet almonds, and pound them in a mortar; then put them in a bowl, and add half a pound of powdered sugar, the yolks of eight eggs, well beaten, and the grated rind of one lemon. Beat the whole together till it becomes white and frothing. Make some light pastry, and line little baking pans with it; pour in the mixture, and bake them in a slow oven.

Almond Wafers.

One quarter of a pound of almonds, half a pound of sugar, the whites of six eggs and two ounces of flour. Make it into a thin batter, drop it on tins, bake, and roll up the wafers while warm.

Wafers.

Nine spoonfuls of powdered sugar, nine of flour and two eggs, beaten up with milk. The batter should not be thicker than for pancakes. The irons must be often greased when new; afterwards one greasing will suffice.

Sugar Wafers.

Beat four eggs in a deep dish; add half a pint of white sugar, sifting it slowly into the pan with the eggs. Beat them well together, and add one pint and a half of flour gradually sifted in. Beat it for five minutes; then add a breakfastcup nearly full of butter, and beat it for ten minutes. Heat the wafer irons, put into each a dessertspoonful of the batter, and bake them in a hot oven till they are of a light brown color. Roll them up as you take them from the iron. They require two minutes to bake.

CHOCOLATE CAKES.

Beat four eggs to a stiff froth; add one pound of sugar, half a pound of grated chocolate, one teaspoonful of cinnamon, half a teaspoonful of powdered cloves, and six ounces of flour. Bake in flat pans.

CHOCOLATE CAKE.

Two cupfuls of sugar, four of flour, two tablespoonfuls of butter, four eggs, two teaspoonfuls of cream of tartar, one of soda, and one cupful of milk. Flavor with vanilla. This will make two cakes of three layers each. The inside mixture, to be spread between the cakes, is composed of half a cupful of grated chocolate, the yolk of one egg, sugar to taste, with milk enough to make it moist. Mix it together, flavor it with vanilla, and heat it very slowly until quite smooth. Make an icing for the top with the white of the eggs, flavoring it with lemon juice.

MACAROONS.

Soak half a pound of sweet almonds in boiling hot water until the skin will rub off easily, and wipe them dry; when the skins are rubbed off, pound them fine with rose water. Beat the whites of three eggs to a stiff froth; stir in gradually half a pound of powdered white sugar, and then add the almonds. When these are well mixed in, drop the mixture in small heaps on buttered baking-plates, several inches apart; sift sugar over them and bake them in a slow oven.

JUMBLES.

Stir together till of a light color a pound of sugar and half the weight of butter; then add eight eggs, beaten to a froth, essence of lemon or rose water to the taste, and flour to make it sufficiently stiff to roll out. Roll them out in powdered sugar, about half an inch thick; cut them into strips about half an inch wide and four inches long, join the ends together so as to form rings, lay them on flat tins well buttered, and bake them in a quick oven.

STRAWBERRY SHORT CAKE.

Make a paste of one quart of flour, one teaspoonful of soda, two teaspoonfuls of cream of tartar, a heaped tablespoonful of butter, a little salt, and milk enough to make the dough soft. Make it up into two cakes, the size of a dinner plate. Split them as soon as they are baked, and butter them well. Have ready two quarts of ripe strawberries, picked and washed and well sugared. Put them between the layers of the cake, as in jelly cake, and a layer on top.

BOSTON WHORTLEBERRY CAKE.

One cupful of butter, two of sugar, four eggs, one cupful of sour milk, one teaspoonful of soda, five cupfuls of flour, and one quart of berries. Bake it in a large shallow baking-pan, in a quick oven.

VERMONT ORANGE CAKE.

Make the cake of one and a half cupfuls of sugar, half a cupful of butter, stirred to a cream, three eggs, reserving one white, half a cupful of milk, two teaspoonfuls of baking powder, and the grated rind of one orange. Bake the cake in a jelly-cake tin, and when done, put between the layers and on top a mixture made of the white of one egg and the juice of one orange, beaten with enough powdered sugar to thicken as for icing.

FLORIDA ORANGE CAKE.

Beat well together two cupfuls of sugar, two cupfuls of flour, and five eggs, reserving the white of one, adding a teaspoonful of cream of tartar, half a teaspoonful of soda, and half a cupful of water, with the juice and rind of one lemon. When the batter is light, bake it in thin layers in jelly-cake tins; then beat the reserved white of an egg with half a cupful of sugar, finely powdered, and add to it the grated rind and juice of a large orange. When the cakes are cool, spread this mixture between the layers and finish it on the top with sugar, finely powdered over it with a sieve.

COOKIES.

Mix well together two cupfuls of sugar, two of butter, beaten to a cream, one of sweet milk, one teaspoonful of soda, and one small nutmeg, grated fine. Make into round or square cakes, and bake a light brown.

CUP CAKE.

Mix three teacupfuls of sugar with one and a half of butter. When white, beat three eggs and stir them into the butter and sugar, with three teacupfuls of sifted flour, and rose water or essence of lemon to the taste. Dissolve a teaspoonful of saleratus in a teacupful of milk, and strain it into the cake; then add three more teacupfuls of the sifted flour. Bake the cake immediately, either in cups or pans.

THANKSGIVING CAKE.

Eight pounds of flour, four pounds of sugar, three pounds of butter, nutmeg, mace and cinnamon to taste; two pounds of raisins, and two pounds of currants. Raise it with yeast,— of this it will require rather more than for the same quantity of bread. Mix in half of the sugar and shortening when you put in the yeast. When well raised, add the remainder with the spice. Work it well and set it to rise again. When it has risen a second time, add the fruit and a teaspoonful of dissolved soda. Put it in the pans, and let it stand only a few moments before baking.

CRULLERS.

Two quarts of flour, six teaspoonfuls of yeast powder, two teacupfuls of sugar, three eggs, six ounces of butter, one pint of rich milk, and a little salt. Warm the butter in the milk. Do not beat the eggs before mixing them with the other ingredients. Knead the dough well, roll it out in a sheet about half an inch thick, and throw the cakes into boiling lard. Be sure that the lard boils. When quite brown they are cooked enough.

FAST-DAY DOUGHNUTS.

Into a pint of lukewarm milk stir a teacupful of melted lard, then enough flour to make a thick batter, and add a small cupful of yeast. Beat it well and set it to rise, and when light, work in three cupfuls of sugar, four well-beaten eggs, and one teaspoonful of salt. Work in gradually flour to make it stiff enough to roll out. Let it rise again, and when very light, roll it out in a sheet about half an inch thick. Cut the cakes out in any shape you fancy, and let them stand for a few minutes before boiling them. Have plenty of lard in the pot, and when it boils, drop in the cakes. When they are a light brown, take them out with a perforated skimmer.

MARVELS.

Rub well together half a pint of sugar, four eggs, and half a teaspoonful of soda; then stir in one quart of flour, and take a separate half pint of flour to roll the cakes out in. Cook them in boiling lard like doughnuts.

Plain Loaf Cake.

Mix together a pint of lukewarm milk, two quarts of sifted flour, and a small teacupful of yeast. Set the batter where it will rise quickly. When perfectly light, work in with the hand four beaten eggs, a teaspoonful of salt, two of cinnamon, and a winglassful of brandy or wine. Stir a pound of sugar with three and a quarter pounds of butter; when white, work it into the cake, add another quart of sifted flour, and beat the whole well with the hand for ten or fifteen minutes; then set it where it will rise again. When of a spongy lightness, put it into buttered cake-pans, and let them stand for fifteen or twenty minutes before baking. Add, if liked, a pound and a half of raisins just before putting the cake into the pans.

New York Biscuits.

Half a pound of flour, half a pound of butter, three-quarters of a pound of sugar, a tablespoonful of caraway seed, and half a teaspoonful of saleratus, dissolved in little less than half a pint of new milk or cream. Roll it into thin cakes.

Rusks.

One pound and a quarter of flour, half a pound of butter, half a pound of sugar, six eggs and a gill of yeast. The butter must be creamed, and the sugar and eggs beaten together and added to it, and beaten until quite smooth; then stir in the flour, next the yeast, and two spoonfuls of rose water. Grease the pan, and set the cake to rise in the same vessel it is baked in. Make it up at night, and very early in the morning stir it well and set it to rise again. Before baking, season it with nutmeg or grated lemon peel.

Sweet Potato Pone.

One quart of grated raw potato, a pinch of salt, one teacupful of sugar, one of butter, one of molasses, two of warm water, and one tablespoonful of powdered ginger. Mix all well together, and bake it in a greased pan two or three inches in depth.

An Old Times Boston Cake for Election Days.

Two cupfuls of the batter of dough raised with yeast, one of sugar, one of raisins, stoned, half a cupful of butter, one egg, and one teaspoonful of cinnamon. Mix all well together, knead, and bake in a loaf.

Kansas Cocoanut Pound Cake.

Bake the cakes in tins, the thickness of jelly cake; spread each one with icing, made rather softer than for loaf cake; strew them thickly with grated cocoanut, and place the cakes in layers, one above another—four in all. Drop occasionally a spot of icing above the cocoanut, on all except the top layer, to make the cakes adhere better.

Molasses Pound Cake.

One cupful of molasses, one of sugar, one of butter, half a cupful of sweet milk, one teaspoonful of saleratus, one cup of stoned raisins, and spices to taste. Bake it in a deep pan.

Common Molasses Cakes.

Two quarts of New Orleans molasses, three-quarters of a pound of lard, and a quarter of a pound of butter, five teaspoonfuls of soda dissolved in one pint of cold water, two small teaspoonfuls of fine alum in just enough water to dissolve it, and enough flour to thicken it; put in last of all. Mix it at night, roll it out in the morning, and bake it in small cakes.

Ginger Pound Cake.

One teacupful of butter, one of sugar, two of molasses, one of cream, with a little soda dissolved in it, four eggs, flour enough to make a stiff batter, three tablespoonfuls of ginger, one of cinnamon and one of cloves, all powdered. Much depends upon the strength of the spices used in portioning the quantity.

Lafayette Ginger Bread.

Half a pound of butter, half a pound of sugar, a pint of molasses, six eggs, of cloves and cinnamon two teaspoonfuls each, and two teaspoonfuls and a half of ginger, (the spices should be powdered,) a heaped teaspoonful of soda, a coffeecupful of sour milk or cream, the rind and juice of two lemons, or of an orange and a lemon, and one pound and a half of sifted flour. Make into small cakes and bake them in pans.

Ginger Bread.

Cut one pound of butter into three pounds of flour, and add three-quarters of a pound of sugar. Stir in two ounces of ginger, eight dozen cloves, ten dozen allspice, half an ounce of cinnamon, all powdered, and one quart of molasses. When mixed, knead it well in small quantities, and afterwards knead it all together. It will require half a pound of flour to roll it out and form the cakes, which must be made not too thin, and baked on tins or sheet iron.

Ginger Snaps.

Melt a cupful of butter and one of lard. Mix with this a cupful of brown sugar, two cupfuls of molasses, half a cupful of milk, two tablespoonfuls of ginger, and two teaspoonfuls of saleratus. Roll it thin, and bake it in a slow oven.

Soft Gingerbread.

One cupful of molasses, one of butter, one of sugar, one of sour cream, one tablespoonful of ginger, three eggs, one tablespoonful of soda, ground spice according to taste and flour enough to make a stiff batter. Mix the butter and sugar to a cream, and then add the other ingredients. Beat the eggs last, very light, whites and yolks together. Bake in a Turk's head or in a common baking-pan in a decidedly slow oven.

Buckeye Cake.

Three cupfuls of white sugar, one of sweet milk, one of butter, four of flour, six eggs, two teaspoonfuls of cream of tartar and one teaspoonful of soda. Beat very light and bake in tin pans.

Hurry Cakes.

One and a half tablespoonfuls of white sugar, two eggs, three and a half cupfuls of flour, one cupful of sweet milk, half a cupful of sweet cream, a pinch of salt, two teaspoonfuls of cream of tartar and one of soda. Beat the sugar and eggs well together first; then add the rest, alternating the milk and the flour. Bake in Gem pans, which should be well heated before filling them. Bake for twenty minutes in a quick oven.

Blueberry Shortcake.

One cupful of sugar, one of sweet milk, two eggs, two tablespoonfuls of melted butter, one and a half pints of flour, two heaped teaspoonfuls of baking powder and one cupful of blueberries well floured. Beat all well together and bake it in a quick oven. To be eaten hot.

Coffee Cake.

One cupful of chopped raisins, one of sugar, half a cupful of butter, half a cupful of cold coffee, half a cupful of molasses, two and a half cupfuls of flour, two eggs, one teaspoonful of cloves, half a teaspoonful of cinnamon and a little soda. Bake it in tins.

ALMOND CAKE.

Blanch one pound of almonds, and beat them as fine as possible in a mortar with a wooden pestle, adding as you beat some orange-flower water; then beat the yolks of twelve eggs and the whites of six for one hour, or until they become quite thick; while beating, sweeten it to the taste with double-refined sugar; when the eggs are in, add the rind of two large lemons, finely rasped. Bake the cake in a tin pan, flouring it well. A few bitter almonds are a great improvement.

COCOANUT CAKE.

One cupful of sugar, half a cupful of sweet milk, one egg, two teaspoonfuls of butter, one heaped teaspoonful of cream of tartar, one teaspoonful of soda; stir in flour to make a batter as thick as for griddle cakes. Bake it in four cakes on jelly cake tins.

Jelly for the same.—One cupful of grated cocoanut, one cupful of sugar, half a cupful of sweet milk and two eggs. Cook for five minutes and put it between the layers of cake. Sift sugar on the top.

HICKORYNUT CAKE.

Two cupfuls of white sugar, half a cupful of butter, one of sweet milk, three eggs, beaten separate, three cupfuls of flour, one of hickorynut kernels, two teaspoonfuls of cream of tartar mixed with the flour, one teaspoonful of soda dissolved in the milk. Bake in small cakes.

Philadelphia Groundnut Cakes.*

Boil two pounds of light brown sugar in a preserving kettle, with enough water to wet it thoroughly, and form a syrup. Have prepared a quarter of a peck of ground nuts, roasted in the shell, and then shelled and hulled. When the sugar begins to boil, throw in the white of an egg to clear it; strain it, and try, by dropping a little of the syrup from a spoon into cold water, if it is done enough. If the sugar hardens and becomes brittle, it is sufficiently boiled, and must be taken from the fire; if not, boil it longer, and try it again. When it has become brittle in the water, remove it from the fire, and stir the nuts thoroughly through the sugar. Then wet with a brush a pasteboard or marble slab, free from all grease, and drop the hot mixture upon it from a spoon, in little lumps, which must be flattened into thin cakes, the size of a tumbler top. When cold, take them off the board with a knife; the white of egg may be omitted if clearness is not desired.

* Many Philadelphians old enough to remember the days when neat colored women, in bright madras turbans, sat on low stools at the market corners, with waiters of these cakes for sale before them, may be glad to recall those memories, and perhaps to learn how the cakes so dear to their childhood were made!

Of the numerous families who fled from St. Domingo during the massacre of 1791, and took refuge in our city, many brought slaves with them as nurses or attendants. It is to these women, in their ready adaptation to new homes and altered circumstances, that we owe the introduction of this small traffic.

The day and generation of this people has passed away. Groundnut cakes—which the little folk called by a less dignified name—are fast becoming myths, and the bright turbans that nodded over the well-stocked waiters are seen no more.

In giving an account of these cakes, it is but fair to add, that one corner of the tempting waiter was always assigned to a collection of rough-looking little preparations called "cocoanut cakes," which no doubt had their admirers, as they were continually reproduced. They never, however, attained the fame of the groundnut cakes, though they cannot fail, thus linked with them, to be remembered, affording another example among the many known in history, of mediocrity lifted into prominence by association!

Cocoanut Cakes.

After the shell is taken from the cocoanut, scrape the brown skin off as much of it as you wish to use. Then grate it on the coarsest grater you can find, or shred it in little pieces the thickness of an ordinary bodkin. To each pound of cocoanut allow three-quarters of a pound of light brown sugar. Put the sugar on the fire in a kettle, with about a tablespoonful of water, only enough to prevent burning. Stir it constantly, and when the sugar is melted, and forms a smooth mass, remove it from the fire, add the cocoanut, and mix it well with the sugar, and then stir thoroughly through the whole the whites of three eggs, beaten light, to bind it all together. Mould the cakes with the hand, using about a tablespoonful of the mixture for each one. Form them in pyramids, and bake them on tins.

Shellbark Macaroons.

To one cupful of kernels, chopped fine, add one cupful of sugar and one egg; stir them well together and add one tablespoonful of flour. Drop this mixture, in little heaps about the size of a large nutmeg, on buttered papers in pans, leaving more than an inch of space between the heaps. When they are baked a delicate brown, take them up carefully with a thin-bladed knife.

Prealaters for Passover.

Take twelve eggs, their weight in fine sugar, and half the weight in flour, and the rind and juice of one lemon. Drop the mixture on sheets of clean white paper, and on each cake sprinkle a little powdered white sugar.

Stickeys.

Beat together a pound and a quarter of sugar, three-quarters of a pound of butter and one egg. Add a glassful of rose water, one of peach water, and some nutmeg. This mixture will not roll. The cakes must be formed in the hand and baked on paper, giving them room to spread.

SAVARIN.

Mix two ounces of beer yeast in a little warm milk, and stir into it six ounces of flour; beat twelve ounces of butter to a cream, then stir in the yolks of four eggs, one at a time, at intervals of five minutes, beating all the time; then add four entire eggs, in the same way; then stir in twelve ounces of flour, and the yeast and flour mixed; three ounces of lemon juice, a tablespoonful of cream, three teaspoonfuls of milk, and two ounces of powdered sugar. Grease two pans, about three inches deep, with butter, and sprinkle them with sugar; put in the batter and let it rise for about two hours When light, put the pans into a quick oven and bake them. When the cakes are done, remove them from the pans. Stir together, over the fire, a teaspoonful of Maraschino and one of Marsalla wine, with a teaspoonful of powdered sugar. When the sugar is dissolved, wash the cake over lightly with this syrup; let it penetrate, but do not wet it too much, lest it should dissolve the cake and make it fall apart. Small, shallow pans must be used to allow the syrup to pass through.

ICING FOR CAKE.

To the white of one egg allow a quarter of a pound of powdered sugar; one pound of sugar and four eggs will ice two good-sized jelly or other cakes. Break the whites of the eggs on a cold china meat dish, add a handful of sugar at once, and keep on beating and adding the sugar until you have poured all in. This icing will require to be beaten for about half an hour. When perfectly thick and smooth, put a layer of it over the cakes and set them in a cool oven; let them stay until the icing is dry, and then add another coat, or they may be dried in the sun. You may flavor your icing with lemon or vanilla.

Icing for Chocolate Cake.

Mix together a pound of sugar and a gill of water. Boil this, without stirring, until it falls in fine threads from a silver spoon. Then pour it in a fine stream into the beaten eggs till all is used.

California Boiled Icing.

To one pound of sugar add half a pint of water. Boil it slowly till near the candy point. Beat the whites of four eggs to a froth that will stand. Pour the hot sugar into the eggs, and beat the whole for fifteen or twenty minutes. Use it as you do other icing.

SAUCES.

LOBSTER SAUCE.

CREAM a quarter of a pound of butter with a teaspoonful of flour; stir this into four tablespoonfuls of boiling water, put it in a saucepan over the fire, with a blade of mace, and stir it until the flour thickens.

Have prepared part of the meat of a lobster, the coral and some of the fat, pounded in a stone mortar, with a little butter and some salt and cayenne pepper. Stir this into the hot butter, give it a quick boil, and serve it.

This sauce is usually eaten with salmon.

MAYONNAISE SAUCE FOR SALAD.

Make a smooth paste of the yolks of eight fresh eggs, half an ounce of good dry mustard, and four ounces of strong vinegar. Dissolve half an ounce of gelatin in two ounces of hot water, and beat it up with four ounces of rich thick cream. Stir steadily into the egg paste a pint and a half of olive oil until perfectly smooth, and then add the cream, stirring it well, also a saltspoonful of salt and a dash of cayenne pepper. Keep it on the ice till wanted.

This sauce is used for chicken salad, lobster, sliced tomatoes, and any other dish of a similar nature.

18

(273)

CELERY SAUCE.

Wash the celery well and cut it up, rejecting the green portions, and boil it well in very little water. When it is soft, and the water much reduced, add a little cream, some mace, pepper and salt. Thicken a large piece of butter—according to the quantity of celery—with flour, and let the whole simmer gently till the flour is cooked; it is then fit to serve. To be used for boiled turkey or chicken.

ONION SAUCE.

Choose white onions, boil them until they are soft, press all the water from them, and chop them fine. Mix a large lump of butter—according to the quantity of onions—with a little flour, put the onions on the fire in a saucepan, with cream or fresh milk, and pepper and salt. Stir in the butter and flour, and when it thickens, it is ready to serve.

ONION SAUCE.

Cut two onions in slices, put them into a saucepan, with as much veal gravy as you will require, and let it simmer till quite thick. Strain it through a sieve, and season it with pepper and salt. If you like it brown, add browned sugar.

EGG SAUCE.

Roll a small lump of beef or veal fat in flour, and put it on the fire in enough cold water for the quantity of sauce you require. Stir it until it boils; then take it from the fire, add a little salt, and when it is cool enough to add the eggs, stir in the yolks of two or three eggs, beaten very light. Set it over a moderate fire, and stir it all the time till the eggs thicken. Just before serving it, add chopped parsley or capers.

This sauce is excellent without the fat.

Sauce for Fish.

Put three or four anchovies, with two large onions, into one pint and a half of water and boil them till quite soft. Thicken them with flour and butter, add two glassfuls of claret or port wine, and, if liked, a little ketchup of any kind preferred.

Sauce for Venison.

To one wineglassful of claret add one of water and one of vinegar; stick an onion full of cloves, and put them on the fire in a porcelain-lined skillet, adding a teaspoonful of pepper and the same of salt. Throw in an anchovy or two, and let them all boil up together. When done, strain it and it is ready to be served.

Sauce for Boiled Chickens.

Beat one egg and the yolk of another, add a tablespoonful of flour, a little pepper and salt, and a soup-plateful of the water in which the chickens were boiled. Stir it over the fire until it is as thick as custard. When the chickens are served, throw the sauce over them.

To Melt Butter.

Keep a saucepan with a cover expressly for this purpose. Simple though it appears, it is nevertheless a very nice and delicate operation to make good melted butter. Rub two teaspoonfuls of flour very thoroughly with a quarter of a pound of butter, and put it into the saucepan with a tablespoonful of water and a little salt. Place it in a large pan of boiling water, and shake it round by the handle of the saucepan constantly, till completely melted and ready to boil. Some cooks use less flour, and stir in at the moment it is taken off the fire the yolk of a well-beaten egg.

White Sauce for Fish or Veal Cutlets.

One pint of milk, one onion, a small head of celery or a quarter of a teaspoonful of celery seed, parsley, salt, pepper, two tablespoonfuls of butter, one dessertspoonful of flour, one egg, and one tablespoonful of cream. Boil the celery and parsley in the milk, and add the salt and pepper. Let the butter liquefy in a saucepan, taking care to prevent it from turning brown, and dredge flour into it until quite thick. Strain the milk and pour it slowly, stirring all the time, into the butter and flour, then stir all over the fire until thick and smooth. It may be made still richer by taking it off, stirring in a beaten egg, and beating it up again.

Sauce for Shoulder of Mutton.

Just before serving the roasted mutton, take the gravy from the pan, and add to it three tablespoonfuls of wine, four of water, a sliced onion, and a small piece of butter; also a spoonful of vinegar or lemon juice. Let all boil up once, strain it, and serve it in a sauceboat.

KETCHUP AND OTHER SAUCES.

Tomato Ketchup.

Take one bushel of tomatoes, boil them until they are soft, mash and strain them through a sieve; add half a gallon of vinegar, one pint of salt, two ounces of whole cloves, quarter of a pound of whole allspice, one large tablespoonful of cayenne pepper (more if it is not strong), two tablespoonfuls of black pepper, and five heads of garlic, skinned and separated. Mix all well together, and boil for three or four hours, or until reduced about one-half, then bottle without straining.

Virginia Tomato Ketchup.

Gather the fruit when quite ripe, cut it in thin slices, put layers of tomatoes and salt, alternately, in a tin or stone vessel, until it is full, then boil it gently for half an hour; pulp it through a hair sieve, and to every gallon of liquor add three or four sticks of horse-radish, a small onion stuck with cloves, some grated nutmeg, one ounce of allspice, and a pod or two of red pepper, or an ounce of black pepper. Boil all well together, and after boiling, add good vinegar at the rate of half a pint to every gallon of ketchup; put it into clean bottles, cork them tight, and keep them in a dry, cool place.

Cold Tomato Ketchup.

Skin and remove the seeds from half a peck of ripe tomatoes, and chop them up; add two sticks of grated horse-radish; three large heads of celery, cut in small pieces; two cupfuls of onion, minced very fine; two red peppers, without the seeds; two-thirds of a cupful of salt; one cupful of sugar; one cupful of mustard seed; one tablespoonful of ground black pepper; one tablespoonful of mace; one teaspoonful of ground cloves. Mix all these ingredients well together, put them in a large jar, and cover the whole with cold vinegar. Six or eight cloves of garlic may be added if the flavor is agreeable. Tie the jar up tight. It will keep well for a year.

To Make Tomato Soy.

The tomatoes must be perfectly ripe. Have a clean stone jar to put them in, and wipe them with a wet cloth; cut them in slices through the middle, put them in layers into the jar two inches deep; cover each layer with salt, until it is full. Let it stand for thirty-six hours, with a cloth spread over it, or until a sufficient fermentation takes place to enable you to strain the juice through a coarse cloth. There is little danger of its fermenting too quickly, and it may require sometimes a few hours longer than the time mentioned. Boil it next in a stone vessel until it is reduced to one-third, skimming it well while boiling. Just before you take it from the fire, add beaten spices, two tablespoonfuls to every gallon, stirring them well in; allspice, cloves, mace and nutmeg. Let all boil for a few minutes after adding the spice; then take it off, and, when cold, put it away in bottles for use. Be careful to cork the bottles very tightly.

To Make Walnut Ketchup.

Lay a hundred walnuts when fit to pickle in salt and water for two days; move them each day; beat them in a marble mortar, put them in a stone jar, with a pint of good vinegar and half a handful of salt, and let them stand for nine days, shaking them every day; then strain off the liquor till they are quite dry; let this boil for about ten minutes, add a quarter of an ounce of mace, a few cloves, a good deal of black pepper, some ginger and five or six anchovies; let it boil for a quarter of an hour; strain it when cold and bottle it. It must be boiled in a pan well tinned, as brass or copper will spoil it. If made of Indian walnuts, fewer will suffice to make the ketchup.

To Make Walnut Ketchup from the Leaves.

Four ounces of garlic, four ounces of ginger, four ounces of horse-radish, one ounce of cloves, one ounce of red pepper, one ounce of sweet orange peel, a pound of salt and one gallon or more of sharp vinegar, poured boiling hot on the leaves. Let it stand for a fortnight in the sun; then strain and bottle it for table use.

Mushroom Ketchup.

Take the large flaps of mushrooms gathered dry. Bruise and put them in layers at the bottom of a stone pan, sprinkling each layer well with salt. Let them stand for a day or two, stirring them up each day. Strain the liquor through a bag, and to every gallon add one quart of red wine, of mace, cloves and allspice, half an ounce each, and a race or two of ginger cut up. If not salt enough, add more. Boil it till about one quart has wasted away; strain it into a pan, and let it become cold before bottling. As the fine flavor of the wine is lost in boiling, it would be as well to add it just as you remove the pan from the fire

Cucumber Ketchup.

Peel and slice a peck of full-grown cucumbers—as for dinner. Cover them with a pint of salt. Let them stand for two or three hours, then drain them; peel and slice a dozen small onions, place them with the cucumbers in layers in a stone jar, cover them with strong vinegar, a teaspoonful of ground black pepper, a gill of sweet oil, a gill of Madeira wine and a couple of blades of mace. Stir them with a wooden spoon, but do not cut the slices. Tie it up tightly.

Cucumber Ketchup.

One dozen large cucumbers, sliced; four onions, sliced. Salt them well and place them in a colander to drain. Add half a cupful each of black and white mustard seed, one tablespoonful of black pepper, and cover them with vinegar. Let them remain thus a week, and then strain off the vinegar and bottle it for use.

Oyster Ketchup.

Pound the oysters well and strain them through a sieve. Mix the juices of the strained oysters with their liquor; put cloves, mace and pepper sufficient to season or flavor it well into a gauze bag, and throw it into the liquor; put in a good deal of salt. Boil and skim it until done; then add a pint of white wine to a pint of liquor. If you put in a glass of brandy, the ketchup will last a long time.

BARBERRY KETCHUP.

One peck of barberries, two quarts of vinegar, four table-spoonfuls of salt, one tablespoonful of allspice, the same of cloves, two tablespoonfuls of cayenne pepper, and the same of mustard. Boil all these ingredients thoroughly; then strain the mixture and boil it again slowly for three hours. Bottle it and keep it well corked.

CHILI SAUCE.

Take nine large tomatoes, two onions, one pepper, two table-spoonfuls of sugar, the same of salt, two cupfuls of vinegar, and of powdered allspice, cloves and mustard, one teaspoonful each. Skin the tomatoes, chop all the ingredients together, and sim-mer it for one hour.

PEPPER SAUCE.

Eight heads of cabbage, seven dozen peppers, seeded and chopped; ten heads of celery, two sticks of horse-radish, grated; of whole cloves, whole allspice, white and black mustard seed, a tablespoonful each; one cupful of sugar, one gallon of vinegar. Cut the cabbage, salt it, and let it stand for one hour; then squeeze all the water from it. Mix all together, and put it in stone jars. Boil vinegar and sugar together; when cold, pour it over the pickles, and tie up tight.

PICKLE SAUCE.

Two gallons of coarsely-cut cabbage; one gallon of green tomatoes; one dozen of onions, cut fine; one ounce of turmeric, one ounce of celery seed, one ounce of whole pepper, half an ounce of whole allspice, half an ounce of whole cloves, half an ounce of ground ginger, one gallon of cider vinegar, one cupful of salt, half a pound of brown sugar, three-quarters of a pound of white mustard seed. Cut up the cabbage, onions and green tomatoes with a cold slaw cutter; put them in a wooden bowl, and chop them fine. Add the above ingredients; put all into a preserving kettle, and boil them for twenty minutes. Put it into stone jars, and keep them in a cool place.

Mint Sauce.

Mix two tablespoonfuls of sugar in half a teacupful of vinegar; then add two tablespoonfuls of mint, chopped fine, and let it stand for ten minutes before serving.

Mustard Dressing.

To a quarter of a pound of the best mustard add one gill of the best salad oil, one teaspoonful of white sugar, one saltspoonful of cayenne pepper and one teaspoonful of salt. The spoons should be heaped. Beat all well together, thickening it to the consistency of paste with vinegar, in which a shred of onion has been boiled. Keep it for a week before using it. It must be very tightly corked.

Horse-Radish Sauce.

One tablespoonful of grated horse-radish, one teaspoonful of mixed mustard, one teaspoonful of salt, two tablespoonfuls of vinegar and three tablespoonfuls of rich cream. Mix all well together. To be eaten with roast meats.

Mint Sauce.

Wash well a handful of mint, and dry it in a towel; then put it in a tumbler; pour as much vinegar as you wish for sauce over it; let it steep for two hours; strain it into a sauceboat, and add as much fine loaf sugar as will make it rich.   It is then fit for use.

PEACH SAUCE.

Scald and wipe the fur from one peck of clingstone peaches, and boil them in water until a straw can pierce them.   Then make a syrup of three pounds of white sugar and one pint of vinegar; put the peaches into this, and boil them until they look clear.   Then put them into jars and pour the hot syrup over them.

CELERY VINEGAR.

Pound two gills of celery seed; put it into a bottle, and fill it up with strong vinegar.   Shake it once every day for a fortnight; then strain it off, and it is ready for use.   This will impart a flavor of celery to everything it is used for.

THYME OR MINT SAUCE.

A delicious flavoring of thyme or mint may be obtained by gathering these herbs when they have arrived at perfection. Pick them fresh from the stalks; put a large handful in a jar with a quart of vinegar or brandy; cover the jar very close. Next day take all the herb out, and put in another handful. Do this a third time; then strain and bottle it for use.   The herb must not remain in longer than twenty-four hours each time, or it will be bitter.

PUDDING SAUCES.

MAPLE SUGAR SAUCE.

Melt half a pound of maple sugar in a small teacupful of water, breaking up the sugar first in small pieces. Put it on a slow fire, let it melt, and then simmer, and remove all the scum. Add a quarter of a pound of butter, mixed with a small teaspoonful of flour, and a little nutmeg grated. Boil all well together. An excellent sauce for any boiled pudding.

HOT SAUCE FOR PUDDINGS.

One cupful of butter, two cupfuls of sugar, four eggs and two wineglassfuls of wine. Stir all well together, and just before sending it to table, pour in one cupful of boiling water and stir it hard.

WINE SAUCE.

Put into a bowl one cupful of butter, two cupfuls of sugar, and one cupful of wine. Set the bowl in a saucepan of boiling water, and let it stand until all is dissolved. Serve it immediately.

PUDDING SAUCE.

Beat to a smooth cream together a quarter of a pound of powdered sugar and a quarter of a pound of butter, and put it in a saucepan in a pan of hot water, or in a farina boiler. Stir it, and when it begins to melt, add the yolk of an egg, well beaten; let it simmer until the egg begins to thicken the mixture, stirring it all the time; then take it from the fire, and stir in a wineglassful of wine in which there is some grated nutmeg.

PUDDING SAUCE WITHOUT BUTTER.

Two eggs, beaten to a froth, with half a cupful of sugar, a little salt, and vanilla to season. The yolks and whites may be beaten separately, and the whites added just before serving.

SAUCES.

Cheap Pudding Sauce.

Melt a piece of butter the size of an egg in a pint of good hot custard, and flavor it with wine or brandy and nutmeg.

Hot Pudding Sauce.

Cream two ounces of butter with four spoonfuls of sugar, and add a little nutmeg; place the bowl in which you have mixed these in a pan of boiling water on the range. Stir it for some time, and add the yolks of two eggs when taking it from the fire. Lastly, throw in a glass of Madeira or sherry wine.

Orange Hard Sauce.

Mix the juice of three oranges with enough soft white sugar to make a hard sauce.

Cold Sauce for Pudding.

Beat a quarter of a pound of butter to a cream, with six ounces of powdered sugar, and add half a nutmeg, grated, half a wineglassful of rose water and the same of wine.

PREPARATIONS FOR THE SICK.

INDIAN MEAL WATER GRUEL.

MIX a tablespoonful of Indian meal smoothly in cold water; stir into it a teacupful of boiling water; let it boil until the meal is cooked, and sweeten it. Add also a little salt.

INDIAN MEAL MILK GRUEL.

A richer and very delicious Indian gruel is made by using milk instead of water; two tablespoonfuls of Indian meal to a quart of milk, and sweetening the milk. This had better be cooked in a farina boiler, as the milk is so apt to scorch. When done, grate nutmeg on the top. The quantity of meal must depend upon the taste of the patient. Some like it thick, and others very thin.

OAT MEAL GRUEL.

Mix a heaped tablespoonful of the best oat meal smooth with a little cold water, and stir this well into a quart of boiling water. Put in a quarter of a pound of raisins (sultanas are the best). Let it boil moderately for three quarters of an hour; then sweeten it, and add grated nutmeg. A little fresh lemon peel may also be added. If the patient can take wine, the raisins may be omitted. If wine is used, it must be added after the gruel is removed from the fire.

(285)

WATER GRUEL.

Boil for ten or fifteen minutes two ounces of oat meal and one quart of water; then strain it, and add sugar and salt to the taste. Wine and nutmeg, if allowed, may be added.

ARROW-ROOT.

Boil half a vanilla bean and a small piece of cinnamon stick, in one pint of milk, leaving three tablespoonfuls to be mixed with a dessertspoonful of Bermuda arrow-root. When mixed quite smooth, pour it gradually into the boiling milk, stirring it all the time. Take it off in a minute or two, and sweeten it with powdered sugar. It may be made with water instead of milk, and seasoned with lemon instead of spices, as the patient may require.

TAPIOCA OR SAGO.

Wash three tablespoonfuls of sago; boil half a vanilla bean and a small piece of stick cinnamon; strain the water, put it on the fire with the sago or tapioca, and let it boil until it jellies, which will probably require an hour. When cold, season it with lemon juice, sugar and nutmeg.

Both of these articles are better for being soaked some hours before using.

BARLEY WATER.

Wash well a quarter of a pound of pearl barley; put it on the fire with two quarts of water, and let it reduce one half. Skim it while it boils, and strain it when done. Sweeten it to taste, and add either lemon juice or wine, as preferred.

Barley requires so long to cook, that it is better to soak it all night. If soaked, it must be boiled in the same water.

Rice Water.

Wash and pick two ounces of rice; put it into two quarts of water; boil it for an hour and a half, and then add sugar and nutmeg, as may be preferred. In cases where wine or lemon can be used, they will be found to improve it.

Toast Water.

Toast water is often very grateful to sick persons, who have become tired of drinks that are sweetened. Toast two rounds of a baker's loaf before a quick fire, letting it brown evenly all over on both sides. If any points have calcined, scrape them off. Put the toast in a mug, and pour a pint of water over it. When it stands for a short time it will become brown, and will then be ready for use.

Apple Water.

Apple water may be made in two ways. Roast two or three fine apples—pippins are the richest—and put them into a quart jug; pour cold water on them, and in a little while taste the water; if it is too strong, dilute it. If the patient likes it sweet, add sugar. If raw apples are used, slice them and pour boiling water over them. When it is cold, it is fit to use. These may also be sweetened if desired, in which case the sugar should be scalded with the apples.

Flaxseed Tea.

Pour three quarts of boiling water on two tablespoonfuls of flaxseed. Set it on the fire, and when it begins to boil, remove it and strain it through a sieve upon some sugar and lemon juice. The hot liquid will prevent any injurious effects from the acid. Sweeten it to taste.

FLAXSEED JELLY.

Sift and clean half a teacupful of flaxseed; put it on the fire in a pint and a half of water, and let it boil down to half a pint. Strain off the seeds, and sweeten it well with loaf sugar. Squeeze the juice of a lemon into it, and grate into it, very lightly, a little of the outside surface of the rind.

BEEF TEA.

Cut into thin slices one pound of lean beef, and boil it in one quart of water for twenty minutes, taking off the scum as it rises. After it is cold, strain the liquor off. This preparation is more nourishing than ordinary broths, and more palatable.

BEEF BROTH FOR THE SICK.

Remove the fat from one pound of lean beef; cut it into small pieces, pour over it one pint of cold water, and let it soak for an hour. Strain the liquid, and wring it in a cloth to extract all the juice; put this over the fire, with a little whole pepper, allspice and salt, and let it simmer for fifty minutes and boil hard for ten. Strain it through a fine sieve or muslin bag. A finger's length of celery, with a scrap of the leaf on it, makes the flavor more agreeable.

ESSENCE OF BEEF.

Take one or two pounds of beef from the round or veiny piece, without fat. Cut it in half-inch pieces, put it in a stone jar, place the jar in a vessel of boiling water, and let it boil for half an hour; a little salt and a blade of mace may be added. This will make about a teacupful of the essence, and must be strained. To be used as directed.

Partridge Tea.

Boil one partridge in a pint and a half of water until it is reduced to one pint. Skim it as long as any scum rises, and add a little salt to taste.

Chicken Jelly.

Joint the chicken and remove all the skin; wrap the pieces in a coarse towel and break them up; cut off the claws and immerse them in boiling water, which will cause the skin to come off like a glove; they contain a great deal of nourishment. Put them, with the rest of the chicken, in a saucepan with two quarts of tepid water, flavor it with a blade of mace, and salt it to taste. Let it simmer slowly until the water is reduced one-half, then strain it through a sieve and set it away to cool. When perfectly cold, remove the grease from the top, and a delicate and nutritious jelly will be found. This may have spices or wine added to it, if needed, in which case the spices must be boiled with the chicken and the wine added after it is strained.

Chicken for an Invalid.

Pound the white meat of a chicken in a stone mortar and moisten it with some of the water in which it is boiled. Pass it through a sieve until about a pint of the water has been used. Season it with salt, a little pepper and a blade of mace; the latter boiled with the chicken. After straining the paste, simmer it over the fire for about ten minutes, then take it off, and when it is cool, not cold, stir in a wineglassful of rich, fresh cream.

Milk Punch.

Put as much loaf sugar in a tumbler of rich, new milk as will be agreeable to the taste; when it is dissolved, add one or two tablespoonfuls of the best brandy; the quantity, of course, being regulated by the condition of the patient. Stir it well,

19

and grate a little nutmeg on the top. If nutmeg is not liked, a little of the rind of a fresh lemon may be substituted. The milk used should come directly from the ice, as adding ice in the glass will dilute the milk and impair its richness.

Milk Punch, to Keep.

Half a gallon of brandy, half a gallon of rum, five quarts of cold water, three pounds of white sugar, two grated nutmegs, two quarts of *boiling* milk, and the juice of eighteen lemons. Soak the rinds of the lemons in the liquor for forty-eight hours. Stir it very well, and strain it through a flannel bag until it is clear. Filtering it through paper will make it bright. Bottle it for use, as it will keep for any length of time.

A Very Fine Bitters for Ague Regions.

One ounce of gentian root, one ounce of orange peel, one of bark, half an ounce of juniper berries, three-quarters of an ounce of cardamon seeds, and one gallon of whisky or brandy. Shake it frequently, and it will be ready for use in a few days. It may be replenished by adding more spirits, as it diminishes by use, to the extent of a quart. If desired, it may be colored.

Blackberry Cordial.

To two quarts of blackberries add one pound of loaf sugar, one ounce and a half of nutmeg, the same of cinnamon, and one ounce and a quarter of cloves or allspice. The spices must be pulverized. Boil all together for a short time, and when cold, add one pint of fourth proof brandy. Dose, from a wine-glassful to a teaspoonful, according to age.

Wine Whey.

Two wineglassfuls of Madeira wine to one pint of fresh milk. When it boils, throw in the wine and let it again come to a boil.

Strain it through a fine sieve without stirring it. The quantity of wine used in making wine whey must be regulated by the condition of the patient or the advice of the physician. Less than one glassful of wine will not turn a pint of milk to whey, and that quantity will sometimes fail. If the wine whey must be very weak, add whey turned with rennet to dilute it.

MULLED WINE FOR THE SICK.

Boil one dozen of whole allspice in water for about ten minutes, or till it is reduced to about a wineglassful. Beat two tablespoonfuls of sugar with the yolk of an egg; then add a winglassful of wine; and lastly, the hot allspice water. Throw all into the saucepan, and keep it on the fire for a minute, watching it carefully, lest the egg should curdle.

ORGEAT, FOR THE SICK.

Blanch half a pound of almonds and powder them, mixing in a little rose water to prevent them from oiling. Then pour over them one quart of boiling water. When nearly cold, strain, sweeten, and flavor it with rose water, according to taste.

TO MAKE ALMOND MILK.

To three dozen fresh almonds, blanched, add two bitter almonds, also blanched, and two lumps of sugar. Pound the whole in a mortar, with a gill of boiling water. Strain it through a cloth, return the pulp to the mortar and pound it, with more water, straining it again, until you have used a pint in all. This is a pleasant beverage for an invalid. It does not keep long, but is easily made fresh when wanted. If you like it sweeter, add more sugar.

Arab Racahout.

One pound of ground rice, one pound of arrow-root, and half a pound of the best chocolate. Mix them thoroughly, and put the mixture into a jar for use. Take a tablespoonful of the racahout and make it into a paste with cold water or milk ; stir this paste into a half pint of boiling milk, and let it boil up for a minute or two. Add sugar if desired, and take it hot like chocolate.

BEVERAGES.

FRUIT SHERBETS.

During the summer heat, a very agreeable and cooling beverage can be made with little trouble from strawberries, raspberries or currants. Mash the ripe fruit, and pass it, first through a coarse, and then through a finer sieve. To every quart of juice add a quart of water, and sweeten it with powdered sugar. When the sugar is dissolved, strain it through a fine muslin bag, put it in an ice cream freezer, and keep a little ice around it until needed. If you have an ice house, put it in bottles, and set them in it. Served in water goblets, sherbet looks very tempting with the rich coloring shining through the dew. The juice of pine apples, cherries and grapes may be used in the same manner. Pine apples must be grated and squeezed to obtain the juice. The Catawba and Scuppernong grape used in this way make a delicious beverage. Even the common wild fox grape is very good. When these are used, mash them and wash out the juice with the water through a sieve.

RASPBERRY VINEGAR.

Put a pound of fine raspberries in a bowl, and pour upon them one quart of white wine vinegar. Next day strain the liquor on a pound of fresh fruit, and do the same on the following day. Do not squeeze the fruit, but drain it is as dry as possible. The last time, it must be passed through a canvas, previously wet with vinegar. Put the liquor into a stone jar with a pound of broken sugar to every pint of juice. Stir it when the sugar is dissolved, put it on the fire, let it simmer, and skim it well. When cold, bottle it. Use no glazed or metal vessel in preparing it.

RASPBERRY VINEGAR.

Pour over two quarts of raspberries one pint of vinegar. Let this stand for twenty-four hours, and then strain it through a hair sieve, taking care not to mash the fruit. This you can accomplish by carefully laying the fruit on the sieve, and placing on top a plate with a weight upon it. Pour this juice over two more quarts of raspberries. Let it stand for twenty-four hours, and then strain it in the same way as before. To one pint of juice thus obtained, add one pound of sugar. Set it on the fire in a preserving kettle, and let it scald, after which, cool it, and bottle it.

RASPBERRY VINEGAR.

Put one quart of ripe berries in a bowl, pour on them a quart of strong vinegar, let it stand twenty-four hours, then strain it through a flannel bag, and pour this liquor on another quart of berries; do this for three or four days successively, and strain it; make it very sweet with loaf sugar, bottle and seal it.

RASPBERRY SYRUP.

Pour two pints of water over four pounds of loaf sugar. Boil it and take off all the scum; then add one pound of raspberries and one pound of currants, and let all boil gently for about twenty minutes. Strain it through a hair sieve; when cold, bottle it, and keep it in a cool place. This is a very pleasant syrup for hot weather. Mix it in tumblers with water and broken ice.

Kentucky Blackberry Cordial.

Wash and pick the berries; put them in a kettle with just enough water to simmer them; when soft, mash and put them in a flannel bag to drain; to one pint of juice add one-half pound of white sugar; clarify it with the white of an egg, and strain. To every quart of syrup add one pint of good brandy.

Blackberry Cordial.

To two quarts of blackberry juice add one pound of loaf sugar, half an ounce of nutmeg, half an ounce of cinnamon, the same of cloves and of allspice. Boil all together for half an hour, and when cold, add a pint of fourth proof brandy. Bottle it and cork it well.

Blackberry Wine.

Pick and mash the berries in a clean tub; to every gallon of mashed fruit add one quart of boiling water. Let it stand open for three or four days, then strain it through a flannel bag. To every gallon of juice add three pounds of good brown sugar; then put it, into demijohns or casks, and cork loosely until autumn; then bottle and seal it and put it in the cellar.

Blackberry Wine.

To every quart of the strained juice of the ripe berry add two quarts of water. Allow three pounds of sugar to every gallon of the liquid, and set it away to ferment. Skim it every day for three weeks, and then strain it through a flannel bag, and put it into a keg or jug. At Christmas it may be drained off and bottled for use. The older it grows, the better it will be. This receipt will serve for grapes, excepting that less water is used—one pint only to a gallon of juice.

CURRANT WINE.

To two gallons of juice add eighteen pounds of sugar, and stir them well together; then add enough water to make the whole six gallons. Leave the bung or cork of the vessel in which you have placed it open until it no longer ferments, which will be several weeks. Close it tight, and leave it until it is settled, or runs clear; then draw it off and bottle it, or put it back in the same vessel after having it thoroughly cleaned.

CURRANT WINE.

Mix well together eight gallons of the expressed juice of the currants, sixteen gallons of water, and fifteen pounds of common brown sugar. Put all into the barrel in which it is to be kept, well bunged up, till cold weather. The wine may then be used from the barrel or bottled; the latter is preferable.

CURRANT SHRUB.

Press the juice from the currants without heating them; put it in a dry, warm place, to undergo a slight fermentation. After a few days, remove the scum from the top, and use the clear part of the juice, leaving the thick portion at the bottom. To a pint of clear juice add two pounds of the best white crushed sugar. When dissolved, scald all together for a moment, and bottle the mixture. This will keep for two years. Mixed with ice water, it makes a most refreshing drink.

After removing the first portion of clear juice, another may be obtained by putting the remainder into a deep vessel, and letting it settle.

ELDERBERRY WINE.

One quart of the juice of the berries, one quart of water and half a pound of sugar. Let it stand in an open vessel for twenty-four hours; then strain it carefully into bottles, and cork them tight.

Rhubarb Wine.

Cut five pounds of rhubarb into small pieces, and put them in one gallon of water. Let it stand for ten days, stirring it twice a day. Then strain it through a sieve, and add four pounds of white sugar to a gallon. Put it in a clean cask, and let it remain for five months; then add the rind and juice of three lemons, half a pint of brandy, and half an ounce of isinglass. In a few days it may be bottled, putting two raisins into each bottle. Cork and seal the bottles.

Lemon Syrup.

To six pounds of sugar add three pints of water, and when dissolved, set it on the fire in a preserving kettle. Mix the whites and shells of two eggs, well beaten, into it. Let it boil until the scum rises, and leaves the syrup below clear. Then take the kettle from the fire, and skim it well. Pour the syrup into an earthen or china vessel, and let it become cold. Squeeze eighteen large lemons; strain them; add them to the syrup, and set it on the fire. Let it come to a quick boil, and skim it well while the scum rises. When cool enough, put it in bottles and cork them well, dipping each cork into hot cement. (See Cement.)

Syrup of Lemons.

To one quart of lemon juice add three pounds of loaf sugar, and boil it to a syrup. When it is boiled thoroughly, pour it very hot over the rinds of the lemons, and let it cool; then bottle it for use. It makes a delicious drink.

Lemonade.

Allow to one quart of lemon juice four pounds of sugar. Three dozen lemons make one quart of juice. Mix and strain it well together. If much ice is used, as will be the case in summer, allow a much smaller quantity of water. If the flavor of the rind is desired, soak one or two of the skins in the mixture.

LEMON PUNCH.

Roll twelve lemons, and pare off the yellow rind very thin; boil the rinds in a gallon of water until the flavor is extracted. Squeeze the lemons over two pounds of loaf sugar, and add them to the water after straining the peel from it. Stir in one quart of the best whisky, and bottle it for use.

MISSISSIPPI POMEGRANATE CORDIAL.

Separate the fruit from the core, and mash it sufficiently to obtain juice enough to keep the fruit from burning. Steam it slowly over the fire in a porcelain kettle until all the juice is extracted from the seeds; then strain the juice from the seeds, and allow two pounds of loaf sugar and half a gallon of good spirits to each gallon of juice. Bottle it close for several months before using.

FLORIDA ORANGE WINE.

Boil sixty pounds of sugar in twenty gallons of water, skimming it until the foam disappears; then let it cool, and when cold, add a pint of orange juice to each gallon,—that is, twenty quarts. Put it in a cask with a piece of leaven, and leave it uncorked to ferment for about six weeks, or until it ceases to work; then cork it tight, and leave it undisturbed for six months, when it is fit to be bottled.

WINE BITTERS.

Two ounces of orange peel; two ounces of sweet fennel; half an ounce of gentian, sliced; one ounce of cardamon seed, bruised; one ounce of chamomile flowers; one drachm of cochineal. Put these ingredients into a gallon of brandy. In one month the bitters will be fit for use. The brandy can be poured off and another gallon of bitters made from the same ingredients.

MINT CORDIAL.

Put two large handfuls of mint into a stone jar with a gallon of brandy, and let it stand for twenty-four hours. Take it out the next morning and press it gently, and again put the same quantity of fresh mint to the brandy, letting it soak for the same length of time; then strain the liquor, and add to each pint three-quarters of a pound of loaf sugar. When the sugar is dissolved, let it stand a little while to settle, and then bottle it.

CHERRY BOUNCE.

Pound the cherries with their stones in a mortar, and strain them through a coarse sieve or cloth. To one gallon of juice add half a gallon of French brandy or rum, a pound of sugar, and a little cinnamon, if you like it. It will be ready for use in four or five months.

CHERRY BOUNCE.

Add four pounds of white sugar to one gallon of juice, and boil it with spice, cinnamon and a few cloves. Let it come slowly to a boil, and in twenty minutes after the actual boiling begins, pour it into stone bottles or jugs, adding one quart of brandy and one pint of rum. Cork the jugs very tight and keep them in a cool place.

SHERRY COBBLER.

Put one tablespoonful of pulverized sugar into a tumbler, with one gill of sherry wine. Add a small quantity of any fruit in season, such as a small slice of pine-apple, a few strawberries or cherries, or half of a ripe peach; then fill the tumbler up with small pieces of ice. Invert an empty tumbler of exactly the same size, and put the rims together. Hold both firmly, and shake the contents briskly, so as to mix them thoroughly. After this, pile on more ice, beaten to the size of hailstones.

In order to partake conveniently of this compound, run a firm rye straw down the inner side of the tumbler, and drink it through the straw.

The sherry cobbler is a delightfully cooling summer beverage, and perfectly safe in hot weather. As it is always taken in the manner above described, it must be swallowed very gradually.

Port wine, Catawba, Scuppernong and champagne can all be used as above instead of the sherry, except that in the case of the champagne a little less sugar is required.

Claret Punch.

One bottle of claret; one-quarter the quantity of ice water; two lemons, sliced and cut into pieces; half a cupful of powdered sugar; half a teacupful of grated pine-apple; half a teacupful of ripe strawberries, mashed. Mix all the fruit together; add the sugar, then the claret, and just before serving it, the water. Put a large lump of ice into the punch bowl, and pounded ice in the glasses.

Mulled Wine.

To one pint of Madiera wine add a pint of hot water, with sugar and spice to the taste. Beat the yolks of six eggs, and when light, add a teacupful of sweet cream. Boil the wine and water quickly, take if from the fire and stir in the eggs and cream.

Egg-Nog.

To every egg allow one tumblerful of cream and milk, half of each, one tablespoonful of brandy, the same of Jamaica spirits, and of powdered sugar. Beat the yolks of the eggs very light first with the sugar, then beat the whites and mix both together. Add by degrees the spirits and brandy, stirring it all the time. Lastly add the milk and cream, and grate nutmeg on the top.

SANGAREE.

To one glass of port wine add a tablespoonful of powdered sugar, a small lump of ice and half a pint of water. Mix all well together and grate a little nutmeg on the top. Porter or ale sangaree is made as above, with the addition of more or less water according to the strength required.

BEER FLIP.

Put as much ale, porter or beer as you require into a tin can and sweeten it to taste. Heat the thick end of a poker, or any piece of iron that is clean and convenient, red hot, and stir the mixture with it until it ceases to bubble. Drink it hot.

SPRUCE BEER.

Mix together two cupfuls of sugar, one cupful of molasses, thirty drops of oil of spruce, thirty drops of oil of sassafras, four quarts of cold and four quarts of boiling water, and one quart of home-made yeast. Let it stand for twelve hours, strain, bottle and cork it tightly.

TO MAKE SMALL BEER.

Boil together for three hours fifteen gallons of water, five gallons of molasses, five of wheat bran and half a pound of hops. Strain the mixture into a clean cask, and when milk-warm pour in a quart of good yeast; shake it well, stop it close, and bottle it when quite clear. The excellence of the beer depends upon putting the yeast in at the proper time; if too hot, or two cold, it will not ferment.

GINGER BEER.

Two and a half ounces of powdered ginger, two ounces of cream of tartar, two and a half pounds of brown sugar and the juice of two lemons or limes. Pour two gallons of boiling water over the ginger, cream of tartar and sugar, and stir it well; then add two gallons of cold water, and when all is dissolved, add the lemon juice. Let it stand in a cask for twelve hours, then bottle it and let it stand for ten days to ripen.

GINGER BEER.

Upon four pounds of brown sugar or two quarts of molasses pour four quarts of boiling water, two ounces of cream of tartar, and half an ounce of ginger root, pounded fine. When quite cool, add half a pint of yeast, and let the mixture stand for twenty-four hours. Then skim it, strain it slowly through a cloth, and bottle it, taking care not to fill the bottles above the neck. Cork them tight, and put them in the cellar for four days before using the beer.

BONESET BEER.

Eight ounces of race ginger, two ounces of boneset, two ounces of horehound, one ounce of sassafras bark, one ounce of hops and eight gallons of water. Pour the water boiling over the other ingredients, and let it stand for half an hour, well covered, to draw. Then strain and sweeten it to taste; put it in a keg, and add a teacupful of yeast. Bung it tight.

CREAM BEER.

Two pounds of white sugar, three pints of water, the whites of three eggs, two ounces of tartaric acid, half a cupful of flour, beaten very smooth in a little water before mixing it with the other ingredients, half an ounce of essence of wintergreen or sassafras, and the juice of one lemon. Boil the sugar, acid, and flour in the water for five minutes. When nearly cold, add the whites of the eggs, essence and lemon. Bottle it and keep it in a cool place. Use two tablespoonfuls in half a tumblerful of water and a little soda.

CREAM GINGER BEER.

One ounce of race ginger, bruised, and boiled in one pint of water for fifteen minutes. As many hops as can be pinched up in the fingers, boiled in one pint of water for fifteen minutes also; slice three lemons and mix them in ten quarts of cold water; then mix three pounds of white sugar and one pint of fresh potato yeast well together, and let it stand for twenty-four hours to ferment. Strain and bottle it, and it is ready for use.

BEER.

Three pounds of brown sugar, two grated nutmegs, one tea-spoonful each of ground cloves and cinnamon and of cream of tartar, and one pint of baker's yeast. Mix these ingredients, then add ten quarts of water; let it stand in a warm place all night, then skim it, and it is fit for use at once.

SASSAFRAS BEER.

One teaspoonful of sassafras, the grated rind and pulp of three lemons, and one pint of hop water. Put all into a vessel, and let it stand until the flavor of the lemon is imparted, then add four pounds of white sugar and four gallons of water. Set it to rise with a pint of good yeast. Strain and bottle it.

TO BOTTLE CIDER.

To fine and improve the flavor of one hogshead, take a gallon of good French brandy, with half an ounce of cochineal, one pound of alum and three of sugar candy; grind them all well in a mortar, and infuse them in the brandy for a day or two;

then mix the whole with the cider, and stop it close for five or six months; after which, if fine, bottle it off. The brandy will prevent the bottles from bursting.

For Artificial Cider.

In one gallon of hot water dissolve one pound of brown sugar and half an ounce of tartaric acid. Pour the mixture into a jug, let stand till only lukewarm, and add three table-spoonfuls of yeast. Shake all well together. When sufficiently worked, which will be the next day after making, cork it tight.

To Mull Cider.

If the cider is "hard," reduce it to a palatable strength with water, and put it to boil with a few grains of whole allspice. While it is boiling, beat the eggs in a large pitcher, allowing eight to each quart of cider; by the time the cider is boiled the eggs will be light; then pour the boiling liquor on the eggs, and pour them from one pitcher to another until it has a fine froth upon it. Grate a little nutmeg on each glass as it is poured out.

Mulled Cider.

Set a pint of sweet cider on the fire, reserving a teacupful of it, with an equal quantity of water. Add a teaspoonful of whole allspice. Beat three eggs very light and then dilute them with the cup of cider you have kept in reserve. Pour this into the boiling cider, and water and stir it till the whole is smooth. Sweeten to taste, and grate a little nutmeg over the top.

PRESERVES.

BEAUFORT ORANGE PRESERVE.

THE oranges must be green—plucked from the trees in September or October. They must be grated all over with a grater, neither too fine nor too coarse. The latter would tear the skin. This process is necessary to extract the oil. Throw each orange, after grating, into salt and water, until all are grated. Then, with a sharp penknife, cut a hole in the stem end of the orange, and cut out all the pulp in the middle which contains the seeds; with a small silver spoon handle or the knife, scrape out as much of the pulp as you can without injuring the orange by breaking it or cutting through the rind. This is the first step in the preparation.

Weigh the oranges, and to every pound, allow two pounds of the best sugar. Measure a pint of water to a pint of sugar. Stir it well, and put it on the fire to boil until it forms a thin syrup; put the oranges into the syrup carefully, one by one, and let them boil steadily, but very slowly, all day. If they boil rapidly, they break and mash. To ascertain when they are done, take up one in a ladle; look at it in a strong light; if there are no opaque spots in it, and it looks clear and transparent, it is done. Try them with a stiff straw; if it goes through easily, there can be no doubt. Shaddocks are preserved exactly in the same manner.

20   (305)

ORANGE MARMALADE.

To one pound of grated orange peel add one and a quarter pounds of sugar. Cut and squeeze the oranges over a strainer, and put the seeds into a pitcher with a pint and a half of water, to stand all night. Boil the peel in several waters until clear and almost free from bitter taste. Let all stand for twenty-four hours; then cut the peel into small thin strips; add the sugar, with a small tumbler of water, to the jelly made by the seeds and juice and boil for one hour, taking off the scum as fast as it rises.

ORANGE MARMALADE.

Weigh the oranges; then grate them, to break the oil vessels. Cut them lengthwise, taking out the seeds and pulp. Put the skins on to boil, changing the water once. When boiled tender, pound two-thirds in a mortar, and cut the rest in narrow strips. Put in the same quantity of sugar that the oranges weighed before grating. Wet the sugar with a little water, and let it come to a boil. Then put into it the juice, and scraped pulp, the pounded skin and the chipped skin, and boil it, stirring it almost constantly towards the last, as it burns very easily when it begins to thicken.

FLORIDA ORANGE MARMALADE.

Grate the oranges slightly, to break the oil vessels. For this purpose the large thick-skinned sour orange is best. Take off the peel, and put it on to boil, changing the water four times. While the peel is boiling, the pulp can be prepared. This is done by slitting down each fig or compartment of the orange with a sharp knife, and scraping the pulp out free from skin and seeds. After the peel has boiled sufficiently, strain off the water, and pound one half of it in a mortar. Cut the other half into fine shreds; mix these with the pulp and measure it. Allow one pound of sugar to every pint of pulp and peel mixed. Put it over a slow fire, stirring it constantly till it is done.

A Fine Receipt for Orange and Apple Marmalade.

Weigh two dozen oranges; peel them, and remove the seeds and all the tough white pulp that adheres to them. Boil the peel for half an hour; then take off all the white inside skin, leaving only the thin yellow rind. Cut this into chips the thickness of a straw, and put them into cold water to extract the bitterness. Change the water several times. Then add to the oranges one pound of grated apples and the weight of the oranges in sugar, with another pound for the apples. Put them over a moderate fire in a preserving kettle, throw in the rind chips, and let the whole cook until it looks clear and thick.

Preserved Sour Orange Peel.

Rasp the peel with a coarse grater, to break the oil vessels, then cut the orange into quarters, taking out all of the inside. Put the peel in brine for several days, then extract the salt by soaking in fresh water for several days, changing it twice a day. Make a thin syrup and boil it down; put in the peel, and boil it until you can pierce it with a straw. When done, put the pieces in glass jars, with plenty of syrup. Allow one pound and a quarter of loaf sugar to every pound of peel.

To Preserve Oranges.

Pare the oranges as thin as possible with a sharp knife; boil them in water until they are soft enough to pierce with a straw; then take out the seeds with the handle of a teaspoon. Make a syrup of two pounds of sugar to one of fruit; skim it; put in the oranges and boil them until they are clear.

Orange Preserve.

Grate the oranges lightly, to break the oil vessels; cut them in half, horizontally; squeeze them carefully, so as not to bruise the skins, and take out all the seeds. Put the oranges in large jars, with half a pint of salt, and cover them with water, placing weights on them to sink them. After they have been in the salt and water for three days and nights, put them in fresh water for the same length of time, and then boil them in water until quite soft. Pour off the water, and boil them a second time to extract the bitterness. Keep a kettle of boiling water near you, so that when the bitter water is poured off, fresh hot water may be added; cold water hardens the skins. Then weigh half a pound of sugar to half a pound of oranges and make a thin syrup; boil the fruit in it until it is quite clear; take the oranges out on a dish and set the syrup aside until the next day; then put them together and cork the jars tightly.

Florida Lemon Preserve.

Grate the lemons, to break the oil vessels, soak them for two days in salt and water, and after this for one day in fresh water. Drain them well and weigh them, allowing each pound of fruit one pound and a quarter of sugar, and one pint of water to every pound of sugar.

Ogeechee Limes.

Boil the limes until soft, and push out quickly the head of each while hot. Then make a syrup of one pound of sugar to three pints of water, and boil it until clear; then throw in the limes and let them boil until transparent.

Mississippi Preserved Figs.

Pick the figs when a little more than half ripe, and peel them very thin. Allow three-quarters of a pound of sugar to a pound of fruit. Make a syrup first, and put your figs into it with a little stick cinnamon. Stir them frequently, and boil them till they look clear.

Florida Preserved Guavas.

Pare and weigh the guavas ; put them in a preserving kettle with just water enough to cover them, and let them simmer gently till they are tender, but not broken. Take them carefully from the kettle and spread them on dishes. Then add to the water in which they were boiled a pound of sugar for each pound of fruit. Boil and skim this syrup well, and then put in the fruit again, gently boiling it all together till they are done. The beauty of this preserve is in having the fruit unbroken.

To Preserve Pine Apple.

Pare and slice thin three pounds of pine apple and lay them on a large dish. Have ready two pounds of finely-pulverized sugar, and as the pine apple is laid upon the dish, sprinkle each layer with sugar. When all are sliced, there will be juice enough to boil the fruit without adding water. Put them on the fire in a porcelain-lined kettle, and let them simmer until they look transparent, then take out the fruit. Put it in glass jars. Boil the syrup for about twenty minutes and pour it hot over the fruit.

To Preserve Pine Apple.

Another very nice method of preserving pine apple is in small pieces, called "chunking it." After paring the pine apple, place it on its thick end, and with a silver fork break off little pieces, from top to bottom, about the size of a small chestnut. This will finally leave behind the stem-like pith that runs through the middle; it is juiceless, and must be rejected. The pine apple must be sugared as fast as it is cut, to enable the juice to flow. Do not add any water. Allow a pound and a half of sifted sugar to two pounds of fruit, and let the fruit and syrup remain on the fire together till the pine apple is thoroughly done.

Pine-Apple Jam.

Twist off the top and bottom leaves of the pine-apples, and cut them in quarters, lengthwise, leaving on the skins. Grate them on a coarse grater; the skin will enable you to hold it firmly and not waste pulp or juice. To every pound of the grated pulp add three-quarters of a pound of powdered sugar. Boil and stir it well till it begins to look of a clear amber color. Put it into tumblers while hot, and paper them when cold.

To Preserve Grapes in Brandy.

Take large full bunches when just ripe, prick each grape with a needle, strew over them half their weight in white sugar, fill up the jars wilh clear white brandy and tie them close. Serve as dessert.

To Preserve Fox-Grapes.

Split each grape and take out the seeds; pour boiling water over them, add a pinch of alum, scatter a few grape leaves among them, and cover them close. Let them stand till they become yellow; then make a syrup, allowing one pound of sugar to one pound of grapes. Drain the fruit and put it into the boiling syrup. Keep the kettle covered while boiling.

Grape Jelly.

Select fine ripe grapes; put them on to boil with water enough to cover them, and let them stew for fifteen minutes; then press them through a jelly sieve or flannel bag. To three cupfuls of juice add two cupfuls of sugar; this quantity is enough to boil at one time. Boil it quickly for fifteen minutes.

To Make Green Sweetmeat.

Take a thick watermelon rind, pare off the outer rind, cut it into any shapes desired, and throw them into a bell-metal skillet, with cold water and a piece of alum the size of an egg to every three pounds of rind. Let it boil until tender, and the rind becomes of a pale green color; then pour off the alum, and let it stand in cold water for twelve hours, or longer, if the alum is not soaked out. Then weigh them, and to every pound of rind add a pound and a half of sugar, and throw them into fresh ginger tea—a pint to the pound. Let it settle, and when clear, add mace and lemon peel. Boil it until sufficiently done, of which you may judge by observing if the sugar has penetrated through the rind; or, if you prefer it, boil it less the first time, and again in a day or two afterwards, taking care to leave syrup enough to cover the rind well. It is neither so good nor so pretty at first as after standing for some time.

Another Receipt for Green Sweetmeat.

Lay as many mangoes as you require in strong salt water for ten days; slit them and take out the seeds, throw them into fresh water and let them remain one or two days; then boil them in vinegar for several hours, after which soak them for a day or two in fresh water, changing the water every day, or until no vinegar remains. Make a syrup of ginger tea and sugar, allowing three pounds of sugar to one of melon. Boil for several hours, or until quite clear.

Watermelon Preserve.

Use the citron melon. Lay the rind in salt water for three days, and then in fresh water for the same time. Make a syrup, allowing a pound of sugar to one of the rind, and let the rind lie in it all night; then boil all together until clear, adding green ginger and lemon peel to flavor it.

Pink Watermelon Preserve.

Cut the pink part of the melon into squares, and remove all the seeds with a penknife. To one pound of fruit allow three-quarter of a pound of sugar, and let it stand for two hours; then remove the fruit and boil the syrup, skimming it carefully; then put in the fruit. Slice a lemon and a few pieces of green ginger root; boil them until tender in a little water, and when they are done, add them to the syrup. Boil it until the melon is tender and clear, and can be pierced by a straw. As soon as it is cool, put it into glass jars and fasten it up tight.

This preserve is not ready for use until it has been kept for a few weeks.

To Preserve Peaches.

Use the clear or open yellow peaches, white at the stone. Weigh the fruit after it is pared, and to each pound of fruit allow a pound of sugar. Put a layer of sugar at the bottom of the kettle, and then a layer of fruit, and so on until the kettle is full enough. Put it in a cool corner of the range till the sugar has dissolved; then boil the fruit until it is clear and done entirely through; then take out the pieces with a per-forated skimmer, and spread them on a dish free from syrup. Then boil the syrup in the kettle until it is quite thick; fill the jars half full with the fruit, and when the syrup is ready, fill up the jars with it.

An Economical and Easy Mode of Preserving Whole.

To fifteen pounds of clingstone peaches allow seven half pounds of loaf sugar. Dissolve half the sugar in as water as possible. Set the kettle on the fire, and when begun to simmer, throw in a layer of peaches. Let ther from twenty to thirty minutes; then take them out free syrup and lay them in a flat dish to cool. Throw in and layer, and so on until all are cooked. After you have boiled two or three layers in this way, the syrup will have increased. By degrees add the rest of the sugar, and when all are done, boil up the syrup till it becomes a little thick; then add, as you take the kettle from the fire, half a pint of alcohol. The peaches may be pared or thrown into a boiling lye made of three quarts of water with a teaspoonful of pearl ash, to destroy the skins, which will come off by rubbing them in a coarse towel. Cork them securely.

PEACH FIGS.

Pare the peaches and cut them in half; weigh them, and allow half a pound of sugar to every pound of fruit; put the fruit and sugar alternately into the kettle, and heat all gradually until the sugar is dissolved; then boil until clear. Take the peaches out with a perforated skimmer, lay them on dishes, without any of the syrup, in the sun, and turn them frequently until dry, putting them on dry dishes as the syrup drains away from them. When dry enough to handle, pack them in drums or boxes, with layers of sifted sugar, beginning and ending with sugar. If you have any syrup left, you may boil more peaches in it.

CANDIED PEACHES.

To four pounds of peaches, cut in quarters, add one pound of sugar. Simmer them in very little water until a straw can pierce them. Take them from the kettle with a perforated skimmer, roll each piece in sifted sugar, place them on dishes, the pieces to lie a little apart, to dry. Put the dishes in a sunny room—not in the sun, but where the air can blow over them. Turn the pieces from time to time and sift a little more sugar over them. They will take some days to dry and crystallize. Use mosquito netting to keep off the flies.

Compote of Peaches.

Blanch the peaches in boiling water, and when soft, take them out on a strainer and put them into cold water. Make a syrup of quarter of a pound of sugar to half a pint of water, and in it boil the peaches for about five miuutes. Skim and lay them on a flat dish and pour the syrup over them. Serve for dessert.

Peach Jam.

To every pound of peaches allow three-quarters of a pound of sugar. Pare the peaches and cut them up in very small pieces; put them on the fire in a preserving kettle with a little water—about a pint to a peck of fruit. Let the fruit boil quickly, stirring it frequently to prevent burning. When it begins to look like a soft pulp, and can be easily mashed, add the sugar. As soon as it begins to boil again, stir it incessantly and do not let the fire be too strong or it will scorch. Stir it till it is a smooth pulp and put it in wide-mouthed jars. When cold, paste the jars up tight.

Brandy Peaches.

Three-quarters of a peck of peaches, six pounds of loaf sugar and one quart of white French brandy. Boil the peaches in strong ley for three or four minutes, until the skins will rub off with a coarse towel. Throw them into cold water to whiten and harden them and put them on a dish to drain. Make a syrup of half the sugar and boil the peaches in it till tender. With the remainder of the sugar and a large breakfast-cupful of water make a fresh syrup, and boil and skim it till it is clear. When it is cold, mix the brandy with it and pour it over the peaches. Cork the bottles tight.

An Easy Way to Brandy Peaches.

Nine pounds of fruit well rubbed, seven pounds of sugar and one quart of white brandy. Pare the peaches very thin and throw them into cold water; boil the parings in water enough to cover them. Strain this water and add the sugar to it. Boil it and skim it well till clear; then throw the peaches in, and let them boil for ten or fifteen minutes, or till tender. They must be kept whole and not lose their shape. Heat the glass jars, and put the peaches into them one by one, without the syrup, directly from the kettle. Then give the syrup a quick boiling, take it off and pour the brandy into it and stir it. Pour this syrup upon the fruit in the jars, filling each jar half full, first, to see how far the liquid will go. If there is not enough syrup to fill all the jars, add more brandy to each till the fruit is covered. Soak some bladders in hot water; cork the jars and cover them with the bladders. Eighteen pounds of fruit, fourteen pounds of sugar and two quarts of brandy will fill fourteen jars containing ten or twelve peaches each.

Brandy Peaches.

Choose the largest and most perfect fruit; have a strong ley boiling; throw your peaches into it, and let then remain for a few minutes only; then with a coarse towel wipe off the down; throw them into cold water, and wash them in several successive waters, until no slippery feeling is left upon them. Then put them into a stewpan, with half a pound of sugar to every pound of fruit; cover them with water, and cover the top of the vessel close; boil them briskly until you can pass a straw easily through them; pour them, liquor and all, into a stone jar, covered closely; let them remain till quite cold; then put the liquor again over the fire (not covered), and stew it half away. Add, while stewing, as much brandy as you have syrup; throw in the blanched kernels, and as soon as they are clear, the syrup will be sufficiently done to pour over the peaches hot. Then cover the jar close. Do not put many peaches into the lye at one time, as they must not remain longer than absolutely necessary to remove the roughness.

To Preserve Quinces.

Weigh, peel and core the quinces, after having washed and wiped them well. Keep the seeds, and put them on to boil with the parings.

Meanwhile, having cut the quinces into halves or quarters, put them into the preserving kettle with enough water to cover them, and let them boil until they are tender enough to pass a fork through them, but do not let them break or lose their their shape; then take them from the kettle. Strain the water in which the parings have been boiled, and add it to that in which the quinces were boiled. Put the parboiled quinces into the kettle, and to every pound of fruit and sugar, add a pint of the quince water. Boil the quinces till they are clear (they become harder and firmer when united with the sugar), then take them out with a skimmer and put them upon dishes free from syrup. Boil the syrup until it jellies. If there is more quince water than is required for the weight of fruit and sugar, it should be added in the beginning, allowing a pound more of sugar to each pint of water. This, from the richness of the fruit, will make more jelly than is needed to cover the fruit, but will be a nice addition to the supply of preserves.

To Preserve Quinces.

Put the fruit in cold water, cover it with a cloth, and let it remain on the fire till scalded. When soft, take them out to cool; then quarter, core, and lastly pare them. Prepare the syrup, pound for pound, and boil it quickly, that it may not turn dark. The syrup must not jelly, or it will make the fruit hard.

To Preserve Strawberries.

Take fine, large strawberries, and to each pound of fruit allow a pound of finely-powdered sugar; place the kettle on a slow fire until the sugar is melted, putting in as little water for this purpose as possible. Then put the strawberries into the syrup, and after they begin to boil, let them remain about twenty minutes on the fire. Take them off, and put them into tumblers or small glass jars. A quart of strawberries will weigh about a pound. Ten quarts, when preserved, will fill about two dozen tumblers.

To Preserve Raspberries Whole.

From five quarts of raspberries cull about three pints of the largest and firmest, and set them aside. Put the remainder in the preserving kettle, and place them on a moderate fire, to extract the juice. When they are boiled enough for this purpose, turn them into a sieve, and let then drip through. Then put the sugar on to boil, allowing one pound to each pound of fruit. Let the sugar boil to a syrup, with only sufficient water to melt it. When the syrup has boiled a few minutes, and all the scum has been removed, throw in the whole raspberries, and let them simmer slowly. As soon as they begin to look ragged, or likely to fall apart, take them from the kettle with a per-forated skimmer, and spread them over a large dish to cool. Throw into the syrup the juice of those previously boiled and strained, and let it boil until nearly a jelly; then throw in again the whole fruit, which has been cooling. Give it a short boil-ing, and then remove the kettle from the fire, and fill the glasses.

Raspberry Jam.

Allow one pound of sugar to one of fruit. Boil the fruit and mash it, boil it again very quietly; then add the sugar, and let it simmer until a fine jam is formed.

To Preserve Green Gages.

Wipe the fruit with a cloth, and boil one pound of gages in a syrup made of water and half a pound of sugar. When the fruit is quite cooked, make a fresh syrup, allowing a pound of sugar to a pound of fruit, and in it boil the fruit until clear. After putting it into the jars, boil the syrup once more and pour over the gages.

To Preserve Damsons.

One pound of sugar to one of fruit. Put on the sugar first, with a little water; when it is hot, add the fruit and let it boil until quite red. Take out the damsons and put them on a dish in the sun, while the syrup boils twenty minutes longer, then fill your jars nearly full with fruit, and pour in the syrup.

To Preserve Egg Plums.

Weigh four pounds of plums and wash them in cold water, leaving the little stems upon them. For every pound of fruit allow a pound of sugar. Put the sugar on a slow fire in the preserving kettle, with as much water as will melt the sugar, and let it simmer slowly; then prick each plum thoroughly with a large needle or a fork with fine prongs, and place a layer of them in the syrup. Let them cook until they lose their color a little and the skin begins to break; then lift them out with a perforated skimmer, and place them singly on a large dish to cool; then put another layer of plums in the syrup, and let them cook and cool in the same manner, and so on till the whole are done. As soon as the first layer is placed upon the dish with a fork and the finger, replace and smooth evenly every piece of broken skin, to preserve the shape of the plum. When the last layer is finished, return the first layer to the syrup and let it boil slowly; when transparent, take them out carefully and let them cool on dishes, replacing as before any broken skin. Do the same with each layer. While the last layers are cooling, place the first in glass jars, carefully keeping them in shape. When all are done, pour the hot syrup over them, and cork them when cold. Four pounds of fruit is the extent allowable at one time, unless the kettle be very large; otherwise keeping the syrup so long over the fire will make it too dark. The jelly, when cold, should be of the color and consistency of rich wine jelly. If great stress is laid upon the color and keeping the shape of the fruit, it would be well to preserve only two pounds at a time.

To Preserve Apples for Daily Use.

Select large firm apples, pare and core them, and allow three-quarters of a pound of pulverized sugar to one pound of fruit. Put the sugar on the fire in a preserving kettle, with as much water as will dissolve it. When the sugar is melted, put the apples into the kettle side by side. Add the rind of a lemon, cut in thin strips, and if the apples are not very sour, add the juice also. Let them simmer slowly, and when the apples begin to look transparent and likely to break apart, remove them carefully to the dish in which they are to be served. Let the syrup boil with the shreds and apple until it is thick and the apple all dissolved, then throw it over the apples and set them away to cool. They will not keep longer than two days.

Apple Jam.

Weigh equal quantities of brown sugar, and good, sour apples; pare, core and chop them fine. Make a syrup of the sugar and clarify it very thoroughly; then add the apples, the grated rind of two or three lemons and a few pieces of white ginger. Boil until the apples look clear and yellow. This resembles foreign sweetmeats. The ginger is essential to its peculiar excellence.

APPLE JELLY.

Cut up as many apples as may be convenient to use. Put them over the fire with water enough to cover them, and let them simmer till they are soft enough to mash ; then pour them into a sieve or colander, and with a large spoon or "masher" press out all the liquid. Pass this liquid through a jelly-bag, and add to it, for each pint, a pound of sugar. Boil it over the fire quickly, as for currant or other fruit jelly. It is easy to find out when it has come to a jelly, by trying a little of it on a cold plate. To make apple jelly, the best apples are required. Pippins, bell-flowers, or other richly-flavored varieties, are necessary ; a sweet dry apple will not do. Some of the early summer apples have a high flavor, and will make good jelly. Fresh lemon peel is often used in apple jelly, but if the apple is fine, it will not require any flavor but its own.

CURRANT JELLY.

Press out the juice of the currants, allowing to each pint one pound of granulated sugar. Wash in clear water the seeds of the currants. To ten pints of pure juice add five pints of the water. Heat the sugar in the oven or range until very hot. Boil the juice for fifteen minutes, take it off the fire, stir into it thoroughly the hot sugar until all is dissolved and put it at once into glasses.

CURRANT JELLY.

One pound of the best white sugar, one pint of cold currant juice. Put the currants into stone jars, and place the jars in kettles filled with water. Let the water boil until the currants are well scalded ; then strain them through a coarse jelly-bag. Measure your juice, and allow one pound of the best sugar to each pint. Put the juice on to boil, and at the same time put the sugar into pans and set them in the oven while the juice is boiling. When it has boiled hard for twenty minutes, stir in the hot sugar until it is all dissolved; then let it boil up once more and take it off. Fill the tumblers at once. Placing a silver fork in the tumbler before filling it will prevent the glass from being cracked by the hot jelly.

FROSTED FRUIT.

Cut the stalks half off from large ripe cherries, apricots, plums or grapes. Have ready in a separate dish some beaten white of egg and finely-powdered sugar. Dip the fruit first into the egg and then into the sugar; then lay it carefully upon sheets of white paper, placing them in the sun or in a warm place until the icing hardens.

PEAR BUTTER.

One peck of pears, five pounds of sugar, half a pint of vinegar. Stir as for apple butter.

PEACH BUTTER.

Two quarts of molasses or four pounds of sugar, and half a bushel of unpared peaches. Stew in water first, and mash with the potato-masher, if hard. If soft, they will cook in syrup. Stir as for apple butter.

TO PRESERVE TOMATOES.

Wipe the tomatoes with a dry cloth, and prick them all over with a large pin. Allow one pound to one pound of sugar; boil and skim the syrup, then add the tomatoes and let them remain for ten minutes. Take them out separately and lay them on a dish to cool; then boil them again separately, repeating this until they are quite clear. Flavor with lemon peel and ginger root, and a very little mace and cloves.

21

Tomato Butter.

Pare ten pounds of tomatoes and cut them up; put them into a kettle and add four pounds of brown sugar and one quart of vinegar; stir them all together until they become as thick as apple butter, stirring often to prevent burning.

To Stew Cranberries.

Wash the cranberries and pick out all those that are defective. To each quart of cranberries add a pound of sifted white sugar and half a tumblerful of water. Stir them frequently, and let them cook till all the berries are done through and burst open. The cultivated cranberries take a little longer time to stew, as they are so much larger than the ordinary fruit. Some persons prefer to remove the skins. In this case stew the cranberries with a little more water than above until quite soft and capable of being mashed; then strain them through a coarse sieve, return the pulp to the fire and add the sugar to it. Let it cook fifteen minutes, and then put it into a form. It will be stiff like marmalade.

For filling shells for tarts the whole cranberries should be used. Many persons think that the delicate flavor of the berry is impaired by straining the pulp from the skin.

CANNING.

The canning of fruits and vegetables in families is not so much resorted to as formerly. The gigantic canning houses now established in the midst of the fruit and vegetable-growing districts have rendered this modern luxury so cheap and plentiful, that it is not worth the trouble to do them at home.

Where fruits and vegetables are hourly brought fresh and ripe from garden and orchard to be canned, they must be in the best condition for that purpose, possessing great advantages over those that are purchased by individuals at markets and elsewhere, as they are suffered to ripen fully before using them, whereas, for transporting them, allowance has to be made for bruising or decay, which, especially in the peach, so soon follows perfect ripeness.

To those living in remote situations who, possessing farms and orchards, have a surplus of fruits and vegetables, these remarks do not apply. For these we give a few simple directions and receipts.

The receipts which accompany the cans are often excellent. The variety of cans made and patented for this purpose is so great, that it would be impossible to decide upon their several merits. Some give the preference to one, some to another.

For delicate fruits, glass jars should have the preference, as the action of acid upon tin causes an unpleasant flavor.

(323)

One thing to be observed is, that fruit not ripe or mellow enough to eat, cannot be made so by being put into air-tight cans. The peach canned crude and unripe, will be crude and unripe when opened. Therefore, to have good canned fruit, it must be ripe when prepared.

If peaches are at all hard, they must be simmered till tender. Plums and strawberries should be scalded several times. In using sugar, each fruit must be treated according to the taste of the family.

Always seal the jars immediately, while the fruit is scalding hot.

If the method adopted is to set the jars in a vessel with water nearly to their tops, allowing the water to boil around them, then the jar itself must be full before sealing.

Hints on Canning.

It is not necessary to have the article boiling just before you close the can, but only to be certain that every part is heated through. Be careful not to fill the cans too full, as moisture in the grooves is to be avoided. When they are filled, put on the lids carefully, and be certain that they are on tight. Then put on the cement by holding a hot iron or poker next to it, taking care to direct the melting stream into the groove. While this is being done, let some one press down the tin lid until the cement is chilled, watching any spots where bubbles may rise.

To Can Tomatoes.

Skin the tomatoes, and remove the seeds. Stew them with pepper and salt for two hours. Boil twelve ears of corn until quite tender, and cut the grains from the cob. To one cupful of the corn thus prepared add two cupfuls of the stewed tomatoes; then boil them together for about ten minutes. While boiling hot, pour the mixture into tin cans, filling them full, so as to leave no space for air. Have them soldered up immediately. When they are used, add a lump of butter the size of a walnut to each can, also pepper and salt if required. Having been already cooked, they will need but a short time to remain over the fire.

To Can Okras and Tomatoes.

Wash carefully one peck of okras; remove the tops attached to the stems, and cut them in slices. Peel and remove the seeds from three-quarters of a peck of fully-ripened tomatoes, and cut them in small pieces. Add one teaspoonful of red pepper and three tablespoonfuls of salt. Put them on the fire in a preserving kettle, and boil them slowly but steadily for three hours. Put them into the cans hot from the kettle; fill them so as to leave no space for air, and seal them up immediately.

Canned Peaches.

Pare the peaches; take the stones out, and cut them in halves. As they are cut, throw them immediately into glass jars (with good screwed lids and gum rings). Have ready a cold syrup of one pound of sugar to half a pint of water. Fill the jars with this syrup, and fasten them up. Put a large boiler over the fire; cover the bottom of it with boards, and on these set the jars of peaches. Fill up the boiler with cold water nearly to the top of the jars, and let them remain until the water boils. Remove them carefully, and give the lids another screwing. Repeat the screwing in a day or two, as they sometimes slip. Keep them in a dry cool place.

PICKLES.

In putting up pickles it must always be remembered that earthenware jars must not be used; the action of the vinegar upon the lead employed in glazing them renders them unsafe. Pickles after being taken out of the brine should be greened with a little vinegar in the water. After they are greened, let them drain several hours before putting them in the jars with the vinegar and spices. The vinegar used for pickles must be of the strongest kind, as it becomes more or less diluted by the water contained in the pickles just salted and greened. Let the vinegar fill the jar some distance above the pickles; if exposed to the air, they are apt to mildew and soften. If the vinegar should in a little while show a tendency to mildew on the top, pour it off, and boil it well with a little fresh vinegar and a few more spices. Horse-radish should not be boiled, but be placed in the jars either shredded or grated, and the vinegar poured over it. Garlic also must not be boiled. If onions are used, they should be parboiled before putting them into the jars. If cucumbers, peppers, &c., are bought already salted and greened, they should be soaked in fresh water before adding the vinegar and spices to them. If it is in the early autumn, when they have not lain very long in brine, an hour or two will be enough; if late in the winter they will require to be soaked all night. When they are soaked, let them drain as long as possible.

In making yellow pickle, be careful not to put in too much turmeric; it is very bitter when soaked in vinegar. It should not be forgotten that in all pickles the acid is to predominate. If pickles have a tendency to soften, add little alum.

Pickles should be kept in dry, cool places. This applies most particularly to pickles in which olive oil is an ingredient. Oil is very apt to become rancid if kept too long.

Poke Melia—A Russian Pickle.

This Receipt was given to Benjamin Franklin on his Departure from Paris in 1785 by a Russian.

Put a layer of white oak leaves and black currant leaves, mixed, at the bottom of an oak cask, and then put in a layer of cucumbers; strew over them horse-radish, garlic, race ginger, whole pepper, allspice and cloves, then layers of leaves, cucumbers and spices successively till the cask is full. Fill the cask with salt and water strong enough to bear an egg, and half a gallon of good cider vinegar. They will be fit for use in about two weeks.

To Pickle Mangoes.

Nine dozen of mangoes require four quarts of horse-radish, grated, two pounds of white mustard seed, two pound of black mustard seed, and of cloves, black pepper, allspice and mace, two ounces each, with a large bunch of garlic heads. Cut a slit down the middle of one end of the melon, and with the handle of a teaspoon take out all the soft inside pulp and seeds. Wash, drain and put them into salt and water strong enough to bear an egg; let them remain in this pickle for eight or ten days, examining them from time to time to see that they are covered by the brine; if the air reaches them they will soften. Remove them from the brine and wash them well in plenty of fresh water, inside and out, then put them in large jars and cover them with vinegar and water, three-fourths water and one-fourth vinegar. Let them remain in a warm place for two or three days to green; then take them out and drain them, and stuff them with the horse-radish and mustard seed, mixed in equal proportions. As each mango is stuffed, add to it a blade or two of mace, two or three cloves, two or three pepper corns, two or three allspice, and a clove of garlic. When stuffed full, tie the slit together with pack thread or sew them up with a coarse needle. Cover the mangoes when in the jars with hot vinegar, cork them tight and set them away. They will be fit for use in six or eight months. Examine the jars occasionally and keep the mangoes well covered with the vinegar.

OIL MANGOES.

Select melons of a medium size, put them in an earthenware jar, and pour boiling salt and water over them. Let them stand till next day; take them out, cut a slit from the stem to the blossom end and remove all the seeds carefully; then return them to the brine, and let them stand for eight days, when they are to be put into a jar and covered with strong vinegar for two weeks; then dry them with a soft cloth. They are then ready for the stuffing, which is to be prepared as follows:

Stuffing for Forty Melons or Mangoes.—Take one pound of race ginger, scald and wash it well, slice it thin and dry it. Mix together one pound of horse-radish, scraped and dried, one pound of mustard seed, washed and dried, one pound of onions, chopped fine, one ounce of mace, one ounce of nutmeg, pounded fine, two ounces of turmeric, and a handful of whole black pepper. Make these ingredients into a paste with a quarter of a pound of mustard and a tumblerful of the best olive oil; then stuff each melon and tie it up with a white thread. Strew some of the stuffing over each layer, and fill the jar with the best vinegar.

Green Oil Mangoe Pickle.

Put the melons into strong brine for a week; take out the seeds, scald them in weak vinegar till green; let them remain in that vinegar one day and then stuff them.

Stuffing for Forty Melons.—One pound and a half of white mustard, one pound and a half of black mustard, two ounces of pepper, well beaten, one ounce of ginger, well beaten, one ounce of whole allspice, three ounces of whole cloves, a handful of garlic, chopped fine, one ounce of mace, well beaten, six large onions, chopped fine. Mix all these ingredients well with an even tablespoonful of salt, one of brown sugar, a breakfast-plate of horse-radish, scraped fine, half an ounce of turmeric, a little red pepper, and a large cupful of sweet salad oil, with vinegar enough to moisten all well.

For the Liquor.—A cupful of pepper, half a cupful of allspice, half a cupful of cloves, a handful of horse-radish, scraped, four onions, a handful of garlic, one ounce of ginger, four ounces of black mustard seed, bruised, an even tablespoonful of sugar, and the same of salt. Boil these ingredients in two gallons of strong vinegar; when perfectly cold, stuff the mangoes and put them in. Great care should be taken that the mangoes are cold when stuffed, and the seasoned vinegar cold when they are put in, as any heat turns the oil rancid and spoils them.

Peach Mangoes with Oil.

Select a peck of soft peaches (the Morris Whites) when just ripe enough to part easily from the stone, and put them in salt and water for twenty-four hours; then take out the stones without breaking them. Make a stuffing as follows: One pint of scalded and peeled onions, one ounce of green ginger, two ounces of celery seed, two of white mustard seed, two of black mustard seed, two of coriander seed and two of turmeric. Mix these ingredients with half a bottle of olive oil and stuff the peaches with it. Place them carefully in a jar and cover them with cold vinegar, into which you have stirred half an ounce of turmeric, a quarter of a pound of brown sugar and a little black pepper.

Oil Pickle.

Wash two dozen large cucumbers and cut them in round slices; sprinkle them with salt, and put them in a perforated vessel to drain for three hours. Take a quarter of a peck of large white onions; peel and slice them; add salt, and let them drain for three hours. Take one ounce of whole cloves and one of allspice; pack in a stone jar a layer of cucumbers, then a layer of onions, then one of spice, until the jar is nearly full. Mix together quarter of a pound of yellow mustard, half a pint of sweet oil, three tablespoonfuls of black pepper; add vinegar enough to cover the pickles, and pour the whole into the jar. Cover tight.

Oil Cucumbers.

Pare and slice, as for the table, two dozen large cucumbers. Put them in a stone pan and sprinkle them with salt. Let them stand in a cool place for twenty-four hours. Drain them well through a hair sieve; then slice four large onions very thin. Put the cucumbers and onions in the jars in alternate layers, and to each layer add pods of small peppers, some cayenne and black pepper, and celery seed. Pour over the whole one bottle of salad oil and one pint of good wine vinegar.

A General Receipt for Pickles.

Put six quarts of good vinegar in a jar, to which add four ounces of mustard seed, powdered fine; six ounces of ginger, soaked in salt and water and sliced and dried; one spoonful of coriander seed, bruised; one nutmeg, and six ounces of garlic, peeled, salted and dried. Close the jar securely and tie a

bladder over it. Set it in the sun or chimney-corner for three
or four weeks, and shake it every day. Soak the pickles in
brine that will bear an egg, and put them in a warm place till
they turn quite yellow; then put some of the liquor they have
been steeped in over the fire and let it boil briskly; put the
pickles into it and turn them with a spoon, and they will soon
become perfectly green, when they must be drained. Put them
in a jar of common vinegar for two days; drain and clean them
and put them into the first-mentioned liquor. If mangoes are
used, stuff them with mustard seed, horse-radish, &c.; cover
them well with the liquor. Pursue the same method with
yellow pickles and cucumbers. At the end of three weeks put
the jars in a cool place and add two spoonfuls of turmeric. As
the pickles are used, others that have been salted may be added
to the liquor.

To Pickle Butternuts.

The nuts must be picked before the shells have begun to
harden. Try them with a knitting needle, and if it will pass
easily through the skin, they are not too hard. Put them in a
large tub, and cover them with lye freshly made from wood
ashes. Stir them vigorously with a stiff hickory broom till the
skins look clean and smooth. Some persons scald the nuts, and
have each nut scraped with a knife or rubbed with a coarse
cloth. When the cleaning and rubbing process is done, put
them in strong brine. In a day or two drain them and add
fresh brine, and let them remain at least ten days in the salt
and water. When they are taken from the brine, soak them
for a couple of hours in fresh water; then drain them and put
them into stone jars. For a hundred nuts take half a pound
of white mustard seed, ten or twelve cloves of garlic, an ounce
of race ginger, half an ounce of cloves, half an ounce of allspice,
half a dozen blades of mace, and half an ounce of pepper—
none of the spices to be powdered. Put this seasoning on the
fire in a porcelain-lined kettle, with as much strong vinegar as

will be required to fill the jar; boil them well, and then throw the vinegar hot over the nuts. Let the vinegar cover the nuts perfectly. Cork them tight. From time to time examine the jar to see if the vinegar has evaporated and left the nuts exposed. If this is the case, the jar must be replenished with fresh vinegar. These nuts, like walnuts, take a long time to become thoroughly pickled; they must be soft and ready to fall apart before they are fit for use. They had better be done for the next year's use. They are a finer pickle than the walnut.

To Pickle Walnuts.

Use walnuts sufficiently tender to pass a knitting needle through them. Rub them with a coarse towel; put a layer of salt, spice and garlic in the jar, then a layer of nuts, and so on until the jar is full. Cover them with strong vinegar and tie them up tight. In a few months add more vinegar, as they soak it up. They are seldom fit for use in less than a year.

To Pickle Walnuts.

Gather the nuts before they are hard, without bruising them; put them in a jar with salt and vinegar, and let them stand for eight days; then shake them and let them stand for eight days longer; shake them again, and in three or four days take them out and let them drain. Mix together two handfuls of garlic, two sticks of horse-radish, ginger, mace, cloves and whole pepper. Put the walnuts into a jar and strew them with the spices. Boil as much strong vinegar as will fill the jar; as it boils, skim it; then take it off and let it stand for a few minutes and pour it over the nuts. Put a round piece of board in the jar, and a weight on it to keep the walnuts down, as all that float above the liquor will spoil. The day after you pickle them, add two or three ounces of mustard seed and fasten the jar up close. About three months later, pour off the vinegar and bottle it up; then boil fresh vinegar and fill up the jar. The walnuts will be much better for this last changing.

To Pickle Nasturtions.

Pick the nasturtions as soon as the blossoms are off; put them into cold spring water with a little salt. Change water for three days successively. Make a very strong pickle of white wine vinegar, mace, nutmeg, shallots, garlic, pepper, salt, and horse-radish. Take the berries out very dry from the salt and water, and put them into bottles. Mix the liquid well, but do not boil it; pour it over the nasturtions, bottle and cork them tight.

Pickled nasturtions resemble the caper, possessing much of its flavor.

Cucumber Pickles.

Gather the cucumbers, and lay them in cold water; rub the mould off lightly with your fingers. Put them in a stone jar; pour a hot brine over them, strong enough to float an egg. Let them stand in the brine for four days, heating it daily. Then use fresh brine, as before, for four days. On the evening of the eighth day, take them out of the brine, and put them in fresh water for twelve hours. Then place them on a napkin in a dish. When drained quite dry, put them in jars; add allspice, black and red pepper, one onion, and some horse-radish, and cover them with cold vinegar. Tie up the jars. If a white scum appears on the top, pour off the vinegar and put on fresh.

To Pickle Cucumbers.

Select good, firm cucumbers, not very large. Make a brine strong enough to bear an egg. Put the pickles in a stone jar, with one large onion in the centre. Heat the brine boiling hot, and pour it over the pickles. Cover the jar very close, and let it stand for twenty-four hours. Pour off the brine, and wash the pickles in cold water. Put them in the jar again with two or three handfuls of whole cloves and allspice, sprinkled between the layers. Scald enough good cider vinegar to cover them, with a cupful of sugar to every two gallons, and pour it, boiling hot, over the pickles. Put a piece of alum the size of a walnut into every gallon of brine and every gallon of vinegar, while boiling.

CUCUMBER PICKLES.

Pour boiling water over the cucumbers; let them stand for five hours; take them out, and wipe them dry. Boil enough vinegar to cover the cucumbers; pour it over them. Do this three times, boiling the same vinegar. Add a teacupful of salt and a tablespoonful of alum, and any spice you prefer, with horse-radish cut in pieces.

SALT AND WATER CUCUMBERS.

Wash some large green cucumbers, and lay them in a stone jar in layers of grape leaves. Fill up the jar with cold salt and water, and let them stand in the sun or in a warm chimney corner for two weeks.

GRATED CUCUMBER PICKLE.

Pare and grate thirty-six medium-sized cucumbers; chop fine or pound in a mortar two small onions; stir in half a teacupful of salt, and let it stand for about three hours. Then put it in a hair sieve, and let it stand for eight hours, or all night, to drain thoroughly. Then add a tablespoonful of black pepper and half a cupful of white mustard seed. Put it in a jar, and add enough strong vinegar to make it as thick as stewed apple.

SLICED PICKLED CUCUMBERS.

Pare and slice the cucumbers before they are too ripe. To every dozen cucumbers add two onions, sliced. Salt them well; cover them close, and let them stand for twenty-four hours; then drain them well through a colander. Boil two quarts of vinegar, one ounce of turmeric and one ounce of mustard. Put the cucumbers and onions in a stone jar in layers; between the layers sprinkle horse-radish, pepper and cloves of garlic. Boil the vinegar, which must cover them, and tie the jar closely. They are fit for use the next day.

Ohio Maetznia Pickles.

Soak the maetznia well in brine for one week, and then boil till tender in weak vinegar. Season them with horse-radish, allspice and pepper. Place them in the jars with slices of onion, in alternate layers. Fill the jars with boiling vinegar, and cover them well. They will be fit for use in six weeks.

Watch the bushes and gather the fruit before they are fibrous. Gather them in the morning while the dew is on them.

Pickled Mushrooms.

Wash well and drain the mushrooms, using only the large ones. To a tin bucketful put two tablespoonfuls of mace and one of cloves, both ground fine, and cayenne pepper. Put all into a stone jar, in layers, sprinkling each layer with salt. Fill the jar to the top with boiling vinegar, and cover tight.

Pickled Artichokes.

Lay the artichokes in salt and water for two days, then take them out and rub them well with a coarse towel to take off the outer skin. As soon as they are rubbed, put them into cold water, to prevent their turning dark. Boil the vinegar, and when cold pour it over the artichokes. Add a teaspoonful of grated horse-radish to each jar to flavor them.

Pine Apple Pickle.

Seven pounds of sliced fruit, three pounds of brown sugar, one quart of vinegar, one ounce of cinnamon, and one ounce of whole cloves. Slice the fruit and arrange it in layers, with the spices between. Boil the sugar and vinegar together, and pour it over the fruit. Do this for three days, and then put it away for use. When in the jars, the vinegar must cover the fruit.

PICKLED CANTALOUPES.

Pare and slice six large cantaloupes not fully ripe, cover them with vinegar and let them stand all night; then take out the fruit, strain the vinegar and boil it, adding three and a half pounds of brown sugar, one tablespoonful of cloves, a few sticks of cinnamon and a little mace. Just before it comes to a boil, add the fruit, and let it boil until it can be easily pierced with a straw.

SWEET PICKLE CANTALOUPE.

Use firm, ripe cantaloupes; peel and slice them, put them in a jar and cover them with strong apple vinegar; let them stand for about twelve hours, then take the cantaloupe out and weigh it, and to every pound of fruit add one pound of sugar. Put it in a porcelain kettle with some water, as there is so little juice in the fruit; let it boil till the fruit is clear and the syrup thick; allow a pint of vinegar to every eight pounds of fruit; scald the vinegar in a separate vessel with a little stick cinnamon, three or four pieces of mace and one dozen cloves. When the fruit is done, lift it out carefully and put it in a glass jar, then add the vinegar to the syrup and pour the whole over the fruit. Seal and put away.

Strong vinegar should be used for sweet pickles, as they are hard to keep.

KENTUCKY SWEET PICKLES.

To seven pounds of fruit add three pounds of brown sugar and one quart of vinegar. Put the vinegar and sugar into a

22

preserving kettle and let them come to a boil. Meanwhile having carefully wiped the fruit, stick them full of cloves, lay them in a stone jar and pour the vinegar and sugar boiling hot over them. Repeat this for four days; each time making the liquid, which will be increased in bulk from the juice of the fruit, boiling hot. During the last boiling add a small handful of stick cinnamon. Peaches, pears, plums and cherries may be done in this way.

To Pickle Apples Sweet.

To seven pounds of fruit add three pounds of sugar, two ounces of cloves, one pound of mustard seed, two ounces of mace and one gallon of good vinegar. Boil all together slowly, keeping the apples whole.

Sweet Pickle.

Pare the rind from the watermelon, cut out the pink part, and lay the white in weak vinegar and water over night. In the morning boil in the same liquid till tender, adding a little salt. Drain them, and to one pint of vinegar add one pound of brown sugar, one tablespoonful of ground mace, half a spoonful of ground cloves, and one stick of cinnamon. When boiled pour this over the melon and set the jar in a cool dry place.

Damson Pickles.

To two pounds of damsons, weighed before they are stoned, add one pound of sugar and half a pint of vinegar. Boil the vinegar and sugar with twenty cloves and a blade of mace; pour this boiling upon the damsons, and repeat the boiling every day or two five or six times, each time throwing the boiling syrup over the damsons.

Tomato Chowder.

One peck of green tomatoes sliced and salted over night, six onions, half a pint of chopped peppers, half a pint of grated horse-radish, a dessertspoonful of white mustard seed, a table-spoonful of yellow mustard seed, the same of ground mace and a half tablespoonful of black pepper. Chop all fine together except the spice, which is to be mixed with vinegar enough to cover all, with several lumps of sugar. Boil the vinegar, sugar and spices together, and when cold, pour the mixture over the pickles, which have been previously packed in stone jars. Cover very tight.

Green Tomato Pickle.

Cut up a peck of tomatoes, sprinkle them with salt, and let them stand for twenty-four hours; then squeeze them very dry and add six sliced onions. If you do not like onions, they may be left out. Then stir in allspice, cloves, ginger, black pepper, an ounce of each, ground, half an ounce of ground mustard, half an ounce of white mustard seed and three pounds of brown sugar. Cover the whole with strong cider vinegar and boil until tender.

Green Tomato Pickles.

Those ready to ripen are the best to pickle. Place them in a large pan and throw on a handful of salt; cover them with boiling water and let them stand till cold; then slice them through transversely once or twice, according to the size, and lay them in a stone jar with onions sliced very thin. Mix the vinegar with cloves, cinnamon and allspice, and pour it on hot; cover and set them away for a few days. They will keep all winter. Those who dislike onions may omit them.

CABBAGE PICKLE.

Cut up two large heads of cabbage, three red peppers, and four onions. Sprinkle salt through them and let it stand for one hour. Meanwhile boil together a pint and a half of vinegar, three tablespoonfuls of white mustard seed, two of brown sugar, and three sticks of cinnamon. Put the pickles into a jar and pour the liquid over them.

PICKLED BELL-PEPPERS.

Core the peppers, and throw them into cold water for one day. Next morning make a pickle of salt, and throw it on boiling hot. Do this every day until they begin to look green; then take them out, wipe them dry, and put them in the sun to dry thoroughly; then pour boiling vinegar over them, season them with mustard seed, spices and garlic, or stuff them like mangoes.

YELLOW PICKLE.

Four quarts of cider vinegar, half a pound of ground mustard, one ounce of white mustard seed, one ounce of bruised mace, a quarter of an ounce of cloves, one ounce of race ginger, three sticks of horse-radish, sliced, two ounces of turmeric, tied in a thin bag, one teacupful of salt. Boil the vinegar and spices for fifteen minutes and add the turmeric. Keep the pickle in a large jar, and put in from day to day, as you gather them, small cucumbers, cauliflower, radish pods, small ears of corn, small green tomatoes, crab-apples, young beans, ripe grapes, cherries, plums, onions, &c. It will be fit for use in three months.

YELLOW PICKLE.

One hard white cabbage, cut as for cold-slaw; one dozen small white onions, sliced. Put these into a deep dish, and expose them to the sun to wilt, throwing in a double handful of salt. After standing for a few days and draining well, wash the ingredients in water and put a layer in a deep earthen dish ; sprinkle in white and black mustard seed, then another layer of cabbage, &c. Prepare vinegar sufficient to cover by throwing into it a tablespoonful of turmeric powder, six tablespoonfuls of ground mustard, two of mace, and two of black pepper-corns. Boil this and throw it over the cabbage and onions. Stir all well together and taste ; if it requires anything, add it and put it away in jars. It will be fit for use in a few days.

MISCELLANEOUS.

Cocoanut Candy.

Grate a cocoanut, and boil it with one pound of white sugar, wet with the milk of the nut. It should boil slowly until thick; then pour it out on buttered plates.

Home-made Cream Candy.

Three coffeecupfuls of white sugar and six tablespoonfuls of water. Boil without stirring, in a bright tin pan, until it will crisp in water like molasses candy. Just before it is done, flavor it with vanilla or essence of lemon, and add one teaspoonful of cream of tartar. When done, pour it into buttered pans, and as soon as fit to handle, pull it until perfectly white.

Taffy.

To two pounds of brown sugar add one pint of water, half a teacupful of vinegar, and two tablespoonfuls of butter. Stir these well together before it is put on the fire, but do not stir it afterwards. Flavor it with mace or nutmeg; boil it until it is brittle, which can be ascertained by dropping a little into cold water. When done, pour it into shallow flat pans, that are well buttered. Score across into squares when it begins to cool.

TAFFY.

Boil in a cupful of water three cupfuls of brown sugar and three or four ounces of butter. Let it boil without stirring till it candies. It is much improved by mixing in it the kernels of walnuts or shellbarks.

MAPLE SUGAR CARAMELS.

Break two pounds of maple sugar into small pieces, and put it in a pan on the fire, with a quart of rich new milk. Stir it with a wooden spoon without ceasing, in order to prevent it from burning. Let the pan be large enough to allow of expansion and boiling over. While boiling, drop a small piece in cold water from time to time ; when it is brittle enough to crack apart, it is done. Pour it out on a marble slab or into pans, and score it across with a knife, into small tablets. Nothing is added to this caramel, as the maple sugar flavor is that which it is intended should prevail.

CHOCOLATE CARAMELS.

Two cupfuls of light brown sugar, half a cupful of grated chocolate, one cupful of milk, one tablespoonful of flour, mixed with the milk, and a piece of butter the size of an egg. Boil it for half an hour. Pour it into flat tins, and with a knife score it over in little squares. When cold, it can be easily broken.

CARAMELS.

One pound of brown sugar, a quarter of a pound of chocolate, one pint of cream or milk, one large teaspoonful of butter, and two tablespoonfuls of molasses. Boil the above, and keep stirring it all the time. Drop a little into cold water, and if it hardens, it is done. It will take about thirty minutes. Just before it is removed from the fire, flavor it with a little vanilla.

To Roast Almonds.

Blanch half a pound of almonds, roll them in fine table salt, and roast them in a pan as you would coffee. These prepared almonds make an elegant addition to a dessert.

Orange Flavoring.

Remove from twelve fine oranges the outside rind without any of the white pulp, and put it into a large bottle, adding half a pint of alcohol and a gill and a half of water. Cork it tight. It will keep a long time, and is an excellent flavoring for puddings and other sweet dishes. Lemons may be prepared in the same way.

To Make Cream Cheese.

Scald the milk, and let it cool a little before putting in the rennet. When the curd is formed, take it out in a ladle without breaking it. Lay it on a thin cloth held by two persons. Dash a ladleful of water over each ladleful of curd, to separate the curd. Hang it up to drain the water off, and then put it under a light press for one hour. Cut the curd with a thread into small pieces, according to the size desired for the cheese. Press them with a cloth between each two for an hour. Take them out, rub them with fine salt, let them lie on a board for an hour, and wash them in cold water. Let them lie to drain, and in a day or two the skin will look dry. Put some grass under and over them, and they will soon ripen.

Cream Cheese.

Put aside a quart of good cream until it is sour and very thick, and stir into it a tablespoonful of salt. Lay a piece of thin muslin in a hair sieve, so as to draw the cheese out in the muslin. Put the sieve on a dish, pour in the cream and let it drain for three days; pouring off the whey every morning.

If the cream will not go in all at once, add it during the day, as the whey sinks. It should be of the consistency of butter when eaten. It may be put into a wooden mould to press, or turned into a bowl or small shallow dish.

CURRY POWDER.

Twelve ounces of coriander seed, six ounces of black pepper, one ounce and a half of cummin seed, three ounces of fœnugreek and six ounces of pale turmeric. Pound these ingredients very fine and dry them well in a dutch-oven, stirring them often. When cold, put the mixture into a dry jar and cork it lightly. The proportion used for cooking must be according to the quantity of meat, and may be determined by tasting it after adding a moderate quantity.

CURRY POWDER.

Two tablespoonfuls of powdered ginger, one of fresh turmeric, three or four cloves, a blade of mace, two or three cardamom seeds, some cayenne and black pepper, and salt to taste.

This is enough for a pair of chickens or a breast of mutton. If you wish to make a quantity and keep it on hand, ready mixed, use the same proportions.

The powder should be bruised in a mortar with onions before using it. This will make a paste, which, with the addition of a dessertspoonful of flour, should be stirred into the gravy and stewed with the meat. Two onions are enough for the quantity above mentioned.

EGGS FOR WINTER USE.

Flake a lump of lime, making the mixture about as thick as ordinary whitewash. Let it stand for three weeks—otherwise the eggs would cook in it. Pack the eggs carefully in a jar, or any vessel that will hold the liquid. Eggs will keep perfectly in this way for a year or longer.

To Preserve Milk.

Bottle the milk tightly, using wine corks; place them in a kettle of cold water. Heat the water gradually till it reaches the boiling point; then remove the kettle from the fire and allow it to cool. The bottles can then be packed for future use. Milk prepared in this manner will keep for six months.

To Test Eggs.

To know whether eggs are good and fresh, drop them singly into a large vessel of cold water. If the broad ends turn uppermost, they are defective.

To Preserve Lime Juice.

Strain the juice, and to every pint add one pound of double-refined sugar. Let it stand in the sun; as the scum rises, skim it off, and when it is quite free from scum, put it into pint bottles and cork it well. It will keep for many months.

To Keep Cider Sweet.

Four pounds of sweet lard, melted down, and half an ounce of oil of sassafras. After racking off the cider and putting it into a sweet barrel, put the sassafras in first, stir it well with a stick, then put in the lard, and stir all well again; then bung the barrel tight, bore a gimlet-hole near the bung, and put a "spill" in to admit air whilst drawing. After racking the cider, it can be improved by adding to every gallon a quarter of a pound of granulated sugar, or good brown sugar.

To Keep Cider Sweet.

To a barrel of cider, which should stand five or six days after making, add ten pounds of white sugar, the whites of twelve eggs, beaten very light, and half a pound of white mustard seed. Draw out of the barrel several gallons of cider before preparing the eggs. Add the eggs when light to the sugar, pouring into the mixture sufficient cider to thin it, so that it can be poured into the bung of the barrel. The mustard seed should be put in thin muslin bags and dropped in the bung, suspended by a tape (for convenience of removal when the barrel is empty). The cider will keep for a year in this way.

CEMENT.

Melt together bees-wax and rosin, the proportions being one-third bees'-wax to two-thirds rosin. Use for this purpose an old skillet or other discarded cooking utensil. Pound the rosin to a powder, and stir it into the melting wax. When the mixture becomes liquid, take it from the fire and add to it powdered brick-dust until it is as thick as melted sealing-wax. Have the bottles or jars corked securely, dip each one into the hot cement, and in a few minutes the mixture will be dry. A piece of soft brick may easily be powdered in a stone mortar and sifted through old gauze or muslin.

INDEX.

CPSIA information can be obtained at www.ICGtesting.com
Printed in the USA
BVOW05s1419280714

360749BV00001B/2/A

9 781557 095695